The Giant Bathroom Reader

The Giant Bathroom Reader

Edited by Karl Shaw

Magpie Books, London

Constable & Robinson Ltd
3 The Lanchesters
162 Fulham Palace Road
London W6 9ER

This edition published by Magpie Books,
an imprint of Constable & Robinson Ltd 2006

A copy of the British Library Cataloguing in Publication Data
is available from the British Library

ISBN-13: 978-1-84529-468-7
ISBN-10: 1-84529-468-8

Printed and bound in the European Union

3 5 7 9 10 8 6 4 2

Read 'em and wipe

The Ultimate Bathroom Reader
The ultimate in bathroom readers was published by Bourne, Jackson & Latimer in 1870 and titled *Stray Leaves From Japanese Papers*. The bound volume contained nothing but 400 blank leaves of toilet paper, "a perfectly pure article for the toilet and lavatory, and a preventative for piles . . . confidently recommended as the best article ever produced for the particular purpose for which it was intended . . . soft, yet so strong as to bear a tight twist".

"Manure Manor"
It was once commonplace for German farmers to stack piles of excrement – animal and human – in front of their farms and dwellings. The size of the farmer's pile was his way of showing off to his neighbours that he had loads of livestock and could afford a huge family.

Thought for the Day

Anyone who claims to see through a woman is missing a lot.

Flying pasties

The expression "flying pasty", coined towards the end of the eighteenth century but now in disuse, described the anti-social act of wrapping excrement in paper and throwing it over a neighbour's wall.

Snow White?

The most reliable indicator of a nation's economy is the quality of the toilet paper it uses: thus argued the Croatian author Slavenka Drakulic in his book *How We Survived Communism and Even Laughed*. In Russia most toilet paper is like cardboard, and in 1993 the Yugoslavian newspaper *Politika* advised readers to use 100-dinar notes as "each sheet of the real thing costs twice as much". In Siberia, where no-one can afford paper of any description, people use snow.

ANIMAL NEWS Pigs Might Fly

A large accumulation of excreted methane gas in a pig shed near Verona in Italy was ignited by a spark from a fuse box. The resulting explosion destroyed the shed utterly and killed all 500 pigs. A witness said: "I saw pigs flying through the air, I thought it was Doomsday."
The Big Issue

Stiff upper lip

Soft top
Until the 1980s all British state-maintained establishments had hard toilet paper with the words "Government Property" stamped on it. Only in the very highest echelons of the Civil Service would you find soft paper.

Hollywood bottoms
The first soft toilet tissue, Andrex, was originally developed from a design for gentlemen's paper handkerchiefs and was sold exclusively at Harrods. It wasn't a big hit until Hollywood gossip columnists revealed that the biggest film stars of the day were insisting that their studios obtain Andrex.

Next Door War
Two lawyers from Encino, California, were severely reprimanded by a judge for bringing the bar into disrepute. The pair were neighbours, and one sued the other for playing basketball noisily, thus interrupting his naps and lowering the value of his property. The other countersued for general damages on the grounds that his neighbour played loud rock music and had harassed him by filming his basketball games for evidence.
LA Times

Space nappies
In the late 1960s NASA scientists were moved to overcome a new personal hygiene crisis – how to defecate in space with the inconvenience of zero gravity. They came up trumps with the "space nappy" – one soiled by Alan Shepard is now in the

British Museum. Modern astronauts now use vacuum toilets which suck away the waste as it leaves the body: liquids evaporate, and solids are freeze dried, sealed in bags and returned to earth.

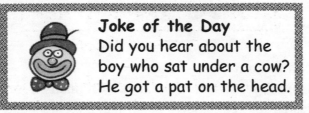

Joke of the Day
Did you hear about the boy who sat under a cow? He got a pat on the head.

The bare-bottomed army
French soldiers at the battle of Crécy in 1346 nicknamed the English "the bare-bottomed army" because they were riddled with dysentery.

Group effort
The daily bowel movements of the eighteenth-century King Ferdinand 1 of Naples were an utterly serious business: he always insisted on having a crowd of people around to keep him entertained while he strained. His father-in-law, the Austrian Emperor Joseph, was one of many who was privy to these unusual audiences and noted later, "We made conversation for more than half an hour, and I believe he would still be there if a terrible stench had not convinced us that all was over." Ferdinand also offered to show his father-in-law the fruit of his labours for closer inspection.

MURDER AND MAYHEM
The "Locked" Room

The first "Locked Room Mystery" was Poe's *Murder in the Rue Morgue*. The first locked room novel seems to have been John Ratcliffe's *Neno Sahib*. This inspired a real murder. In 1881, the wife and five children of a Berlin carter named Fritz Conrad were found hanging from hooks in a locked room. It looked as if Frau Conrad, depressed by poverty, had killed her children and committed suicide. Police Commissioner Hollman was suspicious, and when he found out that Conrad was infatuated with a young girl student, he searched the apartment for love letters. He found none, but came upon a copy of Neno Sahib and read Ratcliffe's account of a "perfect murder", in which the killer drilled a tiny hole in the door, passed a thread through it, and used this to draw the bolt after the murder; he then sealed up the hole with wax. Hollman examined Conrad's door, and found a similar hole, filled in with sealing wax, to which threads of horsehair still adhered. Confronted with this evidence, Conrad confessed to murdering his wife and children, and was sentenced to death.

Edible toilet paper
In order to pass domestic sanitary regulations, British toilet paper has to be edible.

Don't worry, be happy

There are only two ways to live your life. One is as though
nothing is a miracle. The other is as though everything is.
I believe in the latter.
Albert Einstein, 1879–1955

Tons of waste
The average amount of faeces defecated by a human during a
70-year lifespan is 2.6 tons.

Miles of toilet paper
During the course of your lifetime you will use about 15.5 miles
of toilet paper. Or about 18.5 miles if you're a woman and
you're using it to remove your make-up.

The royal bowels
To help keep pace with the royal bowels of Louis XIV, which
were regularly purged with suppositories from infancy (he had
more than 400 enemas and purges in the last year of his life) the
Palace of Versailles had 264 toilets. They were mostly painted
black to signify "courtly distress".

HEROES

Sharing hardships
The final pursuit of Darius, following his capture
by the Bactrian leader Bessus, took place across
the hot, dry and mountainous landscape of what is
now northern Afghanistan and Pakistan. At one
point his men had covered nearly four hundred
miles in eleven days, and many were on the verge of collapse from
thirst. Alexander himself was almost fainting under the heat of the

midday sun when they came across a party of tribesmen bearing water to their camp. They saw the state Alexander was in, and quickly filled a helmet with water and gave it to him; but when the king looked up and saw the haggard faces of his men craning their necks for a sight of the water, he handed it back without drinking a drop. He thanked the men who had offered it, but said: "If I am the only one to drink, the rest will lose heart." No sooner had his troops witnessed this act of self-denial for their sakes than they shouted out for him to lead them on wherever he would, for they could never feel hunger or thirst or any of the weaknesses to which mortal men are subject so long as they had such a king.

Nothing washes whiter than wee
Apart from making wine out of it there are very few uses that human bodily waste hasn't been put to by your forebears. Stale urine and excrement, which both contain ammonia, were commonly used for bathing people and for washing clothing and linen right up until World War II. The urine used on wash day went by different names according to locality: in Lancashire it was called "lant", and every yard had a communal "lant-pot" for collecting it in. In Yorkshire it was called "weetin" or "old waish". Poor people bathed themselves in urine, and more often than not it wasn't even their own: streets and groups of houses in the 1840s frequently collected their urine in a common barrel. The custom continued in poorer working class areas for at least another 50 years. Cakes of animal excrement, added to cold water, also had a cleansing effect and were used instead of, or as an addition to urine. Welsh peasants for example regularly used pig manure as a popular alternative to soap. Women became so immune to the stench of stale urine and shit on wash days that when soap became popular they often complained that the suds made them nauseous. Dung never became quite as popular as

stale urine however, partly because people suspected that it caused something known as "the itch", but mostly because it had so many other uses, as a fertilizer, as a fuel or as a building material. For centuries most poor people used cow or horse dung as fuel: although the smell was incredibly offensive, it was free, easy to collect, simple to burn and gave out a great deal of heat. When coal became more easily available in the late eighteenth and early nineteenth centuries dung fuel became less common, but the practice continued in Cornwall. In the Aran Islands off the west coast of Ireland it was still the main source of heat in the 1930s.

POTTY WISDOM, BULGARIA

Dry pants catch no fish.

The "throne"

Louis XlV had a habit of granting audiences to people while he was sitting on his toilet. Visitors, including the English ambassador Lord Portland, even regarded it as a special honour to be received by the Sun King in this manner. Louis announced his betrothal to his second wife Mme de Maintenon whilst at stool.

Elk dropping earrings

In some parts of the world animal manure is sculpted into

fashion jewellery. Visitors to the 1994 Winter Olympics in Norway were sold souvenir elk droppings at £7 a pair: they were dried, cooked in microwave ovens, painted with lacquer and worn as earrings.

UFOLOGY
Visited by a Spaceman

In England in 1957, a Birmingham house-wife claimed to have been visited by a spaceman in her own home. He did not arrive in a flying saucer, but simply materialized, accompanied by a whistling sound, in the living-room of twenty-seven-year-old Mrs Cynthia Appleton. He was tall and fair and wore a tight-fitting plastic-like garment. He communicated, according to Mrs Appleton, by telepathy, and produced TV-like pictures to illustrate his flying saucer and a large master craft. He indicated to her that he came from a place of harmony and peace. At the end of all this, he simply dematerialized.

Hind Park
In pre-public convenience Britain, London's public parks were notorious for their desperate defecators. When Casanova travelled through St. James's Park he noted with disgust "six or seven people shitting in the bushes with their hinder parts turned towards the publick".

Briny bottoms

In ancient Rome rooms were rarely set aside for individual
toilets. When a Roman needed to relieve himself he would
summon a slave to bring a chamber pot, and he would then do it
there and then irrespective of where he was or who he was with.
By the first century Rome had public latrines, but defecation
continued to be a very communal affair. The Romans wiped
their backsides with brine-soaked sponges on sticks which were
then rinsed out and left for the next user.

Home sweet home

When the Dutch scholar Erasmus visited England in the
sixteenth century, he described the floors of a typical upper-class
English home; they were covered with a twenty-year-old crust
of "filth, spillings of beer, the remains of fish, spittle and vomit,
excrement and urine of dogs and men and other filthiness not to
be named."

Soft sell

Marketing techniques for toilet paper in the 1930s had little to
do with quilts or labrador puppies: it was a war waged over the
terrors of "hard" and "soft" brands. A typical US newspaper
advertisement for "soft" paper confidently asserted that hard
paper was a major cause of what is referred to as "rectal
trouble". An advertisement promoting Scot Tissue ("the paper
that doctors recommend") informed the public that "65% of all
men and women in middle age suffer from troubles caused by
inferior toilet paper".

Curtained off

When Peter the Great's son Alexis went to Dresden in 1712 to
marry a German Princess, the Elector of Hanover Ernst August

noted with distaste in a letter to his wife that the Czarevitch shat in his bedroom and wiped his backside with the curtains.

Fanny paper
In the 1870s American ladies carried a personal supply of toilet paper hidden inside a fan.

An open and sh*t case
The 1883 publication *The Family Physician* blamed poor toilet design as a major cause of constipation in ladies. The ideal surroundings required in order to get the bowels moving freely, the late Victorians were urged, comprised "a bright cheerful little chamber, where you might pass five or ten minutes with a certain amount of comfort, and moralize on things in general".

Parlez-vous Français?
In French polite society, human ordure is referred to as *les cinq lettres*.

Shelf life
The ancient ritual of inspecting one's own faeces in the belief that the consistency and colour of your turds can reveal more about the state of your health than your GP ever could, is still widely observed in Germany. This German fixation with fibrous floaters has led to the evolution of their own unique flat-pan toilet design. The toilet bowl is built so that the faeces, instead of being deposited at the bottom out of sight and out of mind, sit pertly in the middle of a shallow ceramic ledge inviting inspection. Unfortunately, these turds tend to hang around on their little ledge even after a couple of brisk flushes, and instead of whirling off down the drain when they are supposed to, they have to be coaxed off with a stiff toilet brush.

French paper
The French are fussier than any other nation in the world about their toilet paper. In France the toilet paper is said to be of a higher quality than their banknotes.

Sherborne Latrine
Sherborne Lane in the City of London was originally called Shittebornelane, because it was the site of a public latrine.

Stuck up
Britain spends about £70 million per annum on laxatives – more per capita than any other country in Europe.

Fancy that!
For several centuries in Britain, the discovery of a steaming turd in a public place would provoke the popular, but now disused exclamation, "Sirreverence!"

Going for a Harring
Contrary to schoolyard myth Thomas Crapper did not invent the WC. That distinction belongs to Sir John Harrington, godson and privy-maker to Queen Elizabeth 1, who had one of his very first prototype flush toilets, complete with cistern, pan, overflow pipe, valve and waste pipe installed in her palace at Richmond. Sadly, and in spite of the royal patronage, his idea didn't catch on for another 200 years, and the expression "going for a Harring" never entered the English language. Thomas Crapper did however produce something called The Valveless Water Waste Preventer, the forerunner of modern flush toilet systems, which allowed water to flush the bowl only when required.

Fire down below!
Samuel Pepys once noted in his diary that his maid had
forgotten to leave a chamber pot in his bedroom and he had
been forced to "shit twice in the chimney fireplace".

Close stools
Before flush toilets were invented, most ordinary people used
chamber pots, while royalty and the upper classes favoured the
close-stool – an armchair with a strategically placed hole or a
simple box with a hinged lid. Country people however did it in
the fields and townies did it wherever they could.

It's behind you!
Rats can tread water for three days and can easily swim up
waste pipes and enter homes through the S-bends of toilet
systems. In the 1980s a company from Omaha, USA patented a
"plastic rodent stopper" to be fitted in toilet bowls, after dozens
of people reported that they had been bitten on the backside by
rats while sitting on the toilet.

P(ar)issssss . . .
Although France and the court of Versailles was considered to
be the very pinnacle of fashion, it failed to move the Austrian-
born Duchess of Orléans when she became the second wife of
Louis XlV's brother. She wrote home of Paris in 1694, "The
multitude of people who shit in the street produces a smell so
detestable that it cannot be endured." She went on, "There is one
thing at court that I shall never get used to . . . the people
stationed in the galleries in front of our rooms piss into all the
corners. It is impossible to leave one's apartment without seeing
someone pissing."

Plop closets and other little houses

Maybe it's because the modern flush toilet system was a British
invention, or perhaps it's just because the English language has
more words in it than any other, but of all the countries in
Europe Britain has developed the greatest proliferation of
lavatorial euphemisms. The favourite of the sixteenth century
was "Jakes"; in the seventeenth century, it was "closet",
"latrine" or "necessary house"; in the eighteenth century "bog"
grew in popularity, along with "water closet", the "house of
office", the "little house", or the colourful "cackatorium".
"Dunny" was also originally an eighteenth-century British
expression, which migrated to Australia with a few thousand
convicts and took a firm hold down under. It now ranks at the
top of the Antipodean loo lexicon ahead of "diddy", "toot" and
"brasco". Victorian Britons referred to the "bog house", the
"WC" and the "toilet", from the French toilette. The whole
world has since borrowed the English term "WC". By and large
the French are happy to call them *pissoirs*, or occasionally
Rambeteau, after a famous French prefect, or *Vespasienne*, a
reference to the Emperor who established Rome's first public
conveniences. Germany meanwhile has *Abort* (away place),
stilles Örtchen (silent little place), *Abtritt* (walk away), *"D" und
"H"* (*Damen und Herren*) , *Donnerbalken* (thunder board), and
the very silly *Plumsklo* (plop closet). A Russian will usually ask
for the *ubornaya* (adornment place), a desperate Dutchman will
require the *bestekamer* (best room), while an Italian will
confusingly seek the *bagno* (bath) or sometimes the *gabinetto*, a
derivation of the French for cabinet room.

Alien and other strange news

Christ on the Sofa

In 1976, on the back wall of Billsdown Hen House near
Bournemouth, someone noticed what appeared to be an image of
Christ crucified picked out in stains. The *Sunday People* heard
the story and ran a feature article on the "miracle". They invited
readers to examine a photograph of the wall, and then send in
drawings of what they thought they saw. The next week some of
the entries were printed. They included a jug, a candle, a group
of four angels, a scene of rivers and trees, and Christ reclining
on a sofa.
Sunday People

Spiritual Bombardment

A block of flats in Hamilton, New Zealand, was the object of
repeated assaults of hurled bottles. Among the projectiles were
milk bottles, beer bottles and coffee jars. Despite a police
surveillance set up to discover the source of the attacks, some of
which lasted up to four hours, they remain a mystery. Maori
elders explained the phenomena by saying that the building was
erected on sacred land; the spirits of the land were showing that
they were offended.
Sunday Express

Mince Pie Angels

Mrs Jean Hingley of Rowley Regis in the West Midlands
reported a strange visitation to her local police. Answering her
back door one night, she was faced with a blinding
light. As her eyes became accustomed to it, she saw three
figures with corpse-like faces and wings on their backs standing

on her doorstep. Astonished and confused, Mrs Hingley entered into a "close encounter of the third kind" by asking the visitors if they would like some coffee. They refused, but said they would quite like some water. Formalities over, the aliens entered Mrs Hingley's house and enjoyed a glass of cold water. On their way out, they noticed some mince pies and decided to take them with them. They would, they said, be back some time.
Daily Mirror

Twin TV

In July 1979, identical twin sisters Ruth Johnson and Allison Mitchell Erb were reunited. They had been adopted separately in New Hampshire twenty-six years earlier, and had had no contact since that time. Both women were hairdressers. Both had daughters named Kristen. Both had watched a TV programme defending the right of adopted children to identify their families, and as a result each began the search for the other.
Daily Mail

Attack of the Invisible Dwarfs

A policeman called to the home of a man in Toledo found the occupant in severe mental distress because of the invisible dwarfs that were overrunning his home. Obligingly, the policeman mediated: "I told the one dwarf in the kitchen to leave, then went to the cellar to tell the others . . . They didn't put up much resistance and left." Convinced, the man thanked the policeman profusely. The question is, how did he know that they were gone?
Toledo Blade

Unexplained F****** Objects

A farmer from Tout in France reported to astounded police that
a UFO had landed in one of his fields while he was working. A
man and a woman, both naked, had jumped out of the vehicle
and proceeded to have sex three times. When the farmer tried to
approach the copulating couple, he was thrown back by an
inexplicable force. After the third time, the pair jumped back
into the UFO and flew away.
News of the World

Stumping Around

Since 11 January 1976, a mysterious tree stump has been touring
Ridgway, Illinois. The 500-lb stump appears in unlikely places,
including inside a van and various people's houses. It stays for
up to two days then disappears in an equally inexplicable way.
Lebanon Daily News

Bizarre crimes

Cutter Carter

A twenty-three-year-old, bespectacled, Schools' Careers Adviser
named Graham Carter was arrested on 23 June 1977 at Oxford
Circus in London. He was accused of being responsible for a
wave of "clothes cutting" incidents. In the areas around Oxford
Circus, Green Park and Piccadilly tube stations, over the
previous six months, women had been finding that large circles
of material had been removed from the back of their skirts with
sharp scissors. Often the unfortunate victims went on their way
unaware of the crime until either the draught or a considerate
passer-by apprised them of their situation. Mr Carter admitted

the offences, but while he was in custody a small number of snippings continued to occur. "There is certainly one other person, if not more, doing this sort of thing," commented Mr Carter's lawyer.
Daily Express

Foiled Crucifixion
In both 1976 and 1978, British stuntman Eddie Shingler tried to organize his own crucifixion as a spectator event in Nottingham. Witnessing the actual nailing up of Mr Shingler was to cost three pounds whereas just watching him hang there would be a reasonable fifty pence. Both attempts were foiled by the police, who announced that they would arrest anyone trying to nail Mr Shingler to the cross on a charge of assault.
Daily Mirror

Fool's Gold
Rosana Vigil, aged sixty, was attacked by a man in the street in Denver, Colorado. The assailant prised her mouth open and removed her false teeth. Mrs Vigil told the police: "He said, 'There ain't no gold here, so here's your teeth', and he gave them back."
New York Post

Sic Transit Gloria Mundi
Arthur Gloria, a candidate for the Chicago police, was so determined not to let anything go wrong in his entrance test that he stole a car in order to be on time. When he arrived, he parked the car illegally. As he was dragged away by those he so wished to emulate, Gloria commented that he thought he had done well on the test.
Ann Arbor News

Scratching Is Relaxing

In Tokyo, a twenty-six-year-old draughtsman was arrested for
scratching the faces of twelve women with his tie-pin. He
explained that travelling to and from work on crowded tube
trains depressed him terribly, and that disfiguring fellow
passengers helped him to relax. The man had a history of mental
illness.
Straits Times (Singapore)

Wary Fairy

Mr Michael Douglas-Smith was driving back from a fancy-dress
party when he was torn from his car by three large men and
shoved into their vehicle. After having driven a few metres with
their hostage, who was dressed as a fairy, the men had a change
of mind. Mr Douglas-Smith was dumped by the side of the road
and the assailants' car sped away. Subsequently the three men
were arrested and charged with assault. One commented: "There
was a bit of confusion."
Weekend Magazine

Help, Police!

A young police recruit named Paul Williams decided to fake an
assault upon himself. To this end, he stabbed himself repeatedly
with a penknife and hit himself on the head with a brick. After
leaving hospital, Williams was given an award for his bravery in
the "assault". Unfortunately his fraud was detected: the emergency
call for help, as well as other false alarms, was traced to his
extension at the police station. Asked why he had done all this, he
said that he had expected police work to be more exciting than it
was.
Sun

Dodgy Fight
Wendy Bergen, an award-winning news journalist for local
television in Denver, planned a series of reports unmasking the
vicious underground blood-sport rings in the area. The reports
were to be big audience winners, broadcast during the station's
"sweeps", a test week to establish average viewer numbers for
the purposes of selling advertising space. The problem was that,
try as she might, Bergen could not find any illegal blood sports
taking place in Denver. In desperation she organized one herself,
a pit bull terrier fight, and filmed the violent results.
Unfortunately for Ms Bergen, the police were aware of her
activities, and she now faces up to ten years in prison.
Ann Arbor News

Royal Flush

I kid you not . . .
Everywhere the Queen goes, her personal lavatory seat cover
made of white kid goes with her. Whenever her majesty feels
the call of nature a lady-in-waiting guards the door to prevent
anyone else from using the convenience.

The Queen's bowels
Queen Victoria was preoccupied with her bowels and would
summon her court doctor for a discussion on the subject up to
six times a day. While she was away on her honeymoon her
physician was surprised to receive a note from her one day
informing him: "The bowels are acting fully."

The first in line to the throne's line of thrones
Prince Charles once claimed he has a collection of toilet seats.

Horse play
The Queen's favourite royal anecdote, according to those in the know, relates to an occasion when she shared a horse-drawn carriage with a visiting (unnamed) African president. During their trip one of the Queen's horses broke wind so loudly and forcibly that it couldn't be ignored, and so the Queen apologised to her guest. The African president whispered back, "That's quite all right Ma'am . . . I thought it was the horse."

No expense spared
The hellraising actress Tallulah Bankhead once found herself in a cubicle in a ladies' lavatory without any toilet paper. She called out to the next cubicle, "Darling, is there any tissue in there?" The reply came: "Sorry, no."
    "Any Kleenex?"
    "Afraid not."
    "My dear," continued Tallulah, "can you change two fives for a ten?"

Worst Jobs / Occupational Hazards

Cure for dandruff
When Catherine the Great found out that she was suffering from dandruff she had her hairdresser locked in an iron cage for three years to prevent him from telling anyone else about it.

Health and safety solutions

Patent screw manufacturers Nettlefold & Chamberlain, the firm behind British Prime Minister Neville Chamberlain's personal fortune, pioneered an unorthodox approach to health and safety regulations in the 1930s. None of the company's dangerous factory machinery was fitted with safety guards and serious injuries occurred often. Noting that the cries of wounded workers tended to distract other employees from their jobs the management slapped a big fine on anyone who screamed when injured.

The right to be tossed

In March 1992 a 25-year-old French dwarf won the right to be thrown bodily across rooms for a living. Manuel Wachensheim had successfully appealed against a ban on the sport of "dwarf tossing", imposed by the French government because it was "degrading".

Live by the knife, die by the sword

In 1671 the French royal chef Vatel realized that it was just going to be one of those days when the roast beef ran short at Louis XIV's banquet and only two cartloads of fish turned up instead of the 12 he had ordered. Rather than face a lot of awkward and embarrassing questions from the King, he committed suicide by running onto his own sword.

No Curie

Marie Curie's epic work exposed her to such massive amounts of radium that even the notebooks she used are dangerously radioactive to this day. She worked for years on thousands of pounds of radioactive waste in an outdoor shed with no protection from the lethal fumes. Mme Curie expired in 1934 from leukaemia.

First catch your tax collector . . .
In 1901 a Chinese government official sent out to deal with tax-dodgers in the province of Kwan-si was boiled and eaten by the locals.

URBAN MYTHS
True or False – you decide

THE MISSING WIVES

In the early days of commercial air travel, one well-known airline set up a scheme to allow businessmen's wives to fly with their husbands without charge. The aim was to foster the idea that flying was safe. The promotion was widely taken up by businessmen, and records were kept of the names of those who had taken advantage of the offer. Later on the airline sent a letter to the wives, to ask them if they had enjoyed the trip. Over 90 per cent of them replied that they had no idea what the airline was talking about and hadn't flown anywhere with their husband.

The Inept Executioner
The eighteenth-century English executioner John Swift was a convicted murderer who was set free on condition that he did the government's dirty work as an axeman. Thrift wasn't the ideal candidate for the job on account of the fact that he couldn't stand the sight of blood. When he was called upon to execute the Jacobite rebel Lord Balmerino at the Tower of London in 1745, he fainted, then lay on the ground sobbing while

onlookers tried to persuade him to get on with it. When Thrift
finally took up his axe, he took five blows to sever Balmerino's
head. The public never forgave his ineptness. When he died a
jeering mob pelted his coffin and his pall-bearers with stones
and the rotting bodies of dead cats.

Moist as rabbits and twice as nice
Jack Black was Queen Victoria's longest serving Royal Rat and
Mole Destroyer. Although he was nearly killed three times by
rats and once found that a rat had bitten clean through a bone in
his finger, snapping it in two, Black didn't mind because he got
to eat as many rats as he could take home with him. Rats, he
said, were "moist as rabbits and twice as nice".

The dog do collectors
The collection of dog faeces was a lucrative business in
nineteenth-century England. "Pure Finders" sold the dung to
tanners, who rubbed it into animal skins to help "purify" them.
Not surprisingly, the tanners were nearly as far down the social
scale as their suppliers. According to experts the very best
tanning dung was the imported Turkish variety.

Just half a skull for me, please
Workers at the Royal Mint used to be supplied with free
drinking vessels made from the skulls of executed criminals
spiked on Tower Bridge. They were told that ale drunk from the
skulls was a great cure for respiratory ailments caused by
working in a metal foundry.

**POTTY
WISDOM,
GHANA**

Like the turtle, every man
should stick out his neck if he
wants to go forward.

Perk of the job . . .
Monks in the Middle Ages were usually given the job of
keeping vigil over the dead bodies of the wealthy and high
ranking. The custom was stopped after several cases were
reported of monks raping dead women.

Thoughtful employer
Workers in nineteenth-century North Staffordshire suffered from
"potter's rot", a condition caused by severe lead poisoning from
the glazes they handled while making ceramic tiles. One
tilemaker, Maw & Co., brewed a special free-issue beer for its
workforce to counteract the lethal effect of the lead. It contained
sulphuric acid.

Ode to a rat catcher
Lord Tennyson's job as Poet Laureate to Queen Victoria in 1857
earned him less money than the royal rat-catcher.

Hard day at the orifice . . .

Ancient Egyptian embalmers weren't popular at parties, mostly because they usually stank of rotting human flesh, but also because word had got around that embalmers had been caught raping female corpses. Families of female corpses, especially beautiful female corpses, often delayed sending their loved ones to the Necropolis for embalming until they had been dead for several days to discourage rape by the embalmers. The mummification process, which in all took about 70 days, began with the removal of the corpse's brain, usually through the nasal canal with the aid of long brass needles with hooks on the end, or occasionally by removing an eye and breaking through the upper wall of the eye socket. The embalmer would then remove the entrails – intestine, stomach, liver, spleen, peritoneum, kidneys and lungs – by hand. The heart was always left in place. Female genital organs, and sometimes male genital organs, were amputated and mummified separately. The body was then dehydrated and stuffed to give it a more "lifelike" appearance. No trick was ruled out – bundles of cloth, lichen, bitumen, sawdust, sand, mud or baked clay were all used to pad out the gaps left by missing organs.

A skeleton staff

The US Radium Corporation, which made a fortune in the 1920s from producing millions of luminously painted watch dials, fish bait and dolls' eyes, found itself at the centre of a national scandal in 1924 when dozens of their female painters, some only twelve years old, began to fall ill and die, horribly and mysteriously. An independent enquiry into the deaths learned that in order to produce the fine artwork needed on the watch dials, the girls were expected to lick excess luminous paint from their brushes: some of the girls even painted their teeth and lips for a lark. The company meanwhile consistently denied that there was any link between the deaths and the tiny amounts of radioactive material used in the paint. Then in 1925 the company chemist Edwin Lehman, although never directly in regular contact with the deadly paint, also suddenly fell dead. The autopsy found that Lehman's bones were so radioactive that, when left on an unexposed photographic plate, they photographed themselves.

And your point is?
In 1971 a Californian involved in a minor traffic accident confessed to the arresting patrolman that he had recently eaten a social worker. He wasn't hungry, he was just trying to make a point.

Thought for the Day

Anyone who says it's as easy as taking candy from a baby has never tried it.

One man's meat . . .
To humour the Japanese Emperor Hirohito's food-poisoning phobia, every scrap of his food had to be first laboratory tested by scientists for signs of contamination, then served on sterilized plates. Even the royal faeces and urine had to be chemically analysed afterwards. His chef Tadoa Tanak committed ritual suicide when his master died. The Japanese royal ritual of food-tasting before every meal wasn't banned until 1989.

Close enough for you?
From 1956 to 1963 between one quarter and half a million US
military personnel were deliberately exposed to radiation from
atomic test bombs, mostly without any form of protective
clothing or equipment so that they could experience fallout "for
troop training purposes". The US Air Force Brigadier General
A. R. Leudecke once complained that his men weren't allowed
to stand close enough to the blast.

Bison gone
In 1992 six French boy scouts laboured for two hours with
scrubbing brushes to clean up graffiti on the walls of the Grotte
de Mayfrières, a tourist attraction in Southern France. They were
later told that they had erased a 15,000-year-old cave painting of
bison.

Firsts

iPope
Benedict XVI is the first Pope to own an iPod. His version – the
nano – is white and cost around £100.

The presidential nose
Ronald Reagan was the first President of the United States to
have his nasal polyps discussed on live TV.

Rub-a-dub Russell
Earl John Russell (1846–52, 1865–6) was the first British Prime
Minister known to have taken a regular bath.

When not to spit on the floor

Russia's first ever book of etiquette was published by Empress
Anne in 1718. She had revolutionary ideas about good manners
and wanted to keep up with European standards of good taste.
Entitled *The Honest Mirror of Youth*, the slim volume advised
discerning Russians how to use a knife and fork, when not to spit
on the floor, not to blow their noses by applying a digit to one
nostril while blowing down the other, and not to jab their elbows
into their seating partners during formal dinners nor place their
feet in guests' dishes while standing on the dining table.

The world's first bird diaper

In 1959 Bertha Dlugi of Milwaukee, USA, became the first and
only person to realize the major commercial possibilities of a
bird diaper which allowed pet birds to fly freely around the
house without depositing droppings.

Rummaging for heads

The Frenchman Dr Philippe Curtius opened the forerunner to the
Chamber of Horrors, the Caverne des Grands Voleurs in 1783
and taught his talented young apprentice Madame Tussaud how
to model wax. One of her first jobs was to make wax likenesses
from decapitated heads removed from victims of the guillotine.
Curtius acquired his models for her to work on by hanging
around in cemeteries waiting for the arrival of carts containing
the bodies: when Louis XV's former mistress Madame du Barry
was executed, he rummaged through the cart for her head, oiled
her face and applied a plaster mask before tossing her head into
the communal grave.

And his next?
King Louis XlII of France had his first wash on his seventh
birthday.

Is this a bog I see before me?
Shakespeare was the first person to use the word "bog".

The body-snatching anatomist
The Belgian anatomist Vesalius was the first surgeon who could
truthfully say that he knew more about the innards of a human
being than the average butcher. He got his first corpse to
practise on by stealing the body of a hanged man from outside
the city walls of Louvain.

Winning hearts and minds
Peter the Great was the first Russian czar ever to travel West,
but shortly before he left he arranged a small exhibition to
concentrate the hearts and minds of his people in case any of
them had any treasonable ideas while he was away. He had the
ringleaders of a suspected plot against his life arrested and
tortured, then publicly dismembered and beheaded. The czar
then ordered the remains of a famous dissident Ivan
Miloslavsky, who had been executed twelve years earlier, to be
disinterred. Miloslavsky's decomposed corpse was dragged by
pigs to the place of execution, butchered into small segments,
then placed underneath the scaffold in an open coffin. On the
platform above the new plot ringleaders were slowly
dismembered so that their fresh blood irrigated the remains of
the late Miloslavsky below. The severed body parts were neatly
arranged in a large, human meat pie and their heads fixed on
spikes. Peter left express orders that no-one was to remove the
grisly display, which lay rotting and stenching until his return.

A Rolling Stone pays much tax
In 1993 Queen Elizabeth II became the first British monarch
since Queen Victoria to pay income tax. According to her first
tax return she was poorer than Mick Jagger.

Medical advance
The sixteenth-century French surgeon Ambroise Paré earned the
dying, and on a very good day the undying, gratitude of his
patients when he became the first doctor to realize that you
didn't really need to cauterize an open wound by pouring oil on
it, or to stem bleeding during amputation with a red hot iron.

Early "reality" shows
The first circuses were put on by Assyrian and Babylonian kings,
but they had a very limited entertainment value. Usually the main
and only attraction was the sight of up to a hundred very hungry
lions being let loose on a crowd of Bedouin arab prisoners.

Dutch courage
The dodo was the first known species to have been made extinct
by man. The bird, unique to the island of Mauritius, wasn't
killed for its meat, which was tough and bitter-tasting, it was
wiped out for kicks. Bored sailors quickly discovered that the
bird wouldn't run, couldn't fly, was an easy target, and so the
obvious thing to do was kill it. The last dodo was clubbed to
death by a Dutch seaman in 1680.

Eight million bacteria in every drop
The first man to observe human parasites was the Dutchman
Anton van Leeuwenhoek when he looked through a microscope
one day and found them romping in his own diarrhoeic stools.
Leeuwenhoek also disturbed some of the more sensitive

gentlemen of the Royal Society with his brusque announcement:
"there are more animals in the scum of a man's teeth than there
are in a whole kingdom." His fellow scientists were even more
sceptical when the Dutchman, who used as his international
standard of measurement "the eye of a louse" correctly observed
that there are about eight million bacteria in every drop of
drinking water.

Really useful
One of the first inventions lodged at the British Patents Office
was a device for flushing out the Loch Ness monster with a
series of electric shocks.

What a lovely daughter!
Inspired by the belief that the sixteenth-century world would
beat a path to the door of the man who could build a better rack,
the most ingenious method of torture ever created by an
Englishmen was invented by Sir Leonard Skeffington,
Lieutenant of the Tower of London. The regular rack was a
large heavy device, awkward to use, and took up a lot of space
and couldn't be easily transported. In 1534 Skeffington came up
with a cute little contraption which folded the victim in on
himself, rather like a human trouser press. The whole body
would be slowly folded in two until the victim's chest burst and
his lifeblood was squeezed out of his hands and feet, or he
confessed, whichever came first. The device became known as
Skeffington's Daughter.

Cracked Actors

Working girl
When the 1940s Hollywood starlet Frances Farmer was arrested following a drink-drive charge, she signed her occupation as "cocksucker".

And for my next death . . .
The incomparable Robert "Romeo" Coates (1772–1848) is regarded as the worst professional actor ever to grace the English stage. Coates was a late bloomer when he first trod the boards at the age of 37 in 1809, but it was his debut performance in *Romeo and Juliet* in the spa town of Bath about a year later that earned him his first serious notices; from the moment he made his entrance wearing a sequin-spangled cloak, vast red pantaloons and enormous plumed hat, it became obvious to all that they were witnessing a unique talent. Coates was convinced that Shakespeare's original ending was too tame; on one occasion the audience sat open-mouthed as Romeo appeared wielding a crowbar, trying to open Juliet's tomb. If a particular scene went well with the audience, or so he thought, he would think nothing of replaying the scene three or four times over. One of his death scenes was received with such a great ovation that Coates jumped up, took a bow, then "died" all over again. Not even the sound of his audience baying with laughter during a death scene could put him off his stride. At a performance in Richmond, Surrey, he caused several people to laugh so hard that they had to be carried outside and receive medical treatment. Coates died in 1848, aged 75 when he was struck by a London taxi.

Unnatural Causes

Arboreal centenarian
Margaret, wife of the Irish peer Thomas, twelfth Earl of
Desmond, was remarkable for her longevity. According to a
seventeenth-century historian, she died tragically at the age of
one hundred and twelve in 1604 as a result of falling from a
tree.

Who's the dummy?
In 1976 a "dummy" corpse hanging by a noose in a Long Beach,
California Amusement Park turned out to be the real thing. The
figure had been part of a fun-house exhibit for five years until
officials at the park made their gruesome discovery during the
filming of an episode of the *Six Million Dollar Man* TV series.
A cameraman was busily adjusting the arm when it fell off,
revealing a protruding human bone. The corpse, wrapped in
gauze and sprayed with paint, had been bought by the amusement park from a local wax museum, and was never identified.

Joke of the Day
Just before the Ark sets
sail, Noah sees his two
sons fishing over the
side. "Go easy on the bait," he says,
"Remember I've only got two
worms."

Well, I'll die now!
So great was the dread of premature burial in the nineteenth
century that over 200 books were written on the subject and
societies were formed to prevent it. Colonel Edward Vollun of
the US Army Medical Corps offered a practical solution.
Anyone buried without an autopsy, suggested the Colonel,
should be interred with a bottle of chloroform within easy reach
so that if that person should find themselves in the unfortunate
situation of being buried alive, he could commit suicide with the
minimum fuss.

Way to go
Allan Pinkerton, founder of the Pinkerton detective agency, died
of gangrene, after tripping and biting his tongue.

Lucky they hit him at all
Maximilian I, Emperor of Mexico, was shot in the face by a
revolutionary firing squad full of poor shots in 1867.
Afterwards, parts of his body were auctioned off to souvenir
hunters.

Drink can damage your health
When the seventy-eight-year-old Roman Emperor Tiberius fell
ill and lapsed into a coma in 37 AD everyone thought that he was
dead. Just as the court officials were congratulating his young
nephew and successor Caligula, Tiberius sat up and asked for a
drink. Caligula sent his chamberlain in to finish the job off by
smothering the old man with his bedclothes.

An end fit for heroes?

The "processing" of human corpses to create raw material was a British, not a Nazi, invention. On 18 November 1822 *The Observer* reported that the Napoleonic battlefields of Leipzig, Austerlitz and Waterloo had been "swept alike of the bones of the hero and of the horse which he rode" and hundreds of tons of the bones had been shipped to Yorkshire bone-grinders to make fertilizers for farmers. After the siege of Plevna in 1877 a local newspaper farming column casually reported that "thirty tons of human bones, comprising thirty thousand skeletons, have just landed at Bristol from Plevna".

Crouch dead upright

Until 1788 bodysnatching was not a criminal offence: you could however be prosecuted for the theft of the coffin. The undisputed king of the English bodysnatching fraternity was Ben Crouch, who made and lost a fortune from his sales of stiffs to London surgeons. After a long career Crouch was finally found dead sitting upright in a bar near Tower Hill, London.

Two to three guineas for a large small

During the "golden age of bodysnatching" in early 19th-century Britain, the going rate for a corpse was two to three guineas for a body over three feet long, and a guinea or less for dead children or tiny babies, known respectively in the trade as "large smalls" and "foetuses".

Time-share graves

In Belgium, buried corpses are dug up after a few years so that someone else can use the grave.

Into thin air

When the Stevenage grocer Henry Trigg died in 1724 he left
curious instructions to keep bodysnatchers away from his
corpse. His coffin was placed in the rafters of his barn, where it
remained on view for almost 250 years while the premises
changed hands; over the years they were used as an inn, and
later a bank. When the coffin was finally taken down and
opened it was found to be empty: it seems the "resurrection
men" may have got to him after all.

One way to do it

King James I tried to kick-start the British wool trade by making
it compulsory for everyone to be buried in a pure woollen
shroud. The law wasn't repealed until 1814.

Resurrection stones and iron grilles

In order to protect their newly buried dead from the
"resurrection men", Britain's graves were often booby-trapped
or manned by armed guards, and consequently many medical
students were injured by spring-guns or trip wires. The most
drastic measure taken was that by a bereaved parent from
Edinburgh who had a landmine placed on his daughter's grave.
One of the most effective methods, often used in Scotland, was
to have a huge slab of granite over a ton in weight lowered on to
the grave with a block and tackle until it was no longer needed.
In Yorkshire a so-called Resurrection Stone was hired out to the
bereaved at a guinea a fortnight. Another popular security device
was the iron mortsafe – a heavy iron grille which was lowered
onto the coffin, forming a cage around it. As soon as the body
was sufficiently decomposed for the danger to have passed, it
was loaned to the next customer.

If at first . . .

In June 1988 in the Ukrainian village of Zabolotye, a funeral wake was held for a man who had died of poisoning from drinking black market industrial spirit. Unwisely the very same drink was served at the wake, resulting in ten more deaths.

Death decor

For generations the walls of the Convent of Capuccini in Palermo, Sicily, have been traditionally decorated with human cadavers, strung up fully dressed in their normal clothes. The convent is now a major tourist attraction and the nuns will even sell you a postcard on the way out.

1,800th anniversary

The preserved body of "Lindow Man", an Iron Age corpse recovered from a peat bog in the North of England, was dubbed Pete Marsh by the press when it was discovered in 1986. Peat bogs offer excellent opportunities for preserving human tissue, as a northerner discovered to his eternal regret in 1988. When a woman's head was found in the bog he walked into a local police station and confessed that he'd murdered his wife. By the time that archaeologists had figured out that the leathery relic had been lying there since the second century, it was too late for him to change his mind.

The bigger they are, the faster they decompose

Fat corpses decompose more quickly than thin ones. The extra flab insulates and retains body heat, speeding the bacterial action which breaks down body tissue.

URBAN MYTHS
True or False – you decide

TECUMSEH'S CURSE

There is a legend that a death curse from a Native American Indian afflicts American presidents elected in years divisible by twenty.

The origins for this stem from the fact that with one exception, since 1840, Presidents who have been elected in such years have died of natural causes or have been killed while serving their terms. The one exception, Ronald Reagan, came within inches of death when an assassin shot him.

The following presidents died from the "Curse":

William Henry Harrison, elected in 1840, died aged 68 after giving his inaugural address on a cold, drizzly day without wearing a coat. Harrison spoke for nearly two hours, became ill, and died from pneumonia in April 1841, exactly one month later.

Abraham Lincoln, elected in 1860, was assassinated by John Wilkes Booth in 1865 shortly after being re-elected for a second term in office. James A. Garfield was elected in 1880. In July 1881, he was shot from behind in a Washington station waiting room - he died of his wounds in September 1881.

William McKinley was elected in 1896 and again in 1900. He was shot in September 1901, after giving a speech in Buffalo, while shaking hands with members of the public. He died just over a week later.

Warren G. Harding, elected in 1920, was killed by a stroke (or heart attack) in 1923. A rumour that his wife had murdered him did the rounds soon afterwards.

Franklin D. Roosevelt, elected for his third term in 1940, suffered a massive cerebral haemorrhage and died in 1945 – this was soon after he started his unprecedented fourth term in office.

John F. Kennedy was elected in 1960. He was assassinated in Dallas in 1963 – the official explanation was that Lee Harvey Oswald was the marksman, although many conspiracy theories have emerged that give alternative explanations.

Ronald Reagan, elected in 1980, managed to cheat the curse by inches when a bullet fired by John Hinckley just missed his heart in 1981.

The story goes that Tecumseh placed a curse on the Great White fathers after he was defeated by William Henry Harrison in the Battle of Tippecanoe in 1811.

Prostitution and undertaking
Apart from prostitution, undertaking is the world's most recession-proof industry. The world's largest undertaking business, Services Corporation International of Houston, Texas, has an annual turnover of around $600 million.

 Don't worry, be happy
Reflect upon your present blessings, of which every man has plenty; not on your past misfortunes, of which all men have some.
Charles Dickens, 1812–70

Something is rotten in the state of . . . England
Queen "Bloody" Mary's widowed husband Philip of Spain literally rotted to death. In 1598 he fell ill with a fever after a large tumour appeared on his thigh. The court surgeon lanced it, but the infection spread and soon the king's entire body was covered with huge, festering boils. He lay in bed in agony, allowing no one near enough to touch him, let alone change his bandages or place a bedpan under him when he had a bowel movement, and so the king lay for days in his own excreta. The stench from his body became increasingly unbearable until the poor maids who spoon-fed him had to cover their mouths with handkerchiefs, but the cowardly court doctors still refused to allow his servants to move him or change his bedclothes. Soon maggots began to appear in the king's open sores, but when his doctors tried to clean the vermin out he screamed in pain and the doctors retreated again. Eventually the king's body began to putrefy and when he became too weak to put up an argument the physicians moved in and tried to clean him up by applying live

leeches to the wounds. The rotting process was so awful that an eye-witness said that "all that could be seen of His Majesty . . . were his eyes and his tongue." After nearly eight weeks Philip died aged seventy-one.

POTTY
WISDOM
CHINA

After being struck on the head by an axe, it is a positive pleasure to be beaten about the body with a wooden club.

Final curtain call
When Enrico Caruso died in 1921 the great Italian opera singer was laid to rest on show in a glass coffin, allowing his hordes of fans to ogle his corpse for the next five years. Five years and several new suits later his widow decided to give him a more dignified internment in a private tomb.

Strangulation, ma'am, or burial alive?
In Fiji it was once traditional for bereaved wives to be strangled or buried alive with their deceased husbands. A similar custom once prevailed in New Guinea, whereby the widow would request strangulation so that she could accompany her husband on his passage to the next world.

ANIMAL NEWS Dump dining

In the *Cape Cod Times Restaurant Guide* an establishment called "The Sea Gull Café" is listed. According to the description, the café features American cuisine, outdoor dining, and an open buffet. It is open all year round. Unfortunately this pleasant eating place is a hoax played upon the paper: the address given is that of the city's rubbish dump.
National Enquirer

Skeletons in the cellar

The Jivaro people of South America bury their women and children under their floorboards. The men however are placed in a sitting position in a hut, then the corpse and the hut are set ablaze.

From the freezer to the law court

Robert Nelson was the president of a US company which offered a cryogenics service, preserving in capsules of liquid nitrogen the bodies of people prepared to pay out large sums of money in the hope that one day science will find a cure for death. In 1981 Nelson and an employee Joseph Klockgether were successfully sued for fraud by relatives of their clients and ordered to pay $1 million in damages after admitting that they had allowed their freeze-dried loved ones to thaw out.

Not gone, just suspended

In Irian Jaya, Indonesia, deceased leaders and persons of great power were slowly smoked over a fire for several months then hung from the eaves of their houses. From this position they could keep a benevolent eye on the family home for possibly hundreds of years.

Gay funerals
The world's first exclusively gay funeral parlour was opened in San Francisco in February 1984.

You dead yet?
British undertakers got a bad name in the eighteenth and nineteenth centuries for their anti-social practice of mounting a watch on the door of a seriously ill person in anticipation of a new customer.

Care in the community
The Black Death was so called because victims turned black after bleeding into their skin. There were three main main types of plague, of which the most commonplace were pneumonic, the swift death breathed from person to person, and bubonic, which resulted in festering, stinking "buboes", when the lymph glands in the groin and armpits became swollen like rotten peaches. Plague victims in London were often mugged by the nurses sent out to care for them. Some of the more impatient nurses strangled their victims or would rub infected pus into healthy people to ensure another pay day. The physician Nathaniel Hodges described how a greedy nurse hovered around an infected household until the whole family was dead, then she systematically stripped them of their belongings, only to drop dead herself on the street outside, loaded with loot.

Cannibalism, yes – cremation, no
Some South American Indians ate the bodies of their deceased parents, but regarded cremation as a revolting sacrilege.

Remind me to have a word with the undertakers . . .
When Queen Mary attended the funeral of her brother Adolphus, who died in 1927, neither she nor the rest of the mourners could have failed to hear her brother's body explode noisily inside his coffin during the funeral procession.

You don't want to know what they do to the bodies of their enemies
Masai tribesmen leave their deceased relatives out in the open for the hyenas to feed on.

The embalmer's art
When the united Italy's first ever monarch King Victor Emmanuel II died, Rome's daily paper *Opinione* wrote a "live" eye-witness report on the state of their freshly deceased king: "He lies with his face turned slightly to the left. His eyes are closed and his appearance, maintaining a certain look of pride, has taken on an aspect of calm which is enhanced by his natural pallidness. At 7 pm this evening the embalming of the royal corpse will begin." *Opinione* went on to assure readers that the embalming process would guarantee that "the mortal remains of the appearance of our beloved sovereign will be conserved for the benefit of prosperity". This confidence was sadly misplaced: the old king's natural pallidness turned very rapidly into a very natural smell as he quickly decomposed in his new general's uniform, forcing attendants to flee with handkerchiefs covering their noses.

No corpses
Funerals in the US tend to be a lot more sanitized than their European equivalents, because Americans don't like to dwell on what they consider to be the unnecessarily distressing aspects of death. This has been taken to its logical conclusion in California

where it is increasingly commonplace for even the corpse to be
excluded from the funeral.

Stiff arm
When King Francis I of Naples died aged fifty-two, custom
decreed that the royal corpse lay in state in an elaborate cask for
three days. On the third night the two sentries on duty beside
him were startled by a thud. They had a quick peek inside the
cask then ran screaming into the night. Apparently one of the
king's arms had dropped off.

**Thought
for the Day**

Timing has an awful lot
to do with the outcome
of a raindance.

All together now
Some Australian aborigine tribesmen traditionally lacerated
themselves at funerals as a mark of respect for the dead, while
widows would burn their breasts, arms and legs with firebrands.
Occasionally things got so completely out of hand that a
mourner would join the deceased for a double funeral.

Being unhappy makes you unhappy
In 1994 researchers at Ohio State University published their
findings, that bereavement is bad for your health.

Livening up evensong
Under the cover of darkness, on the evening of 22 October 1928
the remains of eight unidentified members of the British royal
family were quietly removed from the royal vault of St George's
Chapel, Windsor and re-interred at Frogmore. It was rumoured
that the coffins were considered a liability after one of them had
exploded during evensong.

Dig up your dead
In rural Greece the women of the family are required to dig up
the bones of their deceased after five years has elapsed and
examine them to see if they are clean enough to be placed in the
communal ossuary.

The fatal king
The ritual governing the French court at Versailles was as strict in
death as it was in life. Within minutes of the expiration of a member
of the French royal family, the royal bedroom would turn into a
crowded abattoir, as six or seven physicians performed an autopsy
on the spot before an audience of lords- and ladies-in-waiting. The
body was slowly cut to pieces, the head sawn open and examined
and the royal entrails placed aside on silver salvers. The doctors
would then make notes and pronounce their verdict on the cause of
death. The death of King Louis XV was an exceptionally traumatic
experience even by Versailles standards. A handful of courtiers,
bound by their official duties, were forced to remain on duty in the
infected sick room while a terrible stench was given off by the
suppurating pustules of the king's body, which was already
beginning to decay at an alarming rate. The corpse had quickly
reached such a state of putrescence that the doctors didn't dare
embalm him. Labourers had to be forcibly commandeered to place
the body in a lead coffin, which was filled with quicklime,

camphorated spirit and aromatic herbs, and quickly sealed. Even then the smell was so overpowering that the pages escorting the hearse had to cover their faces. The king's rotting remains were said to have been so horrible that one of the workmen paid to place them in the box is said to have died from a fit of uncontrollable vomiting.

Playing safe
Australian aborigines in Queensland traditionally removed the knee-caps of the dead to prevent them from returning from the grave.

No fool like a cold fool
An American company who promise immortality through cryogenics offer to keep you hanging around in a vat of liquid nitrogen until a cure is found for a mere $100,000. For less wealthy optimists they also do a "budget" deal: a mere $35,000 will entitle you to have only your head frozen. The company claims that your head contains important genes and memory cells from which the rest of the body can be re-grown.

If the vampires don't get you, the garlic will
In 1973 the body of a Pole, Demetrius Myiciura, was discovered at his home in Stoke-on-Trent. The coroner recorded that he had accidentally choked to death on the clove of garlic he habitually slept with in his mouth to ward off vampires.

Superman ambitions on ice
Twenty-four-year-old Arthur Mandelko had spent a month inside his fridge wearing a Superman costume when his landlord found his frozen corpse in 1970. The landlord explained that Mandelko had long believed he was Superman and spent most evenings

jumping from one roof to another. He was forced to stop this activity when neighbours complained about the thumping sounds.

The Battle Of The Bulge 1944

HEROES

On 16 December Hitler flung his last reserves of 250,000 men and 1,100 tanks into a desperate attempt to strike through the Ardennes and take the ports of Liège and Antwerp, in order to split the Allied forces in the north from those in France with the vain hope of then "rolling-up" the front line. Though checked by the US 5th Corps in the north, the violence of the assault threw back the US 1st Army and 8th Corps. But after the Germans had reached Bastogne in the west on 20 December, they were halted in the south by the US 4th Infantry and 9th Armoured. Patton's 3rd Army then attacked the southern flank of the Germans' salient – the "bulge" – and the German push to the west was halted in front of the Meuse by the British 29th Armoured and American 2nd Armoured. Bastogne was then re-taken, and Allied bombers smashed the German convoys to cut off their supply lines. In January a concerted counterattack pushed the Germans back, and, having failed to re-take Bastogne, they retreated. By the end of January they were back to their starting point, at a cost of 70,000 casualties, 50,000 prisoners, 600 tanks and 1,600 aircraft. The Allies lost 77,000 killed and wounded.

The most famous grave-robber of them all

Leonardo da Vinci was a secret grave-robber and until Pope Leo X put a stop to it, dissected more than a hundred corpses. Da Vinci's resurrectionist activities were undiscovered until the beginning of the twentieth century when his unpublished anatomical studies were revealed for the first time. His *Mona*

Lisa and his *John the Baptist*, which feature the same model, may both have been self-portraits.

Of course it fits, sir
Until the second half of this century, coffins were rarely made to measure. If the body didn't fit the coffin the undertaker would simply break the corpse's ankles and bend the feet back.

Going in style
The nineteenth-century Sussex MP John "Mad Jack" Fuller (1752–1834) builder of follies, declined a conventional burial because of his morbid fear of being eaten by his own relatives. He reasoned, "The worms would eat me, the ducks would eat the worms, and my relatives would eat the ducks." Instead, Fuller had a pyramid shaped mausoleum constructed in which he sits in an armchair wearing a top hat and holding a glass of claret.

"I am recovering well from my fatal wounds . . ."
The author, poet and soldier Robert Graves achieved a unique "double" when he survived World War I and his own obituary. In 1916 Graves was badly wounded in France and left for dead. He was found alive but unconscious the following day and was taken to hospital. By that time however the army's well-oiled bereavement system had already written him off, and his distraught mother was informed that her son had been killed in action. She received the standard letter of condolences, and an announcement was made in *The Times*. Graves responded with his own formal announcement to *The Times*, informing friends that he was recovering nicely from the wounds which had recently killed him. Graves was highly amused to find that some of his worst enemies had written fond tributes to his mother about him.

My ex-husband, the grave-robber
During the reign of Constantine the Great, one of the very few grounds on which a woman could obtain a divorce was if her husband was a grave-robber.

Left . . . or right?
Until 1824 suicides were banned from burial in consecrated ground, and were buried instead at a crossroads with a stake through the heart. The belief was that suicides returned as malicious ghosts unless they were tethered to one spot by a stake. If the spirit did get free, the choice of roads would confuse it.

Footloose and fancy free
The tenth Duke of Hamilton, Alexander Douglas, outbid the British Museum when he paid £11,000 for a magnificent ancient tomb which had been originally made for an Egyptian princess. Douglas housed it in a fabulous mausoleum at his ancestral home, Hamilton Palace. It wasn't until his death in 1852 that it was discovered that he was too tall to fit inside it; the only way they could get him in was by sawing his feet off.

Night of the visiting dead
A freak storm in the early 1980s washed up more than a hundred coffins from a local cemetery in Verdugo Hills, Los Angeles and onto the city streets. Rotting coffins were swept along on the crest of a mudslide and plunged corpses, some of which had been buried for decades, through windows and into houses and stores. A local newspaper photographer found one body wedged upright in the doorway of a supermarket.

Iron soup

After the Great Fire of London in 1666 the remains of the
deceased former Dean of St Paul's, John Colet, were rescued
from the cathedral where they had lain since 1509. Although
protected by a lead-lined coffin, it was noted by two gentlemen
named Wyld and Greatorex that the Dean's remains had become
cooked in his preserving fluids and had dissolved into a soupy
substance like "boiled brawne". They tasted the "soup" and
declared that it tasted "only of iron".

Head overboard!

By 1869 so few natives survived in Tasmania that when William
Lanne died he became a subject of a bizarre battle between local
scientists and London's Royal College of Surgeons. Both parties
believed that Lanne was one of the last of his race, and each was
determined to acquire the corpse for study. A doctor representing
the Royal College severed Lanne's head and stole the skull, but not
before craftily skinning it and substituting another skull to try to
delay discovery of the theft. When the Tasmanian officials realised
they had been tricked, they cut off the hands and feet to prevent the
Royal College from stealing the whole skeleton. The body was
buried, but later quietly exhumed by agents of the Royal College
and shipped off to London. Lanne's head didn't survive the
journey: it had been wrapped in leather, and was thrown overboard
when the ship's crew finally found the smell too much to handle.

The headless artist

In November 1888 the remains of the Spanish artist Francisco
Goya were exhumed from the cemetery in Bordeaux where he
had lain for sixty years in order to return him to his native
country for re-burial. When the coffin was opened however,
Goya's head was missing.

Cross robbers

Crucified criminals in the Roman empire were often liable, while still hanging on their crosses, to be mutilated by practitioners of black magic. Some historians claim that the body of Jesus was guarded after his death, not as Matthew suggests, to stop his disciples from taking him away, but to prevent graverobbers from despoiling the body of its extremities.

Stiff

Dead men can have "erections" – a condition which results from bloating, with decomposition, of the sexual organs. This fact contributed to the ancient myth of the vampire, which was generally depicted as a highly sexed creature.

Rasputin's penis

After Rasputin was variously poisoned, shot, drowned, castrated and shot again, his penis was hacked off and preserved in a small velvet lined box. The 30-cm penis is today preserved and on display in a museum of erotica in St Petersburg, Russia.

Bodies don't burn easily

Because of the high water content of the average human adult, cremation is extremely difficult without modern day furnaces. In Greece and India bodies were first wrapped in layers of animal fat to aid combustion. In India many families couldn't afford enough firewood to do the job properly and half-burned bodies were regularly thrown into the river. The City of London Crematorium in Manor Park burns around 4,600 corpses a year, making it Britain's busiest.

URBAN MYTHS
True or False – you decide

ROMAN RAILWAYS

The English railways were built by the engineers who had also previously built tramways. The tramway builders used the same jigs and tools as for building wagons - these used a particular wheel spacing. This was to avoid the wagon wheels breaking on some of the old, long distance tracks in England, by following the wagon ruts that had been left over centuries.

The first long distance straight roads in Europe (and England), were built when England was part of the Roman Empire – the Romans used them to move chariots pulled by horses. The idea of a standard gauge for wheel spacing was invented by the Romans – they kept a standard chariot wheel size so that the wheel ruts would be consistent. The same roads have been used ever since. Thus the standard railway gauge of 4 feet, 8.5 inches is derived from an Imperial Roman war chariot's specification. The final irony is that this width is equivalent to a measurement of two horse's rear ends, as Imperial Roman war chariots were designed to the width of the back ends of two war horses.

One way of showing respect

The Biami head-hunters of New Guinea never bury their dead. The corpses are left to rot on platforms in the open, and female mourners smear themselves with excrement from the bodies as a sign of respect for the deceased.

Resurrection Shuffle

Gravestones were originally intended to prevent the dead from rising. For hundreds of years gravediggers and mortuary workers have reported sightings of long-dead corpses apparently sitting up – a phenomenon due to commonplace biological, rather than supernatural causes. The human body has its own post-death system which switches on to prepare the corpse for decomposition. The corpse contains chemicals which continue to function and cause organs to contract. Muscles and tissues within the stomach and lower digestive tract are reduced, and the body arches forward into the sitting position.

The living dead

When the Russian court official Count Karnice Karnicki witnessed the premature burial of a young Belgian girl he was so shocked by the experience he tried to patent a new type of coffin which would ensure that such a mistake never happened again. His contraption involved a long tube which extended from the coffin to six feet above ground. The uppermost part of the tube led to a sealed box, while at the other end a glass ball, attached to a wire spring, was placed on the deceased's chest. The coffin was also fitted with an interior electric light bulb. The slightest movement would activate the spring, and the sealed box would fly open and release air into the coffin. At the same time a flag would extend outside the coffin, the interior light would switch itself on and a bell would ring for thirty minutes.

Legal News: Cough Up, Congress!

The descendants of Jacob DeHaven are suing the US government for 141.6 billion dollars. They claim that this is equivalent, with interest, to the 450,000 dollars that their ancestor lent to the Continental Congress for the purpose of rescuing George Washington's troops at Valley Forge.

LA Daily News

The king's cutlery

When King Henry VIII was interred in the royal vault at Windsor, a workman removed one of his finger-bones and used it to make a knife handle.

Stop that!

While Cardinal Espinosa, the prime minister to Philip II of Spain, was being cut open in preparation for embalming, he sat up and grabbed the knife out of the hand of the dissector before finally expiring.

Ensuring doctor-patient privilege

When the tenth Sultan of the Ottoman dynasty Suleiman the Magnificent was injured in the field, his body was taken to a tent where his doctor struggled valiantly in the midst of battle to save his life. When the Sultan eventually died his followers were so desperate to keep it a secret that they strangled the doctor to avoid a leak before the Sultan's son Selim could be told.

A much-loved king

Queen Anne, George IV and William IV all died of cirrhosis of the liver due to alcoholism. George IV was very badly embalmed and his body became so swollen that it almost burst through the lead lining in his coffin. It became necessary for someone to drill a hole in it and let out some of the putrid air. His death was exactly like his reign, as an eye-witness Mrs Arbuthnot recorded, altogether a thoroughly unpleasant experience. *The Times* wrote, "There was never an individual less regretted by his fellow creatures than this deceased King."

Scottish gunnery
When King James II of Scotland was inspecting his troops' artillery in 1460 one of his own cannons exploded and a piece of shrapnel sliced the top of his head off.

Food for thought

Dog dumplings
The Chinese are still the world's biggest dog lovers, especially when they are fried, minced, stewed or served with chilli. Although it is now illegal to eat them, dogs in China are still divided into three traditional categories – hunting dogs, watch dogs and edible dogs. Two great favourites today are dog dumplings and braised dog in brown sauce.

A diet fit for a king
The Danish King Frederick VII lived his entire life on pea soup and bacon washed down with vast quantities of lager.

Day in, day out
Every day for eighteen years the elusive and probably late Lord Lucan ate grilled lamb cutlets for lunch.

Now, did I take my chocolate-covered garlic balls, or not?
US First Lady Eleanor Roosevelt ate three chocolate-covered garlic balls every morning. Her doctor said it would improve her memory.

MURDER AND MAYHEM

A Death Foretold

Elizabeth Short, known as The Black Dahlia, was to meet a horrible end, beaten and stabbed nearly to death and cut in half at the waist. During her early days in Hollywood, she visited a fortune teller on Hollywood Boulevard with a friend called Marjorie Graham. Marjorie recalled later that Beth Short had been in high spirits before they went to the fortune teller, but that when they left the gypsy, she seemed "saddened and uneasy". "Whatever that woman told her had disturbed Beth. She seemed to have other things on her mind the rest of the day and was depressed."

Ketchup Krazy
One hundred and seventy-eight tons of tomato ketchup are eaten daily.

This little piggy went . . .
In December 1993 a 47-stone Argentinian was rushed to hospital and placed on a respirator in an intensive care unit in a hospital in La Plata, near Buenos Aires, after he had eaten a whole piglet for dinner.

And your point is?
The Pogues lead singer Shane MacGowan, in order to demonstrate the cultural inferiority of the United States, once ate a Beach Boys album.

And champagne too?
During the Crimean War, British soldiers were supplied with a daily ration of caviar.

Famous gluttons
Excess in the appetite department has been met with astonishment since ancient times. Astydamus the Milesian Olympic athlete was once invited to a banquet for nine people and ate the ration for the entire party. Milo the Crotonian wrestler bore an ox on his shoulders for a furlong, then ate it. The extraordinary Roman Emperor Claudius Albinus was reported to have eaten for breakfast "as many apples as no man would believe, five hundred Greek figs, ten melons, twenty pounds of grapes, one hundred gnat-snappers, and four hundred oysters".

***Bocatitos*, anyone?**
During widespread food shortages in Cuba in 1994 the cat population fell by 400,000.

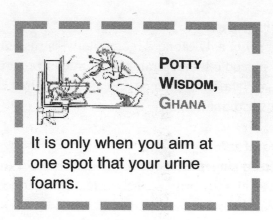

POTTY WISDOM, GHANA

It is only when you aim at one spot that your urine foams.

Sandwich-eating champion
In 2006 an American woman ate twenty-six sandwiches in ten minutes to scoop the World Grilled Cheese Eating Championship. Sonya Thomas said she was disappointed in her performance, adding that she was aiming for thirty sandwiches. She soaked her sandwiches in water to make them easier to swallow.

Survival rat-ions
The only animal excluded from the Special Air Service survival manual as a potential meal, even in the most dire of circumstances, is the common rat.

I love the way you eat that . . .
In parts of Asia fresh ape brain is still regarded as a delicacy and an aphrodisiac. The animal is killed immediately before the meal and the brains are eaten raw.

One man's meat . . .
Rat meat sausages are considered a delicacy in the Philippines.

Could this have been the beginning of the end of the relationship?
When Prince Charles and Princess Diana visited Korea in 1992 they were fed roast dog, but it could have been worse; Koreans have such a high regard for Spam that there is even a black market for it.

UFOLOGY
Witnesses to a crop circle being made

In August 1991, a British couple were present when a circle was formed. They were Gary and Vivienne Tomlinson, and they were taking an evening walk in a cornfield near Hambledon, Surrey, when the corn began to move, and a mist hovered around them. They reported a high-pitched sound. Then a whirlwind swirled around them, and Gary Tomlinson's hair began to stand up from a build-up of static. Suddenly, the whirlwind split in two and vanished across the field, and, in the silence that followed, they realized they were in the middle of a crop circle, with the corn neatly flattened.

Rodent roast
At a state dinner during the Queen's visit to Belize in 1985 she was fed roasted rodent. Royal-watchers noted that the Queen appeared to "pick" at her food.

Pesticide homicide

In 1985 a building worker in Bangkok died after eating his favourite lunch-time snack, four bags of locusts. An inquest recorded that it was the DDT in the locusts, not the locusts themselves, that had killed him.

Would you like some coal with that kettle "fur", darling?

The odd food cravings experienced by some pregnant women are caused by a temporary hormone imbalance. A survey into these odd tastes revealed cravings for jelly babies with salad cream, fried eggs on cake, lemon curd with salt and vinegar crisp sandwiches, biscuits coated with carbolic soap, potatoes smeared with mud, marzipan with pickled onions, silver paper, kettle "fur" and lumps of coal.

You didn't use the canned salmon, did you, darling?

Apart from in the comfort of your own home, the places in which you are most likely to be poisoned by food are restaurants or buffet receptions, followed by hospitals, institutions, schools and works canteens.

You must be choking!

Every year 2,500 Americans choke to death on food. It is the sixth most common cause of death in the USA.

A real short straw

"The custom of the sea" was the British navy's nineteenth-century euphemism for eating your shipmates – a legitimate and almost routine method of keeping alive when sailors were shipwrecked and starving. The order of priority on the menu was decided by the drawing of straws.

Cow cruelty
Your daily pinta comes to you from a dairy cow which is being
slowly milked to death. Dairy cows are only built to produce
about five litres of milk a day, but intensive farming often forces
them to yield five to eight times that amount. Although the cow
should have a lifespan of about thirty years, she is physically
broken and prematurely decrepit at the age of six or seven. By
this time she is considered useful only as burger plant fodder:
her head is thrown away and the rest of her goes into a giant
crusher, to be mashed into a pink slurry.

Newsflash: Pie contains steak and kidney!
A unique case of food contamination happened in October 1992,
when nine people complained that Linda McCartney's brand of
vegetarian pies had been spiked with steak and kidney.

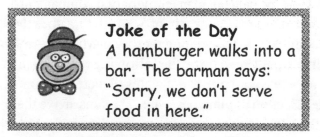

Joke of the Day
A hamburger walks into a
bar. The barman says:
"Sorry, we don't serve
food in here."

Give us this day our daily bread . . .
In Paris in 1594 during a siege by Henry of Navarre, starving
townsfolk fed themselves by making bread from the ground
bones collected from the crypt of the the Holy Innocents.

Would you like some food with your additive, sir?
The average Briton eats about 9 lb of chemical food additives
every year.

The coffin in the Frenchman

The Frenchman Michel Lotito, who worked by the stage name Monsieur Mangetout, had a unique digestive system which enabled him to make a living from eating metal, wood, glass and anything else that tickled his fancy. His diet included ten bicycles, several supermarket trolleys, 80 ft of steel chain, TV sets and a whole Cessna light aircraft. Monsieur Mangetout has also eaten a brass handled 6 ft 6 in x 3 ft coffin: according to *The Guinness Book of Records* this is the only known case of a coffin ending up inside a person.

The condom in the loaf

In March 1992 an American bread company was taken to court after a woman in Los Angeles found a used condom in a large loaf.

That's all clear then

When in 1978 the canteen management of a company in Morden, Surrey found a caterpillar in a tin of Spanish tomatoes they wrote a letter of complaint to the canning factory in Murcia. Any misunderstanding was cleared up by the following reply : "Tins are running for a line with plenty hot water til were the women are doing the selection of tomatoes, when the cans arrive there and to take off the hot water that maybe you can fine in, the same line turn off the tins so everything inside go out. One tins arrive then women full it by hand, mens tomato by tomato, so is impossible to get any foreing matter into any of our tins but if women do not so a proposal, thing that is unbelieve."

Frog cruelty

The frog's legs eaten as a traditional French delicacy are bullfrogs from the Indian sub-continent. The legs are the only valuable part of the frog, so they were traditionally ripped off while the still-living discarded torso was left to crawl away. This practice was banned in 1985 and the frogs are now killed by electric shock.

Civet dropping coffee
The world's most exclusive coffee is made from a bean which has passed through the colon of a civet cat.

Good old Victorian values
Although it is widely held that modern-day food is relatively less "natural" than it used to be, meal-times in Queen Victoria's day were a far more risky and often lethal activity because business morals in the catering industry were never lower. Deliberate food adulteration, with no effective laws to stop it and the incentive of a quick profit, grew to horrific proportions as food suppliers cheerfully ripped off and poisoned their customers at the same time. The most common well organized frauds included the use of ground Derbyshire stone instead of flour, fake Gloucester cheese coloured with red lead, baked horse offal from the knacker's yard in coffee, lead chromate in mustard and even iron bars baked in loaves to make weight. People died after eating green blancmange coloured with copper sulphate and yellow Bath buns which owed their coloration to arsenic. Fifteen people died after buying sweets from a Bradford market which were found to be laced with white arsenic. Beer drinking was possibly the most dangerous pastime of all: over 100 convictions were obtained in one year for contaminating beer with dangerously poisonous substances, including sulphuric acid which was added to "harden" new beer, and iron sulphate, added to give it a good frothy head.

Fatty paté
Paté de foie gras is produced exclusively from the livers of force-fed geese. Some geese have their feet nailed to boards while they are forced to eat 5.5 lb of salted fatty maize a day.

Slug soup and curried lice
In 1992 the London Natural History Museum re-issued a Victorian booklet called *Why Not Eat Insects?*, which included tempting recipes for slug soup, curried lice, fried wasp grub caterpillars and moths on toast. Entomologists point out that by the middle of the century food shortages will force us all to change our attitudes to what we eat anyway, so we may as well get used to the idea of popping out for a Big Mac cockroachburger.

Japanese balls
The Japanese eat dolphins' testicles as a highly prized delicacy.

Thought for the Day

The voices may not be real, but they have some pretty good ideas.

Testes on toast
Before every major Spanish bullfight there is a pre-fight "bulls' testicles on toast" party.

Rats, only one ducat each

The ancient sailors of Spain and Portugal regularly ate rat on
long voyages. The crew on board Magellan's ship during his ill-
fated attempt to circumnavigate the world sold rats to each other
for one ducat each.

Eating potatoes can seriously harm your health

When Sir Walter Raleigh brought tobacco and potatoes back
with him from the New World they got a mixed reception.
Spuds were immediately branded a health hazard because they
were supposed to caused syphilis, scrofula, flatulence and
unnatural carnal lust. Tobacco on the other hand was thought to
be completely harmless.

Twenty-eight cockroaches in four minutes

Although *The Guinness Book of Records* now refuses to publish
unusual gastronomic records, acknowledging that such feats are
not only very dangerous but also in dubious taste, it hasn't
stopped people from trying. Records held include the eating of
cooked dog (3 lbs of dog meat in 18 minutes 10 seconds), baked
beans (4 lbs 13 oz in 10 minutes), eels (2 lbs in 32 seconds),
cockroaches (28 in 4 minutes), earthworms (60 in 3 minutes
6 seconds), raw eggs (13 in 1.4 seconds), live maggots (100 in
5 minutes 29 seconds) and slugs (12 in 2 minutes).

Famous vegetarians

One of the most persistent arguments in favour of vegetarianism
was that a meatless diet bred peace-loving, gentle people. That
was until the Second World War when it was discovered that
both Hitler and Mussolini were vegetarians.

The final . . . screwdriver
In 1998 Turkish surgeons removed twenty-seven screws, twenty
nails, a screwdriver, six magnets and several pieces of wire from
the stomach of twenty-year-old Cem Demeza after he
complained of stomach ache. The handyman from Ankara noted
later: "These things haven't given me tummy ache before. It
must have been the screwdriver."

A macaroni and cheese habit
In 1995 Rob Watkins, thirty-five, of Odessa, Ontario claimed to
have eaten 10,000 Kraft macaroni and cheese dinners over his
lifetime, including many days when he ate Kraft macaroni and
cheese for breakfast, lunch and dinner. He added, "I don't
consider it an addiction."

Headless rabbit
Cat meat is served in Belgian restaurants as *lapin sans tête*, or
"headless rabbit".

Long pig
According to people who have tried it, there is absolutely no
difference between the taste of cooked human flesh and pork.
The Fijian language makes the point succinctly: the phrase for
"pig" is *puaka dina*: the phrase for "human" is *puaka balava*,
literally "long pig".

Saliva soup
The main ingredient of the popular Chinese dish, bird's nest
soup, is saliva.

Pig cruelty
Factory reared piglets are taken from their sows when they are a couple of weeks old and made to spend the rest of their lives in a "growing section", where boredom leads to aggression and often cannibalism against other pigs. When the pigs are moved to larger pens the shock often kills them.

Anti-flatulence biscuits
Digestive biscuits were originally made in 1892 as an aid to control flatulence.

Melt-in-your-mouth meat
Meat starts to rot the moment the animal has been killed. The practice of hanging meat is done to allow the bacteria to break down the tissue and cellular walls: the more rotten and decomposed a piece of meat is, the more it will melt in your mouth.

Turnip sex
Whenever you find a hole in a turnip, you may want to pause to consider the female turnip eelworm, which mostly lives inside the vegetable. You may wish to consider also the male of the species, which mates with her by poking his penis through a hole in the turnip skin.

I can see clearly now the battle is won . . .
To help them see better, Maoris ate the eyes of men they slew in battle.

Oops!
The puffer fish, considered a great delicacy in Japan, is lethal if it is not cooked and prepared in precisely the right way and no chef with less than three years' experience is allowed to serve it.

Killer Cans
The Botulism bacterium *Clostridium botulinum* can resist being boiled at temperatures of 212° F and produces a fatal toxin in canned products. One ounce of the germ could theoretically kill one hundred million people.

Tasty morsels
Chihuahuas were originally bred by the Chinese for their meat.

Killer cooking oil
The single biggest ever case of mass food poisoning occurred in Spain in 1981. Cooking oil manufacturers Ramon and Elias Ferrero along with thirty-six other company executives were convicted on 585 counts for their part in the deaths of 600 people, by contaminating their product with "denatured" industrial colza or rapeseed oil. The Ferreros and their colleagues were jailed for a total of 60,000 years.

A bit of lead helps the food go down
The ancient Romans put lead in their food to make it easier to digest.

Fatal food
10,000 Britons suffer from food poisoning every week and 100 people die from it every year.

Lions' balls
In Regency London the rich and fashionable ate lions' testicles for their alleged aphrodisiac properties.

Don't worry, be happy
Use what talents you possess. The woods would be very
silent if no birds sang there except those that sang best.
William Blake, 1757–1827

Vermin cuisine
When crops failed all over Europe in the early fourteenth
century troops were posted on gibbets in France and Germany to
prevent people from rushing the gallows and cutting down and
eating the corpses of hanged criminals. In England the famine
was so great that horsemeat was considered a delicacy suitable
only for noble tables. Most ordinary people ate dogs, cats and
vermin.

A "good" death
A "good" English butcher, while slitting the throat of a pig,
would make sure that it died slowly because a lengthy bleeding
improved the flavour of the meat. At one time it was common
practice for butchers to whip sheep and pigs to death because it
was supposed to make the meat more tender.

A glass of tap water, please
The parasite cryptosporidium which can cause severe diarrhoea,
occurs naturally in British tap water. About 10,000 cases are
reported every year, including about 2,000 requiring hospital
treatment.

URBAN MYTHS
True or False – you decide

MUSSOLINI MADE THE TRAINS RUN ON TIME

All political leaders, even tyrants such as Italian dictator
Benito Mussolini, need public support, because power
ultimately derives from public support. One way to gain
public support is to do something that clearly benefits
them. Other than that, the next best thing is to persuade
them that you *have* done something that benefits them, true
or not (here lie the origins of political spin). This is the
case with Mussolini and the Italian railways.

After the "march on Rome" in October 1922, which
resulted in King Vittorio Emanuele anointing Mussolini as
Prime Minister, Mussolini needed to convince the Italian
people that fascism was a system that would benefit them
directly. This led to the myth of fascist efficiency, which was
symbolized by the train. The story was put out that Mussolini
had turned round the ramshackle Italian railway system,
making it into one that would be envied across Europe, with
trains that were dependable, punctual and clean.

There was only a fragment of truth in this. The Italian
railway system had become very run-down after the
1914–1918 war. It did improve a good deal during the 1920s,
but most of the repair work had actually been performed
before Mussolini's fascist party came to power. And the
fabled punctuality of the trains was simple propaganda, not

borne out by passengers who actually used the system at the time – in fact the trains were as late as they ever had been. This myth came to be remembered as the "one saving grace" of Mussolini. Sure, he may have been a tinpot despot who became involved in ruinous wars, bullied, tortured and imprisoned many of his own people and political opponents; but "at least he made the trains run on time." There could hardly be a better example of how a good story tends to survive longer than the actual facts.

The cocoa moth

Ephestia Elutella, more commonly known as the cocoa moth, lives in chocolate. It reaches the chocolate factory hidden in the raw materials and lays eggs in the finished goods which in turn produce worms.

Steamed camel, with all the trimmings

A recipe once favoured by Indian princes involved the following: take one whole camel, and put a goat inside it. Stuff the goat with a peacock, which in turn should be stuffed with a chicken. Stuff the chicken with a sand grouse, the sand grouse with a quail, and the quail with a sparrow. Put the camel in a hole in the ground and steam.

Never on a Sunday

In Iraq it is illegal to eat snakes on a Sunday.

Maggot meals

The Chinese diet could soon include maggots from the common house fly. Scientists at Beijing's Agricultural University have

developed a high-nutrition, low-fat maggot and are currently
negotiating with food and pharmaceutical firms to put them into
mass production. Evidently, just 35 ounces of maggots produces
17.5 oz of pure protein and 7 oz of low-fat oil and amino acids,
and one fly can produce millions of maggots every week – just
the thing when you've got 1.2 billion mouths to feed.

A spider sandwich

In the 1830s doctors tried to cure consumption by handing out
pills made from cobwebs. Today, Kentuckians eat spiders on
bread and butter as a cure for constipation.

POTTY WISDOM, FRANCE

He who fondles you more than
usual has either deceived you
or wishes to do so.

Drugstore ketchup

Tomato ketchup was first sold in the USA in 1830 as a patent
medicine.

The Dancer in the Rye

In the Middle Ages an outbreak of mass hysteria known to
contemporaries as "dancing mania" , caused men and women to
dance around, screaming and begging to be freed from demons
inside them. It was in fact probably caused by food poisoning. A

mould called ergot would often infect bread made from rye, and contained small amounts of LSD, which in turn caused hallucinations. A similar outbreak of ergot poisoning took place in France in 1951.

Baker's top ten
The ten most gruesome foreign bodies reported found in a British loaf are: human toenail (Humberside, 1989); a whole mouse (Preston, 1980); a toupée (Humberside, 1975); surgical support hose (Glasgow, 1977); a glass eye (Bristol, 1972); a rat's tail (Stoke-on-Trent, 1887); rat excrement (East Staffordshire, 1976); half an adult rat (Plymouth 1988); 3 feet of soiled bandage (Tayside, 1986); a condom (West Midlands 1988).

Famous for fifteen minutes
Andy Warhol predicted that in the future everyone would be famous for fifteen minutes, but some people aren't prepared to wait that long. In 1994 the Channel 4 TV programme *The Word* put to the test their cynical hypothesis that some of their viewers were stupid enough to do just about anything to get on to British television for about forty-five seconds. They were absolutely right. In spite of an increasingly nauseating range of gastronomic tasks devised by the show's production team there was no shortage of takers. Some of the more vivid highlights included a girl who was required to place a live garden slug in her mouth, a student called Adam who was shown eating a quarter of a pound of lard, and another who ate from a bowl of breakfast cereal liberally laced with human veruccas, corns and toenail clippings. The feature arguably reached a nemesis when viewers saw a twenty-year-old named Chris eat into a very live worm buttie.

Love Hurts

The long and the short and the tall . . .
According to the Kinsey Institute, the biggest erect penis on record measures thirteen inches. The smallest is 1 inch.

Not soon enough
Hitler and Mussolini probably both had syphilis. Churchill didn't, but his father Randolph did.

We pray for tall, straight crops
Circumcision probably began as a harvest ritual. Some ancient peoples believed that the penis contained magical life-giving properties, and regularly planted cut off foreskins in their fields to produce better crops.

Spoilsports
There are now twenty-five known types of venereal, or sexually transmitted, diseases which are harmful to mankind, variously caused by viruses, bacteria, parasites, mites, yeasts, chlamydiae and fungi.

ANIMAL NEWS Frozen Zoo
The Anderson Hospital and Tumour Institute in Houston, Texas, has cell cultures of over 300 rare animals stored in liquid nitrogen in preparation for the day when gene science will allow them to be cloned into complete specimens.
Daily Courier Democrat

Start now!
Given the average frequency of sexual intercourse, it would take a typical couple more than four years to try every one of the five hundred and twenty-nine positions described in the *Kama Sutra*.

The Elixir of Youth
A seventy-two-year-old doctor caused a sensation in 1889 when he gave a lecture to the French Society of Biology claiming to have discovered the elixir of youth. Dr Charles Brown-Séquard described how he chopped and ground up the testicles of puppies and guinea pigs, then injected himself with the resulting compound. He announced that he was now physically thirty years younger and boasted that he was able to "visit" his young wife every day without fail. The lecture caused a stir in the medical establishment, albeit briefly. Soon afterwards his wife left him for a younger man, and shortly after that the doctor dropped dead from a cerebral haemorrhage.

Vengeful king
The first Hanoverian to ascend the British throne, George I, divorced his wife then had her locked up in a German castle for thirty-two years. His particularly vindictive approach to separation was probably because she had infected him with syphilis and he wanted revenge.

Stretch or cheat
The Caramoja tribe of northern Uganda tie a weight on the end of their penises to make them longer. The Mambas of New Hebrides cheat by wrapping theirs in yards and yards of cloth, making them look up to 17 inches long.

Foreskin royale

King Louis XVI of France did not consummate his marriage
with Marie Antoinette until nearly seven years after their
wedding day because of a freak disorder of the royal penis.
Louis suffered from an abnormally overgrown foreskin – a
major drawback which made erections painful and sex
completely out of the question. He reluctantly agreed to undergo
corrective surgery, and lost his virginity on his twenty-third
birthday.

VD extra

During the First World War, one in three British servicemen
suffered from venereal disease – a much higher percentage than
other European nations, largely because the British soldier alone
was completely denied counselling on the avoidance or
treatment of the disease. Not that too many soldiers minded: as
VD was usually a passport away from front-line service, many
tried to catch it deliberately. Back in England, prostitutes found
they could charge Tommies extra because they offered the hope
of invaliding them out of service. Some soldiers were caught
selling venereal discharge to their comrades, while others
deliberately infected their eyes, unwittingly risking permanent
blindness.

Penis Locking and Lacerating Vaginal Insert

The US Patents Office currently holds plans for five anti-rape
devices designed to horribly mutilate the assailant. In 1977
inventor Charles Barlow of Arizona patented a device designed
to be inserted into a woman's vagina. It contained three spears
with harpoon-like barbs which would embed themselves into the
penis of a would-be rapist. Anna Pennystone's anti-rape device,
patented in 1983, also involved a rigid sheath inserted into the

woman: the inside of the device was coated with adhesive and contained a pouch of chemicals which would burn the flesh. Others included Alston Levasque's "Penis Locking and Lacerating Vaginal Insert", and George Vogel's "Female Protective Device" – a large lump of metal with a solid spear in the centre. A creation devised by Joel Rumph and Lynda Warren meanwhile offers to inject the assailant's penis with a fast-working sedative thus rendering him unconscious. None of them ever got off the drawing board largely because of a basic design flaw – each device would have to be big enough to house an erect penis and would make wearing them extremely uncomfortable, not to mention highly dangerous if any of them went "off" spontaneously.

Post-coital snack

After sex, the female marine bristleworm eats her partner's sex organ.

And that comes to . . .

The most expensive one night stand in history took place in 1850. The prostitute and part-time evangelist Laura Bell, who lived in Grosvenor Square London, charged Prince Jung Badahur, Prime Minister of Nepal , £250,000 for services rendered.

You've lost that lovin' feeling

In central Europe until the late eighteenth century, if a betrothed girl died before the marriage the prospective bridegroom was expected to consummate the marriage by having intercourse with the corpse. A similar custom existed in Burma and parts of India.

Impressionism, Cubism . . . Syphilism?

Nineteenth-century Paris was such a hotbed of prostitution that for virtually every great artist and writer who lived and worked there, life-threatening social diseases were accepted as an occupational hazard. Renoir once fretted that he couldn't possibly be a genius, because unlike Manet, De Maupassant, Dumas and Baudelaire he hadn't yet caught syphilis. Paul Gauguin's best known paintings were achieved in Tahiti while he was hoping to find a cure for his syphilis in the sun.

A round of applause

The term "clap": is derived from the sixteenth-century French *clappoir*, which describes the buboes or groin swellings sported by gonorrhoea sufferers.

Le vice anglais

Thanks largely to their public school system which in the seventeenth and eighteenth centuries was described as "a charter for sodomites", the English acquired a reputation across Europe for homosexuality. In spite of this, English laws against homosexuality have always been more severe than anywhere else. In 1553 Henry VIII introduced hanging to punish "the detestable and abominable Vice of Buggery committed with mankind or beast". In France homosexuality and flagellation are still referred to as *le vice anglais* – "the English vice".

Slug love

Siberian women used to flirt with the opposite sex by lobbing slugs at them.

Porcupenis
Porcupines are capable of sex about ten times a night, all year round.

That's got to hurt
Between his first encounter with Dr Johnson in 1763 and his death thirty-five years later, Johnson's biographer James Boswell caught gonorrhoea nineteen times. His first dose was caught from a minor actress named Sally Forrester. Although Boswell was a strict Calvinist Presbyterian, he continued to sleep with prostitutes long after his marriage in 1769 and fathered five illegitimate children. In Boswell's day gonorrhoea was a much more painful and debilitating disease than it is now: the only recognized treatment up until the last century involved inserting curved metal rods into the penis.

Collect your peasants on the way out
The going pension rate for Catherine the Great's ex-lovers was about 9,000 Russian peasants apiece.

Oscar and Dorian
Oscar Wilde suffered from tertiary syphilis and was renowned for his mouthful of rotten teeth, which could have been a symptom of either the disease itself, or the mercury treatment he took for it. His novel *The Picture of Dorian Gray* was allegorical of his disease. The horrible illness Gray suffers from, the "leprosies of sin", turn him into "a monstrous and loathsome thing with hideous face, misshapen body and failing limbs" with "warped lips" and "coarse, bloated hands".

Golden showers
For a randy squirrel monkey, foreplay involves urinating in your partner's face.

Ménage à trois
The actress Sarah Bernhardt claimed a unique treble by sleeping with Edward VII, his bisexual son "Eddy", the Duke of Clarence, and the French Emperor Napoleon III. The favourite gossip around London at the time was that Ms Bernhardt and Edward VII enjoyed copulating in a special silk-lined coffin which she kept in her bedroom for special "guests". Given the King's elephantine girth it was a fair bet that she was on top while Edward played dead.

Peach bottom
During the British Raj more than half the British troops serving in India suffered from venereal disease, so commanding officers set about organizing army-run brothels containing only infection-free whores. Army quartermasters received requisitions which read "please send young and attractive women". Many of the officer classes however, ex-public schoolboys to a man, had other diversions. A popular refrain in the mess lamented: "There is a boy across the river with a bottom like a peach, but alas I cannot swim."

66,795 women
Saudi Arabia's first king Ibn-Saud is reputed to have had sex with three different women every night from the age of eleven until his death in 1953 aged 72.

Whatever floats your boat

The nineteenth-century poet Charles Swinburne admitted he once copulated with a monkey which was dressed in women's clothing.

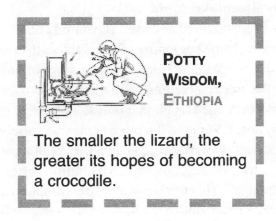

POTTY WISDOM, ETHIOPIA

The smaller the lizard, the greater its hopes of becoming a crocodile.

Biblical leprosy

Most of the people in the Bible who are described as lepers were probably syphilitic. The outward signs of advanced syphilis are almost identical to those found on lepers: Biblical "leprosy", however, was nearly always described as a highly contagious disease – a description inappropriate to leprosy but which fits syphilis perfectly. Unlike syphilis, leprosy requires prolonged body contact and a healthy person can live among lepers for years without becoming infected.

Mad King Herod

Herod, the King of Judea, probably suffered from syphilitic insanity: he was described as having private parts which were "putrefied and eaten up with worms".

Heroic harlots

For services rendered to an isolated garrison of troops in the late 1940s during the war in Indo-China, France awarded two prostitutes the Croix de Guerre.

Flying the regimental colours

Coloured, scented, textured and even flavoured condoms are not a recent invention. At the beginning of the eighteenth century Mrs Phillips of Leicester Square, London sold a range of prophylactics designed for the more discerning gentleman about town, including condoms hand-fashioned on glass moulds, in sheep or goat gut, pickled and scented. Some of the more exclusive variety were tied on at the neck with ribbons available in a variety of regimental colours. For extra-safe sex, however, Mrs Phillips offered her "Superfine Double". This double-strength contraption, about eight inches long, was advertised in the *Tatler* as "an engine for the prevention of harms by love-adventurers".

The condom laundrette

Condoms made from offal were all the rage in early-eighteenth-century London, but they were heavy and expensive passion killers and many people preferred to use the old variety made of linen, which needed to be dampened first – James Boswell used to wet his by dipping them in Hyde Park canal. Linen sheaths were also more economical because unlike the sheep gut variety you could take them to the condom laundrette in St Martin's Lane. Condom sales didn't really get a lift until Mr Goodyear vulcanised rubber in 1843.

Good branding

The US Ramses brand condom is named after the great pharaoh Ramses II who fathered over 160 children.

Venereal Disease I
During the first world war the British Army suffered 416,891 VD casualties.

Contra-contraception
The Romanian dictator Nicolae Ceaucescu tried to double his country's population – and economic growth along with it – by completely banning all forms of contraception. Romanian women were forced to undergo monthly body searches to prove that they weren't secretly using contraceptive devices.

Starting young
The poet Lord Byron had sex with his nanny when he was nine years old.

Thought for the Day

Sex is not the answer. Sex is the question. "Yes" is the answer.

Anything to confess?
Like most Bourbons the French King Louis XV had an unnaturally high sex drive, but he was terrified of catching syphilis. This was why he preferred to sleep with very young girls, some only fourteen years old, and would often bed several at a time. Before he died on 10 May 1774 Louis made his first confession to a priest for thirty-eight years: a courtier timed it at a full 16 minutes.

Duelling donors

Duelling is legal in Paraguay as long as both parties are registered blood donors.

Crabs

Pubic lice – *papillons d'amour* to the French and "crabs" to the English – are passed through sexual intercourse but don't live exclusively in pubic hair: they also like taking up residence in beards and eyelashes.

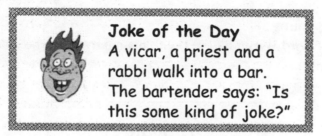

Joke of the Day
A vicar, a priest and a rabbi walk into a bar. The bartender says: "Is this some kind of joke?"

Rebel with an itch

James Dean's pubic lice were a major distraction on the set of *Rebel Without a Cause*. The film's director had to drag him away to a chemist after Dean's co-star Natalie Wood complained that he constantly scratched at his genitals.

Bleed or starve

The queen bee has sex only once in a lifetime, an arrangement with which the male bee is perfectly happy. When his job is done his organ snaps off inside her as a plug to prevent sperm leakage. He then bleeds to death. At least he dies happy: the Queen's unsuccessful suitors return to the hive to die of starvation.

Poo shoe

Two of the most popular anaphrodisiacs in medieval times were pigeon dung and snail excrement. It was also widely believed throughout Europe that a man hopelessly in love with a woman could suppress his sexual urges by placing some of her excrement in his shoe and wearing it.

Can I cut you another slice, darling?

The eighteenth-century manual *Grimorium Verum* advised the following as a useful aphrodisiac: "Go to a stews (public baths) and stay in the hottest part of it until you are sweating profusely. Dust yourself with sufficient white flour to absorb fully the sweat and then brush off the flour into a bag and take it home with you. Place the flour into a bowl, add to it clippings from your nails (finely chopped, of course), and add a few hairs from both the scalp and pubic area. Then make a cake mixture from your favourite recipe and add the previously compounded unpleasantness to it before baking. Serve it to your intended lover or mistress, who will then find your approaches irresistible."

Sip and spit

For the lucky male giraffe foreplay involves drinking the female's urine to find out whether or not she will be receptive to his advances.

Love potion

The Chinese regard black chow meat as an aphrodisiac.

URBAN MYTHS
True or False – you decide

KING JUAN CARLOS OF SPAIN ACCIDENTALLY KILLED HIS BROTHER

In 1956, two Spanish princes entered a room with a loaded gun. Only one of them came out alive. King Juan Carlos is the only person who knows what really happened on March 29th 1956. He was 18, his brother Alfonso was 14. They were on holiday at the exiled royal family's home in Estoril, Portugal.

The royal household's official statement claimed that the two princes were cleaning a revolver when it discharged, hitting Alfonso in the forehead and killing him. How the shooting came about may never be known – although Juan Carlos was said to have admitted to friends and family that he felt it was his responsibility. He had been a military cadet and knew the danger of cleaning loaded guns. The two boys had been very close throughout their childhood in exile from Franco's Spain. Hundreds of thousands of Spanish royalists risked crossing to Portugal, many carrying Spanish earth to place on Alfonso's grave. Even after Franco's death and the restoration of the monarchy, this shooting was usually referred to as a chance accident. However, staff of the royal household at the time have referred to a pistol and shotgun and the rumour persists that the full truth of the incident is not known.

PM Treat
Until the eighteenth century, many Germans believed that
menstrual blood was an aphrodisiac: women would mix some of
their menstrual blood into their husband's food and drink.

Can't keep my eyes off of you . . .
Despite being one of showbiz's best known homosexuals,
Liberace successfully sued the US magazine *Confidential* (for
$40,000) and the *Daily Mirror* (for £8,000) for implying that he
was gay. When Liberace had his final face-lift the plastic
surgeon accidentally removed so much wrinkled skin from his
patient's face that he could no longer keep his eyes closed, even
when he was asleep, and he had to use eyedrops through the
night to keep his eyeballs from drying up. Liberace later had the
face of his male lover reconstructed by plastic surgery to make
him look like his twin.

Metal nightie
In the Middle Ages the Christian Church grudgingly admitted
that sex was necessary, but drew the line at enjoying it: they
decreed that any pleasure derived from sexual intercourse was
the devil's work and contact with the female body should
therefore be reduced to the absolute minimum. The most
extreme result of this was the passion-killing *chemise cagoule* –
an armour-plated nightie with a strategically placed hole.

Tonight's the night
Stentor Coeruleus is a primitive organism capable of repro-
ducing without coupling, but after one year a male and female
enjoy a thirty-six-hour orgy which kills them both.

A Rolling Stone gathers . . . women
Former Rolling Stone Bill Wyman says he slept with over 1,000
women. Elvis Presley claimed he had slept with about 1,000
women before he married Priscilla.

One-legged lover
Sarah Bernhardt, said to have been France's finest actress, had
more than 1,000 lovers but only one leg.

Dinner for one
For many species of male spider sex is a deadly business. During
or shortly after intercourse the female mantis spider bites off her
lover's head then eats the rest of his body. The male's sex drive is
so strong he continues on the job even while he is being eaten
alive. Some female crickets have a similarly abrupt post-coital
manner. The female scorpion takes part in a touching courtship
ritual, but as soon as fertilization is successful she makes a meal of
her partner. The male wheel-web spider usually dies of exhaustion
and starvation after a marathon sex session, then the female
immediately leaps on his body and eats him. The female antlion
not only eats her partner after sex, but also any other passing male
ant she can catch. More wily male partners resort to bondage
before sex to ensure they escape with their lives. Some tropical
spiders offer their intended a pleasant-tasting secretion, taken
from a gland in the thorax – a desperate tactic to prevent the female
from killing him during copulation. The idea is that she is less
likely to eat his spermatophore if her mouth is already full.

Malodorous monk
The sex-mad monk Rasputin (the name is Russian for
"debauchee") was leader of a pseudo-religious cult called
Khlysky, which carried out orgies of bloody self-mutilation

followed by mass copulation. Rasputin is said to have bedded
every female aristocrat in St Petersburg (including in all
probability, the Czarina herself) more than once, even though he
smelled like an open sewer. He didn't believe in bathing and
often went for months without washing even his hands or face,
offering the excuse that water sapped his libido. Rasputin's body
odour was so bad that women literally bathed themselves in
perfume before sleeping with him to try to overpower it.

Le petit mort
A mouse-like marsupial called the swamp antechinus copulates
so enthusiastically that it usually drops dead afterwards from
exhaustion or starvation.

Retired at nineteen
The personal brothel of Louis XV was said to have been the
biggest ever to accommodate the needs of one man. Set in the
grounds of his palace at Versailles, it employed a huge staff and
cost £200,000 a year to maintain. The king's procurers were
expected to make a constant supply of girls aged between nine
and eighteen available for the royal bed, although it was only
during the last three years that they were obliged to be on
"active service". When the girls outstayed their welcome by
reaching the ripe old age of nineteen they were either married
off or dispatched to a convent. Over a period of thirty-four years
a steady stream of girls passed through Louis's brothel and there
was no shortage of volunteers. Families considered that a few
years of shame was a price well worth paying for the guarantee
of lifelong security for their daughters thereafter.

The love worm
Nymphomania was believed in the Far East to be the result of
worms in the vagina.

Engorged
When the female bumblebee eelworm mates it always results in
the death of the male. The female doesn't get off lightly either:
she then undergoes an incredible transformation, as her sex
organ inflates until it is 20,000 times bigger than she is. Her
body then withers away and dies.

Gropecunt Lane
London's Coppice Alley and Grape Street, both formerly
famous for prostitution, were originally called Codpiece Alley
and Gropecuntlane.

Size matters
More than 40,000 penis implant operations are performed
annually in the USA but not all are successful. One of the most
regular side-effects is Peyronie's disease, which results in a
permanently bent penis. Cosmetic surgeons in Miami offer penis
enlargement operations for as little as £2,000. Augmentation
phalloplasty will lengthen the penis by up to 1.5 inches: while
circumferential autologous penile enlargement makes a penis
thicker.

That should work
Ancient Egyptian men rubbed crocodile dung into their
phalluses to make them bigger. Elsewhere in the Middle East
some developed their own method of penis enlargement by the
application of hot pitch, leeches and the boiled private parts of
an ass.

Thirty vasectomies an hour
To celebrate the fifty-seventh birthday of King Bhumibol of
Thailand, on 8 March 1985 1,200 loyal subjects had vasectomies
performed on them by a team of sixty doctors working at a rate
of one vasectomy every two minutes.

Penis decoration
The Dayak tribe of Borneo decorate their phalluses by inserting
metal rods through them with golden balls at each end. Aboriginal
tribesmen in Australia traditionally slit their own penises open so
that they imitate the forked penis of the kangaroo.

Here's my spout . . .
Although extremely short, the artist Toulouse-Lautrec had an
enormous penis and was known to his friends as "Teapot".

Until death do us part . . .
The greatest known age difference between a married couple is
eighty-eight years; in Bangladesh in 1983, sixteen-year-old
Marium Begum became the fifth wife of one-hundred-and-four-
year-old Amin Ali Azam.

Nasty
At the turn of the century the rate of VD infection was so great
in the British Army in India – around 50% – that General
Kitchener issued a memorandum to his troops to try to stop
them from sleeping with Indian women. Venereal disease,
explained Kitchener, "assumes a horrible loathsome form . . .
the sufferer finds his hair falling off, the skin and the flesh of his
body rot, and are eaten away by slow cancerous ulcerations, his
nose falls off, and he eventually becomes blind; his throat is
eaten away by foetid ulcerations which cause his breath to

stink". There was little danger of the great general himself being tempted by the the local whores; it was widely rumoured that Kitchener shared a bed with his male military secretary.

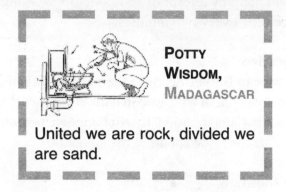

POTTY WISDOM, MADAGASCAR

United we are rock, divided we are sand.

Monkey business
In 1987 Japan's Nippon TV station reported that an actress Hitoko Tagawa had volunteered to have sex with an ape called Oliver "in the interests of research". Oliver's owner was so offended by her offer he filed a £750,000 lawsuit against the TV station.

Political oddities

The glorious Second of August
Only two people signed the Declaration of Independence on 4 July – John Hancock and Charles Thomson. Most of the rest signed on 2 August; the last signature wasn't added until five years later.

Wanted: dead or alive
In 1986 the electors of San Mateo county, California, voted in Brendan Maguire as sheriff with an overwhelming 81,679

majority. It was only after the results were announced that
someone pointed out that he had already been dead for two
years.

The dead vice-president
Although US vice-president James Sharman died of uremic
poisoning a few days before election day in 1912 he still
managed to win almost three and a half million votes. The
incumbent ticket of Taft and Sharman came in third, and
Sharman's eight electoral votes for vice-president were cast for
Nicholas M. Butler.

An explanation
In 2005 Thailand's prime minister, Thaksin Shinawatra, refused
to answer reporters' questions because the alignment of the
planets was not in his favour. "Mercury is not good, so I am
going to request not to speak until next year," he explained.

No worries
In 1974 a town in Western Australia accidentally re-elected a
mayor whose death had originally caused the election. The town
clerk was forced to admit later that this had been "a bad mistake".

Lousy elections
A novel variation on the more conventional electoral processes
was observed in the Swedish town of Hurdenburg. Once a year
the town's most eligible bearded personages would sit around
the table, allowing their beards to rest on it. A head louse was
then dropped in the middle and the person whose beard it chose
to climb into got to be mayor for the next twelve months.

The Iron Duke

The Duke of Wellington, British war hero and prime minister from 1827–28, had many affairs throughout his marriage to Kitty Pakenham. Wellington's famous retort "Publish and be damned" was his response to the blackmailer Joseph Stockdale, who threatened to print the memoirs of Wellington's favourite prostitute Harriette Wilson. Stockdale did publish and so the whole of London was able to read about the Iron Duke's prowess between the sheets, which according to the high class tart was "most unentertaining" and "very uphill work". Wellington's stance wasn't quite as brave as it is often painted: he threatened to sue for libel, but the writ did not materialize. The Duke went on to have an affair at the age of eighty-three.

Westminster shenanigans

George Canning was Britain's shortest ruling Prime Minister; he took office on 10 April 1827 and died of pneumonia just under four months later. Although he was eventually married to an heiress who gave him four children, Canning was reputedly bisexual. As a young man his name was often romantically linked with the sexually ambivalent William Pitt, the Younger. Canning was also alleged to have had an affair with King George IV's estranged wife Caroline.

Tory Antichrist

In 1995 a thirty-six-year-old Briton, David Griffiths, was expelled from the Twickenham branch of the Conservative Association after telling a meeting that he favoured the death penalty for all crimes, that homosexuals should be encouraged to commit suicide and that people who claim social security should gun each other down on the street. Griffiths returned to politics a year later however when he ran for the Twickenham seat in the

1996 general election as the Antichrist. He explained that he had been aware that he was the Antichrist for some time, but had kept quiet about it in case it damaged his career in the Conservative Party.

Oh, and I was president for a while too

Thomas Jefferson is credited with several inventions, including the swivel chair, a pedometer, a machine to make fibre from hemp, a letter-copying machine, and the "lazy susan". He wrote his own epitaph however without mentioning once that he served as President of the United States.

The height of effeminacy

The Norwich MP John Fransham (1830–1910) fought his parliamentary campaign promising to prohibit people from making their beds more than once a week. He believed that daily bed making was "the height of effeminacy".

Bennett, Wisconsin – capital of the world

In 1975 Emil Matalik put himself forward as a candidate for the US presidency, claiming there was an "excess of animals and plant life, especially trees". He advocated a maximum of one animal and one tree per family. Matalik's bid for the presidency was apparently merely a stepping stone towards his long term plan to become president of the world. "The problems of the world are building up to an explosive point," he explained. "The only solution is a world president." His choice of world capital? Bennett, Wisconsin.

Well, only one thing to hide

The American artist Louis Abalofia ran as a nudist candidate for the US Presidency in 1968. His sole item of campaign literature was a poster of him naked but for a bowler hat covering his genitalia above the slogan "I have nothing to hide". This uninhibited approach to the White House earned him 300,000 votes.

Start the day right
The American President Calvin Coolidge liked to eat breakfast in bed while having his head rubbed with Vaseline.

Bed politics
Thomas Pelham-Holles, 1st Duke of Newcastle, served as prime minister during the reign of King George II during the critical years when France and England fought over their possessions in North America. Newcastle was also a hypochondriac and was terrified of catching a cold. At the funeral of King George, the Duke of Cumberland, finding that he was unable to move, looked over his shoulder to discover that Newcastle was standing on his robes to keep his feet warm. Newcastle once visited an ailing William Pitt at his bedside to discuss important matters concerning the Seven Years War. As there was no fire in the room, Newcastle climbed, fully clothed, into a second bed. The Under Secretary entered the bedroom to find his two senior ministers shouting to each other from under the bedclothes of adjoining beds.

 ### Don't worry, be happy
You can search the world for happiness, but you won't find it. Happiness is the way you travel, not a destination.

One long bad dream

The 8th Duke of Devonshire (1833–1908), was considered one of the most staggeringly boring politicians of his era – a fact he readily acknowledged. The Duke was once caught yawning in the middle of a speech in the House of Lords; he immediately apologized, explaining that what he had to say was "so damned dull". He fell asleep everywhere – at dinner, on the stairs, in cabinet meetings. He once fell asleep in the House of Lords, woke up with a start, looked at the clock and exclaimed, "Good heavens! What a bore . . . I shan't be in bed for another seven hours!". The Duke once told of an experience he had at Westminster; "I had a horrid nightmare. I dreamed I was making a speech in the House of Lords and when I woke up I found I was!"

If at first you don't succeed . . .

Robert, Lord Clive of India, the English soldier and administrator who went to India in 1743 as a servant of the East India Company, but transferred to military service and eventually became governor of Bengal, twice failed to shoot himself in 1744. After the second attempt he declared, "It appears I am destined for something. I will live." Thirty years later however he succeeded in slitting his own throat with a pen knife.

Embrace and be damned

The eighteenth-century Tory Party leader Viscount Bolingbroke was as well known for his debauchery as his oratory. He once described a perfect day: "Got drunk, harangued the Queen, and at night was put to bed to a beautiful lady, and was tuck'd up by two of the prettiest young Peers in England, Lord Jersey and Bathurst." The radical MP John Wilkes was also an infamous and rampant bisexual. When the Earl of Sandwich once said to him, "I don't know whether you'll die on the gallows or of the pox", Wilkes replied: "That depends whether I first embrace your Lordship's principles or your Lordship's mistress."

Most corrupt prime minister ever?
Britain's first Prime Minister Sir Robert Walpole, a foul-mouthed little man with dirty clothes who only stayed awake during debates in the House of Commons by eating apples, was also possibly the most corrupt prime minister ever. He lined his pockets and those of his friends with public funds, bought contraband goods and smuggled spirits through customs.

 ## You Should Have Arrested Me!
In 1982 John Crumpton IV and Jane Berry robbed a bank in Los Angeles. While trying to escape, Crumpton was shot dead by the police and Berry was shot and seriously wounded. Subsequently, Berry decided that she would sue the police for not having arrested her on a previous warrant, thus indirectly causing her wounding.
LA Daily News

AC/DC PM
Britain's seventh Prime Minister the Earl of Bute (1762–63) was variously alleged to have had an adulterous relationship with the Prince of Wales' wife Augusta and a homosexual affair with the young King George III.

Mad as a prime minister
Most of the family of the Earl of Chatham (Prime Minister 1766–68) suffered from mental illness, and he was no different. He had several mental breakdowns and his appearances in the

House of Commons became increasingly rare and eccentric. Eventually he became a total recluse and spent all his time locked in his bedroom while food was passed to him through a hatch.

Not the first lady
The Earl of Grafton (1768–70) wasn't the first adulterous prime minister, but he was the first to flaunt his mistress in front of the reigning monarch and the first known to have slept with his mistress, Nancy Parsons, at Number 10 Downing Street.

A little stiffener
Henry Addington, British Prime Minister from 1801 to 1804, did not dare face the House of Commons until he was drunk and would prepare for his speeches by downing about five bottles of wine.

Brandy and laudanum
Lord Melbourne, Queen Victoria's first prime minister, suffered at the hands of his scandalously unfaithful wife Lady Caroline Lamb, but was also involved in two court actions brought against him by the husbands of Lady Brandon and Caroline Norton. Lord Melbourne was also addicted to flagellation and was a heavy drinker who spent Queen Victoria's entire coronation in a drunken stupor. He later offered the excuse that he was suffering from violent constipation and tried to get through the ceremony by swigging large quantities of brandy and laudanum. He didn't attend Cabinet meetings after that for a week.

Way to go

Viscount Palmerston, British Prime Minister 1855–8 and
1859–65, was an habitual womanizer who was cited as
co-respondent in a divorce case at the age of seventy-nine.
Palmerston forced himself on one of Queen Victoria's ladies-in-
waiting while he was visiting Windsor Castle. He defended his
behaviour by claiming he was blind-drunk on port and had
entered the wrong bedroom. The whole matter was hushed up, but
Victoria never believed his story nor did she forgive him.
According to rumour, he died of a heart attack while having sex
with a young parlour maid on his billiard table on 18 October
1865.

The rescuer

The Liberal Prime Minister William Gladstone spent his
evenings prowling London's brothels "rescuing" prostitutes and
used to flog himself afterwards with a whip. He admitted he was
a pushover for a pretty face and probably succumbed to
temptation more than once.

"Three-in-a-bed" Dilke

The late-nineteenth-century Liberal cabinet minister, Sir Charles
Dilke, was widely known as "Three-in-a-bed" Dilke. He
resigned his post after being named as co-respondent in a
divorce case. During the trial it was revealed that he had slept
with the young wife of a fellow MP and persuaded her to allow
his maid to join them, teaching the MP's wife "every French
vice".

URBAN MYTHS
True or False – you decide

HOW TO WORK OUT IF A MIRROR IS 2-WAY OR NOT

This story comes from a policewoman who travels the world giving personal safety seminars to businesswomen who travel alone:

When you visit a toilet or bathroom, or stay in a hotel room, or use a changing room, can you be sure that the apparently ordinary mirror on the wall is a real mirror? Or could it actually be a two-way mirror? There have been many documented cases where people have installed 2-way mirrors in female changing rooms in health clubs and clothing shops. It is very hard to positively identify the surface by just looking but this test will enable you to be certain. Put the tip of your fingernail against the surface of the mirror – if there is a gap between your fingernail and its reflection, then it is a normal mirror. But if your finger-nail directly touches the reflection of your nail, it is a two-way mirror.

"Squiffy" Asquith

Herbert Henry Asquith, Prime Minister from 1908 to 1916, admitted to "a slight weakness for the companionship of clever and attractive women": a slight understatement as he was a compulsive womanizer. At the age of sixty-two and married, he had an affair with the twenty-seven-year-old friend of his

daughter, Venetia Stanley. Asquith bombarded his young
mistress with alarmingly indiscreet love letters, sometimes three
a day, often scribbled during Cabinet meetings. He was
devastated when she jilted him for a younger man in the middle
of the Dardanelles crisis. Asquith was also a heavy drinker and
once appeared on the front bench during an important debate too
drunk to speak.

Robert Browning and Elizabeth Barrett
Robert Browning was asked by his future
wife Elizabeth Barrett, what an exceptionally
obscure passage in one of his poems meant.
Having puzzled over the passage for some time, Browning gave
up the struggle. "Miss Barrett," he said, "when that passage was
written only God and Robert Browning knew what it meant.
Now only God knows."

47,000 perverts, adulterers, nymphomaniacs, drunks and homosexuals
In 1917 the right wing MP Pemberton Billing was accused of
libelling a well known dancer by calling her a lesbian. During
his trial he claimed to have assembled a list of 47,000 perverts,
adulterers, nymphomaniacs, drunks and homosexuals in high
places. He was acquitted, and wildly applauded in court and by
thousands outside. It was believed that the judge and Prime
Minister Asquith were both on his list.

Honours for sale
David Lloyd George, Prime Minister from 1916 to 1922,
charged £10,000 for a knighthood, £30,000 for a baronetcy and
up to £100,000 for a peerage.

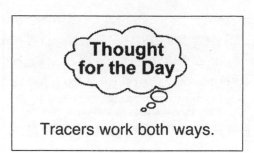

Thought
for the Day

Tracers work both ways.

The Welsh Goat

David Lloyd George (Prime Minister 1916-22) was married with
five children but, according to his son Richard Lloyd George,
where women were concerned "as much to be trusted as a
Bengal tiger with a gazelle". The "Welsh Goat" survived a
number of near-disastrous scandals. He twice bribed his way out
of being named in divorce suits, once in 1897 then again in 1909
when, in the middle of a climactic budget debate, the London
tabloid *People* revealed that he had bought his way out of being
named as a co-respondent in a divorce trial. At forty-nine Lloyd
George began an affair with his daughter's twenty-four-year-old
tutor Frances Stevenson, whom he later made his private secretary. For several years he lived a double life, spending half his
time with his wife and the other half with his mistress. The press
turned a blind eye to the affair even when she gave birth to his
daughter.

Grey lover

John Major (Prime Minister 1990–97), derided as Britain's most
boring politician, owned up to a passionate four year affair with
Tory backbencher Edwina Curry, while he was a chief whip.
Said Mrs Curry, "He may have been grey to the world, but he
was a very exciting lover."

MURDER AND MAYHEM

Murder and Mayhem: The Elusive Earl

Practically everybody but his closest friends and a few reporters are convinced that Richard John Bingham, seventh Earl of Lucan, is a murderer. The evidence is strong that on the chilly night of 7 November 1974, John Lucan burst into the expensive London townhouse occupied by his estranged wife and children, attacked and injured his wife, and killed, probably by accident, the children's nanny, Sandra Rivett. The mystery is that Lord Lucan then disappeared, and though he was one of the most sought-after men in the world, no trace of him has ever been found.

POTTY WISDOM, ROMANIA

Kiss the hand you cannot bite.

"Be men, not mannequins"

The first Labour prime minister Ramsay MacDonald (1924, 1929–35) was accused of being a class traitor when he had an affair with a leading Tory "hostess", the Marchioness of Londonderry. MacDonald began to lose his mind while he was in office, suffering from what he called "brain-fog" – probably the slow onset of premature senile dementia. As he deteriorated his speeches became more and more incomprehensible and towards the end of his career he dreaded appearing at the despatch box because he hadn't a clue what he was supposed to be talking about. At a disarmament conference in Geneva he again lost the thread of his speech and told his puzzled audience, "Be men, not mannequins."

Fair trade

Sir Winston Churchill was a major piss artist, but at least he was quite open about his problem. He once tried to persuade Saudi Arabia's strict Moslem King Ibn Saud that he drank alcohol because it was part of his religion. Although it wrecked his health and he suffered several minor strokes, he claimed, "I have taken more out of alcohol than alcohol has taken out of me."

"How is it with you, Harold?"

Prime Minister Harold Macmillan's term in office (1957–63) was bedevilled by a series of sex scandals including the infamous Profumo affair. In 1958 Macmillan's junior Foreign Office minister Ian Harvey resigned after he was caught behaving in a manner "likely to offend against public decency" with a nineteen-year-old Guardsman under a tree in St James' Park, London. On the way to the police station the MP gave a false name and tried to run off. Another prominent member of Macmillan's government Sir Ian Horobin sexually assaulted young boys after inviting them to see his stamp collection; he admitted ten charges of indecency with young men and boys at the Old Bailey in 1962. All this was taking place at a time when Macmillan's own wife was having an open affair with one of his Tory cabinet ministers, Bob Boothby. One day the US President John F. Kennedy confided to Macmillan, "If I don't get a woman for three days, I get a terrible headache . . . how is it with you, Harold?"

The toilets of Westminster

The homosexual Labour MP Tom Driberg (or "William Hickey" to *Daily Express* readers) admitted a liking for "rough trade" . When he joined the House of Commons he was given a formal tour of the "most important rooms" in the Palace of Westminster by the Tory MP Henry Channon: they turned out to be the men's toilets. Driberg, who was also on MI5's payroll, admitted using his status as British spy to get him off the hook every time the police caught him importuning in public lavatories.

Fuss about nothing

The fifty-one-year-old Parliamentary Under-Secretary of State at the Defence Ministry in Edward Heath's Tory government Lord Lambton resigned after admitting taking drugs, including opium, and regularly visiting prostitutes while married. He said later, "I can't think what all the fuss is about, surely all men patronize whores."

"Pillow biter"

Former Liberal Party leader Jeremy Thorpe's evidence during a trial in which he was accused of conspiring to murder his gay lover Norman Scott gave the English language the phrase "pillow biter".

UFOLOGY
Bender's Bureau

Albert K. Bender, who founded the International Flying Saucer Bureau, and who disbanded it in 1953, claimed that he had done so after an interview with a "spaceman" who warned him that he would be killed if he continued to delve into the mystery of flying saucers.

Seven years later, Bender finally told the story, and also said that he asked the space being – whom he called the "Exalted One" – various questions. Asked if he believed in God, the Exalted One replied that "they" had no need to believe in things as Earth people did. Asked if there was life on Mars, he said that there had been, but it was destroyed by invaders. The Martians had built beautiful cities and developed vast canals, but had not been as technologically advanced at the time of their destruction as Earth civilization is now. According to the Exalted One, Venus was now developing life.

Asked by Bender if Earth people would reach the moon, he was told "yes". Seven years later, the prophecy came true.

World's Sexiest Woman
In 1993 a Japanese opinion poll voted Margaret Thatcher the
World's Sexiest Woman, ahead of Brooke Shields, Michelle
Pfeiffer and Sharon Stone.

AIDS spread by sheep
Peter Bowen was an unsuccessful candidate for governor of
Missouri in 1998. During his campaign Bowen told voters that
rock music "stimulated sexual frenzy", lambasted sheep for
spreading AIDS by coughing and attacked Buckingham Palace
for holding "homosexual parties upstairs". He added that the
birthmark on former Soviet leader Mikhail Gorbachev's
forehead was the Satanic mark of the Beast, citing as conclusive
proof the fact that Gorbachev hardly ever agreed to be
photographed without his hat.

Loony dictators

A suitor for Princess Anne
When Idi Amin became ruler of Uganda the occasion passed by
without a murmur of dissent from the international community,
who believed him to be semi-literate, stupid and arrogant, but
harmless. It didn't dawn on them that Amin was also
dangerously insane until he volunteered to marry the Queen's
daughter Princess Anne.

A tidal wave of human flesh
Francisco Lopez, President of Paraguay from 1862 to 1870, was
not only the craziest, but also the ugliest and the most obese of
all South America's dictators: one of the more flattering

descriptions of him was "a tidal wave of human flesh". Lopez spent most of his reign waging a hopeless war against Paraguay's neighbouring enemies Argentina, Brazil and Uruguay, and trained his men so hard that many didn't live long enough to see a battle. This, combined with Lopez's refusal to allow any of his men to surrender, reduced the male population of Paraguay by nine-tenths. Lopez's incompetence meant that the military situation grew ever worse, so he organized a spying system which encouraged every third man in his army to spy on his comrades, and to shoot anyone, including officers, who showed any sign of cowardice. The resulting widespread paranoia among the ranks led to many of his men marching into battle backwards because they feared their own side more than the enemy. When his senior commander found himself surrounded and facing certain defeat, he opted to blow his own brains out rather than face his president, but missed and only shot one eye out.

Snowball, the genital-biting dwarf
Rafael Trujillo, the Dominican Republic's longest serving president, was a torturer *par excellence* in whose name a variety of methods were employed, including slow-shocking electric chairs, an electrified rod known as "the cane" – especially effective on genitals – nail extractors, whips, tanks of blood-sucking leeches and "the octopus", a multi-armed electrical appliance strapped to the head. Trujillo's most respected torturer however was a dwarf known as "Snowball" who specialized in biting off men's genitals.

Joke of the Day
A man walks into a pub and sees a gorilla serving behind the bar.

"What's the matter?" says the gorilla, realizing he is being stared at. "Have you never seen a gorilla serving drinks before?"

"It's not that," says the man. "I just never thought the giraffe would sell this place."

Ba'athist barbarity

Saddam Hussein's chastisements followed a clearly defined scale of medieval barbarity. Deserters had an ear cut off; thieves had fingers or hands cut off, depending on the source and value of stolen goods; liars had their backs broken – offenders were tied face-down on a wooden plank between two cement blocks and another block was dropped on the victim's spine. Informants who supplied the state police with tips that proved false had a piece of red-hot iron placed on their tongue. Homosexuals were often bound then pushed off the roof of a building. Traitors, spies, smugglers and occasionally prostitutes paid the ultimate price, beheading with a 5-ft broadsword known as al-Bashar. Saddam also executed underlings himself by shooting them on the spot, sometimes giving his gun to someone else and ordering them to shoot, thus making them his accomplices.

ANIMAL NEWS Free the Jinja One!

In August 1978 a strange rumour spread through Uganda, at the time ruled by the murderous dictator Idi Amin. According to whispered accounts, a tortoise had wandered into a small Ugandan village and explained to anyone that would listen that it must be taken to the town of Jinja, on the River Nile, near the country's capital Kampala. There, in the presence of the Regional Governor and the Police Commissioner, it would reveal its dark knowledge. The rumours did not reveal the reptile's news, but they did tell of the unfortunate creature's immediate imprisonment: it was not seen again. This story was widely believed. It was brought to international attention when several departments of the Ugandan government held crisis meetings at which they strenuously denied the existence of the "politically imprisoned" tortoise. A spokesman commented that the Ugandan populace was "always drunk with rumours". But the story would not disappear. Finally Amin himself held a press conference at which he threatened to shoot anyone caught mentioning the animal again.

Guardian

Touring taster

When Nicolae Ceaucescu visited the Queen at Buckingham Palace in 1978 he took his official food taster with him to make sure he wasn't being poisoned.

Who's crazy?

In the late 1960s China's communist leader Chairman Mao confessed to his aides that he secretly hoped the USA would drop a nuclear bomb on a province of China and kill between ten and twenty million Chinese people. Then, said Mao, it would show the rest of the world just how crazy the Americans were.

Emperor Faustin I

Faustin Soulouque, the nineteenth-century Haitian dictator and self-styled Emperor Faustin I, established a secret police force, known as the zinglins, to keep dissenters in line and took part in cannibalistic rites, drinking the blood of his late rivals and keeping their skulls to use as drinking cups on his desk. Faustin once had a suspected enemy called Similien arrested and shackled to a dungeon wall. Later a report came to Faustin that the man's legs were turning gangrenous from the pressure of his fettles. Faustin sent word back: "Tell him not to worry. When his legs drop off I'll chain him by the neck."

Stalin's boots

The Soviet leader Joseph Stalin was never seen without his high, heavy, black riding boots, even on the most inappropriate occasions and in the most uncomfortable conditions. He once had one of his bodyguards sent to the salt mines for not wearing boots. It turned out that the bodyguard had taken to wearing slippers so as not to wake Stalin when he was sleeping. Stalin had him arrested for plotting to assassinate him. A guest once asked Stalin why he never took his boots off even on a stiflingly hot day. The Russian leader replied, "Because you can kick someone in the head with them so hard he'll never find all his teeth."

Bandleader Heath
To mark the anniversary of his military coup in 1977, Idi Amin
invited the former Prime Minister Edward Heath to fly to
Uganda "with his band" to play before him during the
celebrations. Amin said he regretted that Mr Heath had been
demoted to the obscure rank of bandleader, but noted that he'd
heard that Mr Heath was one of the best bandleaders in Britain,
and offered to assist the ex-PM with a supply of goats and
chickens. By now the British were used to Amin's philanthropic
gestures: he once offered to send a shipload of vegetables to
England to solve the recession.

Face to face
The North Korean leader Kim Il Sung compelled the entire
population of his country to wear lapel badges with his face on
them.

Boots for Amin
Idi Amin once refused to attend the Commonwealth Games
unless the Queen sent him a new pair of size-thirteen boots.

Brooke Shields stands in for the Pope
In 1980 Imelda Marcos had a "mystical vision" which prompted
her to blow $100 million on a bizarre attempt to create a
Filipino version of the Cannes film festival. Most of the money
was spent on an extravagant new film theatre. The builders and
everyone else associated with the Marcos family were so corrupt
that no-one was particularly surprised when in 1982, two months
before the official opening, half of the building collapsed killing
at least thirty workers. To avoid delaying construction Marcos
had concrete poured over the dead men and had the theatre
exorcized to appease the superstitious. The grand opening went

ahead almost exactly as Imelda had planned, with just one minor
setback: she had invited the Pope, but in the event had to settle
for Brooke Shields.

Let's swop
Before he became President of Haiti "Papa Doc" Duvalier spent
two years in hiding from the government of the day dressed as a
woman and at mealtimes habitually switched dinner plates with
his "friends" to avoid being poisoned.

The Palace of Sighs
Over 500 people died building Louis XIV's monumental folly,
the Palace of Versailles, mostly from fevers and epidemics
caused by the insanitary conditions his workers were expected to
live and work in and numerous fatal building site accidents.
Louis was embarrassed by the death toll and banned his
courtiers from discussing it.

Private jets and peasants
In 1992 Namibia's President Nujoma appealed for foreign aid
after his country's worst drought this century, then spent £16
million on a private plane.

Head to head
"Papa Doc" Duvalier claimed he could predict the future from
late-night conversations he had with a severed human head,
which he kept in a cupboard in the presidential palace. It
belonged to one of his former army officers Blucher Philogenes,
who had led a doomed CIA-backed invasion of Haiti in 1963.

Keep your friends close, and your enemies closer
The Ethiopian dictator Colonel Mengistu Haile Mariam kept his
under the floorboards of his office. This was where police found
the remains of the man he ousted, former Emperor Haile
Selassie, in 1992.

Favourite hobbies of Idi Amin
One of Idi Amin's two favourite hobbies was erecting statues all
over Uganda to his two greatest idols, Queen Victoria and Adolf
Hitler. The other was crushing the genitals of his victims with
his bare hands.

Bulletproof bra
In addition to the 1200 pairs of shoes that the Philippine government confiscated from Imelda Marcos, they also swiped her only
bulletproof bra.

An excellent way to resolve a conflict
The dictator Idi Amin was a former heavyweight boxing champion
of Uganda. When his country was being overrun by Tanzanian
troops in 1978, he suggested that he and Julius Nyerere settle the
war between them in the ring with Mohammad Ali as referee.

"Saint" Francisco Lopez
In 1870 the Paraguayan dictator Francisco Lopez declared
himself a Saint of the Christian Church. When the matter was
put to the bishops of Paraguay, the twenty-three who did not
agree were shot. "Saint" Francisco was duly anointed and that
date officially entered into the Christian calendar. His final act
was to have a new medal minted which he awarded to the entire
population of Paraguay, or at least what was left of it.

A death foretold

Idi Amin handed out a mass murder contract to his private police force, the implausibly named State Research Bureau. The SRB simply rounded up candidates and murdered them, then informed the families that for £150 they would lead them to the body. The scheme became such a huge success that neighbours complained about the ceaseless din of machine gun fire at SRB headquarters. To keep the noise down, Amin bribed his prisoners to execute themselves by clubbing each other to death with 16-lb sledgehammers. Amin's favourite place for disposing of his enemies was Lake Victoria: it was said that when the lights went out in Kampala, everyone knew that the hydro-electric generators on the Lake's Owen Falls Dam was once again clogged with human bodies. The scale of Amin's campaign of terror against his enemies was so immense it was bound to run into logistical problems. A former government employee Francis Kalimazo recalled that he was at a wedding when he learned of his own "death" on the radio. He then realized that he was part of the backlog.

Papa Doc's prayer

"Papa Doc" Duvalier had the Lord's Prayer rewritten for use in Haitian schools: "Our Doc, who art in the National Palace for life, hallowed be thy name by present and future generations. Thy will be done in Port-au-Prince as it is in the provinces. Give us this day our new Haiti, and forgive not the trespasses of those anti-patriots who daily spit upon our country . . ."

Unsportsmanlike plot

A British diplomat who proposed an easy way of assassinating Hitler with a sniper's bullet had his plan turned down by the British government because it was "unsportsmanlike". General

Sir Noel McFarlane was military attaché at the British Embassy in Berlin in 1938 when his plan was turned down by Whitehall. He calculated that the shooting could be easily done during one of Hitler's frequent public appearances.

Purge of the sparrows

After victimizing everyone else he could think of, Chairman Mao mobilized the entire Chinese nation to take it out on the sparrows. Sparrows eat cereal crops, and so over a period of forty-eight hours about 80 million Chinese took to the the streets and fields and banged woks and gongs until the birds dropped dead of exhaustion. It was a popular move with most people because the Chinese loved fried sparrow. Without the sparrows to control worms and other pests however, agricultural disaster followed. With the natural food cycle altered, 43 million people starved to death over the next three years.

Marriage of convenience

In 1978 Idi Amin planned a full-scale invasion of neighbouring Tanzania, but first decided to lull Tanzania's President Julius Nyerere into a false sense of security. He sent Nyerere a telegram which read, "I love you so much that if you were a woman I would consider marrying you."

Life in the Kim lane

Kim Il Sung had every road in North Korea built with an extra lane for his sole private use.

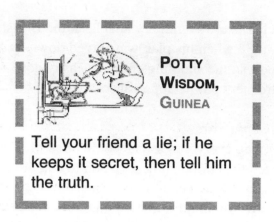

POTTY WISDOM, GUINEA

Tell your friend a lie; if he keeps it secret, then tell him the truth.

Ask the goat

When "Papa Doc" Duvalier needed advice on matters of state he mostly got it by sitting in his bathtub wearing a a black top hat while consulting the entrails of a dead goat.

What a bastard!

The Paraguayan dictator Francisco Lopez had his seventy-year-old mother publicly flogged then executed because she confessed to him that he was a bastard.

Hang him

The Shah of Persia, Nasir ud-Din, became well known to the British public in Victorian times for his visit to Buckingham Palace and his enormous moustaches. He once visited an English prison and when he was shown the gallows, asked if he could see someone being hanged. When he was politely told that this wouldn't be possible as there was no one about to be executed, the Shah pointed to his entourage and said, "Take one of my suite."

URBAN MYTHS
True or False – you decide

MOBILE (CELL) PHONES CAN CAUSE EXPLOSIONS

Oil companies have supposedly issued warnings about several incidents where mobile phones ignited fumes while drivers were refuelling their cars, and the phones rang or were answered.

In one incident, a driver were severely burnt and his car seriously damaged when fuel vapour ignited and exploded while he was talking on his mobile near an attendant who was pumping gas. Electronic devices at gas stations are protected by explosive containment devices, but the danger from cell phones is that they are not so protected. Mobile phone makers protect themselves from legal action by printing warnings in their user handbooks against use in "gas stations, fuel storage sites, and chemical factories", although many people do not read these warnings.

The cause for this danger is the sparks generated by the battery inside the phone. Any mobile phone that lights up when switched on, can release enough energy to provide an ignition spark. As well as filling stations, according to this urban legend, you should turn your phone off when fuelling lawn mowers, boats or barbecues.

Adrian Heller
The Contemporary History Conference in Braunau-am-Inn,
Austria, birthplace of Hitler, once held a conference to discuss
the plight of people with problem names. Among the guests
were Adolf Hitler, retired bus driver and Heinrich Himmler,
bricklayer. The lesser known Herr Hitler complained that
frequent jokes at his expense had contributed to the break-up of
his marriage and caused many work-related problems. Once,
when required to drive a coachload of Jewish tourists, he had to
have his name changed for the day to Adrian Heller.

Manners maketh man

It's an ill wind, that blows no good
When the Earl of Oxford, Edward de Vere, accidentally broke
wind while bowing to Queen Elizabeth I he was so embarrassed
by the incident he decided to keep a low profile and threw
himself into extensive travelling abroad. When he finally
returned to the court after a seven-year absence, the Queen
greeted him with "My Lord, I had forgot the fart."

The green sickness
The famous German physician Carl Ludwig wrote a pamphlet
explaining why so many ladies in the nineteenth century
suffered from chronic constipation. Women, he explained, had a
fear of accidentally farting after eating, and suffered from too
much tensing of the buttocks. He called it "the green sickness".

As the Bible tells us

The Old Testament book Ecclesiasticus recommends clearing
the stomach by throwing up before or during a big meal to make
room for more food.

Death by peacock feather

The Romans were prolific meal-time vomiters, finding that it
was an effective way of preventing a hangover the next day.
They even evolved a special technique to encourage it, tickling
their gullets with peacock feathers. The Emperor Claudius I tried
it and choked to death in the process.

No beans for the clergy

For centuries the Church actively discouraged priests from
eating beans in case they broke wind during solemn holy rituals.

Compliments to the chef

In some Latin and Mediterranean countries, loud public belching
is a sign of appreciation after a good meal.

Pinkie picker

Tibetans used to grow the fingernail long on the little finger of
their left hand so that they could use to it to pick their ears and
noses clean.

Lost but not forgotten

Found in the lost property department of the Scotland to
Midlands rail line in 1947: three artificial limbs, a glass eye, a
two-headed carp and a three-legged chicken.

Better out than in
Aristophanes, Chaucer, Rabelais, Swift, Ben Franklin and Mark
Twain have all written about farting. Erasmus once wrote a
treatise about flatulence and belching, and warned that a stifled
fart was a health hazard.

Spittoon chair
Nineteenth-century English gentlemen had "smoking chairs"
designed with secret drawers under the seat into which a chap
could spit.

Pots and pans
The ancient Greeks made elaborate bronze pans for vomiting
and urinating at meal times.

It is the law
The Roman Emperor Claudius was so troubled by the notion that
thousands of Romans were risking their health by stifling farts, he
passed a law permitting people to break wind freely in company.

The Battle of the Atlantic 1940–44
This is the name given to the great four-year
struggle to keep open Britain's supply routes
from America, upon which it was utterly
dependent. It cost the lives of 30,248 merchant
seamen, and 51,578 Royal Navy personnel. By
the Summer of 1941, Britain and its Allies had lost over 1,200
ships, and imports had fallen by a third. It was the work of
U-Boats. Although the Allies sank 31, the Germans soon had
100 new submarines in the Atlantic. In 1942 U-Boats sank 1,160
ships and almost brought Britain to its knees. But the
introduction of "Asdic" underwater detection, radar and new

escort systems reduced losses and began to make inroads into the submarine fleet. Though the Germans had 250 U-Boats operating in 1943, 67 of them were sunk between March and May, and Admiral Doenitz was forced to recall them to rest and repair. By the time they returned to the attack, Allied merchant production was exceeding its decreasing losses. Morale was further raised when the Royal Navy sank the German battle cruiser *Scharnhorst*, which had ravaged merchant shipping. By the end of 1944, the battle was won, though the U-Boat commanders struggled on until the end, then scuttled 221 of their surviving craft.

Dead wrong

The British soldiers who went over the top at the battle of the Somme on 1 July 1916 were told that, after heavy bombardment of enemy positions, the only Germans they would meet would be dead ones. Some officers advanced armed only with swagger sticks or umbrellas, while others kicked footballs towards the German lines and charged after them.

Not palace trained

When the Shah of Persia arrived at Buckingham Palace in 1873 for a brief stay with Queen Victoria, it was noted that he repeatedly failed to use the royal lavatories and went wherever the spirit moved him.

Arse about face?

Casanova was offended by the sight of Londoners dropping their pants and urinating openly in busy streets. He suggested that the very least they could do was face the street so that their backsides were not exposed to passers-by.

A Rolling Stone pisses anywhere

Rock 'n' roll's most celebrated three pints of urine, released
against a garage wall on 18 March 1965, helped cast the Rolling
Stones as Britain's public enemy No.1. The notorious leak took
place at a service station in Stratford, east London, after a
garage attendant refused them admission to the toilets. Mick
Jagger explained, "We piss anywhere, man." Jagger, Bill
Wyman and Brian Jones, described in court as "shaggy-haired
monsters", were charged with insulting behaviour and fined £5
each.

Peter the not so great

The crowned heads of Europe held their breath when Peter the
Great travelled west in 1697. Peter was noted by nearly
everyone he met to have been incredibly dirty and smelly even
by seventeenth-century standards, and blissfully unaware of
rudimentary personal hygiene, table manners or even basic potty
training. For the duration of the czar's visit to England he and
his friends were accommodated in a mansion belonging to Sir
John Evelyn. Sir John later presented a bill for £350 to the
British government for damage to his property, which included
vomit and excrement smeared on the walls and floors.

World domination by constipation

The eighteenth-century Chinese Emperor Qianlong planned to
bring the whole of Europe to its knees by banning rhubarb
exports, thereby creating a constipation epidemic.

Great sporting moments

Spending 200,000 pennies

When nature called the Spanish First Division footballer David Billabone during a game between his club Bilbao and Cadiz, he decided he couldn't make it to half-time and discreetly urinated behind a goalpost. Unfortunately he wasn't discreet enough to escape the attention of a 20,000 crowd and a local photographer who splashed a picture of the leaking Spaniard all over Spanish newspapers. Billabone was fined £2,000.

Thought for the Day

If at first you don't succeed, destroy all evidence that you tried.

Pissing on the pitch

The Yorkshire slow left-arm bowler Bobby Peel (1857–1941) played cricket for England from 1884 to 1896. Peel was frequently inebriated during matches, often drinking himself into a state tactfully interpreted by the cricketing bible Wisden as "unwell" or "gone away". During one county game the Yorkshire captain Lord Hawke was forced to suspend Peel from the side for "running the wrong way" and "bowling at the pavilion in the belief that it was the batsman". Peel was eventually sacked from the Yorkshire team after his performance against Warwickshire at Edgbaston in May 1896. During an unbeaten partnership of 367 with Lord Hawke, Peel relieved himself on the pitch.

The Papal football
The skull of Pope Clement VI, who died in 1352, was later used by the Huguenots as a football.

Some recovery
In 2005 a Belgian football team lost 50–1 after their regular goalkeeper missed the game to attend a music concert. "At half-time the score was 27–0, but after half-time we were able to recover," said SK Berlaar's substitute goalkeeper.

In 2012 perhaps
The Greek Peregrinus, nicknamed "Proteus", set himself on fire during the Olympic games of AD 165 to prove his faith in reincarnation. He hasn't reappeared at any subsequent Olympic meetings, although he did have a small cult following after his death and his staff was treated as a religious relic.

Winning is everything
The deadliest ever ball game was Tlachtli, once played by the Maya Indians of Central America. Two teams struggled violently to force a rubber ball through their opponents' goal – vertical stone rings on elevated pedestals at either end of the court. Players often died during the game. The losing team players were decapitated and their heads put on display.

Become strong, with boar dung
Professional chariot racers in ancient Rome used to build their muscles up by drinking dried boar's dung in water.

Pinioning the prepuce

The supposition that professional sportsmen, especially boxers, should avoid sex before a contest because it might sap their strength has a long tradition. In ancient Greece top athletes were prevented from having intercourse by having their foreskins tied up.

Curse of the hole-in-one

Emil Kijek of Massachusetts achieved his first ever hole in one at the age of seventy-nine at the Sun Valley Golf Club in December 1994. The shock killed him several minutes later.

A real water hazard

Golfer Whitney McIntosh from Edinburgh drowned in 1994 while attempting to retrieve his ball from a water hazard.

A bad day on the golf course

Frenchman Jean Potevan threw his golf bag into a lake in disgust in May 1995 after a poor game at a course near Lyon. Realizing however that his car keys were still in the bag, Potevan dived in after it but drowned when he became entangled in weeds. His golf partner Henri Levereau revealed that his last words were, "I'm going for the keys, but the clubs stay down there."

The cart of death

Golf widow Diana Nagy filed a lawsuit in Charleston, West Virginia, against the manufacturer of the golf cart from which her husband fell to his death during a tournament at the Berry Hills Country Club. She admitted that her husband had been drinking heavily but complained that the cart should have been fitted with seat belts and doors.

The links killer

Japanese golfer Takeo Niyama was arrested in January 1995 after beating his playing partner to death with a 5-iron. Niyama, forty-three, reacted when Aioa Sakajiri laughed at his slice into the Tokyo course lake. Niyama had two previous convictions for golf course assaults including a six month prison sentence in 1994 for a links assault.

Death on the oval

The only English cricketer convicted of manslaughter on the field of play was William Waterfall, at Derby Assizes in 1775.

Better than Graham Taylor

Romania's deranged King Carol II was a sex-mad autocrat whose personal harem and tacky private life were the talk of Europe. He abolished all political parties and declared himself Royal Dictator, and had some of Bucharest's finest buildings demolished so that his machine-gunners had a clear field of fire in the approaches to his home. He also insisted on personally picking Romania's football team for the 1930 World Cup Finals, where they beat Peru 3–1 and failed to reach the semi-finals by going out to the hosts and eventual winners Uruguay. History will therefore remember King Carol II as a dangerous, sex-mad despot whose record in competitive international football, nevertheless, was much better than that of former England manager Graham Taylor.

 Don't worry, be happy

You won't be happy with more until you're happy with what you've got.

Bad horse

The Indian Maharajah Jay Singh of Alwar, a personal friend of George V and the king's guest at Buckingham Palace in 1931, was a keen big game hunter; he was said to use live babies or elderly widows as tiger bait. The Maharajah was also a polo player. In 1933 after a particularly bad game he blamed his horse, which had stumbled and thrown him. As an audience of British VIPs watched, the Maharajah poured a can of petrol over the polo pony and set fire to it.

Keeping it in the family

The head of the family

After the execution of Sir Walter Raleigh in 1618, his head became the Raleigh family heirloom. His widow Elizabeth kept it for twenty-nine years before passing it on to their son Carew, who looked after it until 1666 when it went with him to his grave.

POTTY WISDOM, BULGARIA

Thrash your apprentice while he has not yet broken the water jug.

Where there's a will . . .

The wife of an eccentric London dentist Martin van Butchell (1735–1812) decided to repay her husband for years of marital misery with a spiteful will which decreed that her fortune pass to a distant relative "the moment I am dead and buried". Her resourceful husband quickly found a loophole in the will by keeping her body well above ground. Van Butchell, a skilled embalmer, fitted her out with a new pair of glass eyes, and filled her veins with oil of turpentine and camphorated spirit of wine. She was then dressed, propped up in the drawing room and put on public display from 9 am to 1 pm, from Monday to Saturday. The rush to see the corpse was so great that van Butchell was forced to restrict viewings to private appointments only.

From father to son

Pills made from the toxic metal antimony, highly esteemed in medieval times as great bowel regulators, were handed down from father to son and from mother to daughter as precious family heirlooms. The pills irritated the intestinal tract and worked their way out again.

Heady profits

Maori tribesmen often preserved the elaborately tattooed heads of their deceased relatives as "auto-icons" to keep alive the memory of the dead. The heads would be steamed several times in an oven, smoked dry, and their hair carefully combed into a top-knot. In 1770 the British explorer Sir Joseph Banks acquired the first specimen Maori head ever seen in Europe and heads suddenly became fashionable, highly collectible items. The Maoris quickly overcame their early objections to selling off the heads of their loved ones when they discovered that British museums and private collectors were prepared to pay generously for good quality, highly decorated specimens. As heads became scarce, unscrupulous Maori dealers would supply the untattooed heads of recently deceased slaves: few Europeans could tell the difference between a genuine antique relic and that of a recently dead slave which had been freshly tattooed post-mortem. By this time the greedy dealers were only one short step away from depriving living Maoris of their heads. In 1832 the gruesome practice had reached such horrific proportions that the head trade was finally made illegal.

Sawney Beane, the Scottish cannibal

A radical experiment in self-sufficiency was effected by Britain's second most prolific mass murderer, Sawney (Sandy) Beane, who was born in fifteenth-century Scotland in East Lothian, near Edinburgh. Beane married young and eloped with his bride to set up home in a cave on the wild west coast of Scotland and the couple had eight sons and six daughters, who then incestuously increased the Beane family to include eighteen grandsons and fourteen granddaughters. At first Sawney Beane provided for his clan by stealing sheep but soon the growing family took to murdering passing travellers, cannibalism being the best way to fill their stomachs and dispose of the evidence – the family that slays together, stays together. In 1435 Scotland's King James I led a posse of 400 men to flush out Beane and his murderous family and came across several members red-handed, attacking a man and his wife. When they finally discovered the Beane lair they found evidence of hundreds of murders including a well-stocked larder containing dried, pickled and salted human body parts. Sawney Beane and the adult members of his family were put to death following a show trial at Leith. The men had their hands, feet and sexual organs cut off and were left to bleed to death. Their wives were forced to watch, then burned at the stake.

Military eccentrics

"Look after Dowb"

During the Crimean War the British chiefs of staff were
delighted to find themselves equipped with the state-of-the-art
communications plaything, the electric telegraph. One day Lord
Panmure cabled General Simpson, "Captain Jarvis has been
bitten by a centipede. How is he now?" The General was not
amused to find that he had been awoken in the middle of the
night by a dragoon who had been required to ride two miles
under enemy fire to deliver such trivial news. Nevertheless the
next morning General Simpson sent a mounted dragoon to
enquire after Captain Jarvis, four miles away, only to discover to
his disgust that Jarvis "has never been bitten at all, but has had a
boil, from which he is fast recovering". Simpson received a
second telegraph from Lord Panmure, this time on behalf
of his Lordship's favourite nephew Captain Dowbiggan:
"I recommend Captain Dowbiggan to your notice, should you
have a vacancy, and if he is fit." Confusingly, the message was
relayed by the telegraph operator as "Look after Dowb."
Subsequently "Look after Dowb" became the standard
catchphrase for nepotism in the army.

Operation Foxley

The British scientist Bertie Blount spent the Second World War
working for the government's undercover "dirty tricks"
department, the Special Operations Executive (SOE). Blount
was required to invent ingenious methods of assassination,
including a plan to kill Hitler using anthrax – Operation Foxley.
The devilish plan was hatched in December 1944 when Blount
was asked by his senior officers to come up with an

assassination method employing chemical or bacteriological agents. Blount pondered ways of hiding the lethal agent; he suggested the assassin could wear glasses or false teeth, or perhaps should have a "physical peculiarity such as wearing a truss or a false limb". He also advised, "Guns and hypodermic syringes disguised as fountain pens are usually not a bit convincing and are likely to lead to the death of the operator before he has had any opportunity of making his attack."

Kaiser Wilhelm II, the uniform fetishist
Many of the Hohenzollern Kings of Prussia were military uniform fetishists, none more fanatical than Kaiser Wilhelm II. He had over four hundred uniforms stashed away in his mahogany wardrobes. In the first seventeen years of his reign the Kaiser redesigned the uniforms of his German army officers thirty-seven times, and had a squad of tailors in his palace on permanent standby. He had uniforms for every occasion: uniforms for attending Galas, uniforms to greet every one of his regiments, uniforms with which to greet other heads of state, uniforms for eating out, even "informal" uniforms for staying in. It was said that he even had an admiral's uniform which he only ever wore to see performances of *The Flying Dutchman*.

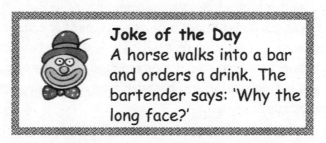

Joke of the Day
A horse walks into a bar and orders a drink. The bartender says: 'Why the long face?'

The Blunt Duke

The Duke of Wellington, victor of Waterloo and later prime minister of his country, was a blunt man with little time for small talk. When an aristocratic lady enquired whether the great man had been surprised to discover he had won the Battle of Waterloo, he replied icily, "Not half so much surprised as I am right now, ma'am." Wellington also had little time for music, especially anything remotely contemporary. In Vienna he once sat through a performance of Beethoven's *The Battle of Vienna*. When asked by a Russian diplomat whether the music resembled the real battle, the Duke replied, "By God, no. If it had, I should have run away myself." During the Battle of Waterloo in 1815 the British cavalry commander Lord Uxbridge had his horse shot from under him nine times. Eventually, as he was riding beside the Duke of Wellington, he himself was hit by French grapeshot. "By God, sir, I've lost my leg", he informed Wellington. "By God, sir," the Duke replied in his usual deadpan manner, "so you have."

The Potsdam Giant Guards

Prussia's eccentric King Frederick William I was obsessed with creating a regiment of very tall men. He established a regiment of freakishly tall grenadiers known as the Potsdam Giant Guards. The minimum height requirement for the Potsdam regiment was six feet, although most were over seven feet and the tallest were almost nine feet tall. All of them wore special pointed headgear which sometimes reached a height of ten feet. Height was the only criterion, because many of them were mentally retarded.

Frederick "the Great"

The Prussian King Frederick "the Great" was renowned for his
military genius but had a complete disregard for casualties or
human life, including his own. Wounded men were expected to
find their own way off the battlefield and back to hospitals as
best they could and were denied rations. As only one in five
who entered a Prussian military hospital came out alive, men
deserted by the thousand rather than risk being buried alive in
one and hundreds more committed suicide. When his campaign
funds ran short Frederick saved money by skimping on his
soldiers' uniforms: there was so little material in them they
couldn't even be fastened and so many of his men froze to
death. Frederick would always open a vein before a battle to
calm his nerves and when the tide turned against him he fought
on with a phial of poison ready for suicide. He drank up to forty
cups of coffee a day for several weeks in an experiment to see if
it was possible to exist without sleep. It took his stomach three
years to recover. One day, he was surprised to find one of his
best soldiers shackled in irons. When he asked why this was so,
he was told that the man had been caught buggering his horse.
Frederick ordered: "Fool – don't put him in irons, put him in the
infantry", then apologised to the soldier for taking his horse
away from him.

Shuffling soldiers

Austria's Emperor Franz Josef was in office for so long that
many of his subjects came to venerate him as the nearest thing
to a god on earth. When the Emperor became old and senile he
tended to shuffle along with his head thrust forward and his
shoulders slumped; when his soldiers marched, they too
shuffled, in respectful imitation of their Emperor's walk.

URBAN MYTHS
True or False – you decide

THE THIEVES' THANK-YOU NOTE

The natural politeness and formality of the Japanese knows no bounds. Two weeks after one of the biggest bank heists in Japan's history (over $5 million), the Kobe branch of Fukutoku Bank received a letter of gratitude from the robbers. The note said *"Thank you very much for the bonus. We can live on this loot for ever."*

Legs of glass

The Greek commander General Hajianestis, who led his country's army in the war with Turkey in 1921, was believed at the time to have been completely insane, but in fact showed a keen sense of self-preservation. Rather than rouse himself to command his troops he lay in bed pretending to be dead. Another ploy he used was to claim that he couldn't get up because his legs were made of glass and that they might break if he moved.

Mad MacMahon

The French military hero Marshal Macmahon crushed a Paris left-wing uprising in 1871 and went on to become President of France from 1873 to 1879. One day he was visiting a field hospital when he came across a soldier who lay ill with a tropical fever. "That's a nasty disease you have there,"

sympathized the great man. "You either die of it or go crazy.
I've been through it myself."

But what if it rains?
The British Second World War officer Digby Tatham-Warter,
company commander of the 2nd Battalion Parachute Regiment
won a Distinguished Service Order for his part in the Battle of
Arnhem in 1944 after famously leading a bayonet charge
equipped with an old bowler hat and a tattered umbrella.
Although a fine company commander, Tatham-Warter was not
quite so gifted at handling alcohol. He got into several wild
drunken fist fights in the mess with his friends, but remembered
nothing of the incidents on the following morning, although he
would always return to his unit, fresh and impeccably attired. He
was worried about the unreliability of the radio sets he was
required to use and so had trained his men in the use of bugle
calls that were used by the British during the Napoleonic Wars
of the early nineteenth century. Tatham-Warter's trademark
brolly became a symbol of defiance to the British at Arnhem
who stubbornly held on to the north end of a road bridge,
although outnumbered and short of ammunition, food and water.
During the heavy fighting that followed, Digby could often be
seen calmly strolling about the defences with his brolly, obliv-
ious to the constant threat of mortar barrages and sniper fire.
When a fellow officer commented, "That won't do you much
good", Tatham-Warter replied, "But what if it rains?"

The emperor's diapers
The French Emperor Louis Napoleon III, who suffered from a
variety of ailments including dysentery, gonorrhea and a huge
bladder stone, commanded his troops at the Battle of Sedan in 1870
with towels stuffed inside his breeches to act as king-size diapers.

The most damned bad-tempered and extravagant bitch in the kingdom

At the age of fourteen James Thomas Brudenell, the Seventh Earl of Cardigan, was thrown from a horse and struck his head on a gate, emerging from a weeks-long recuperation with a much changed disposition and given to flights of extraordinary rage. He later became famous for two scandalous marriages and "the charge of the Light Brigade" at Balaclava in 1854. His first wife Elizabeth was already married to one Captain Johnstone when she met Cardigan in Paris and eloped to Versailles. Johnstone later described her as "the most damned bad-tempered and extravagant bitch in the kingdom". When Cardigan offered Johnstone the chance to fight a duel to obtain satisfaction, the cuckolded husband declined and said that by taking Elizabeth off his hands, Cardigan had performed the greatest service one man could do for another. The second Lady Cardigan, the cigar-smoking Adeline de Horsey, outraged Victorian society, not least the Queen herself, by openly living with Cardigan as his mistress for years before they were eventually married. Lady Cardigan was also known for her unconventional dress sense. She went cycling in red military trousers and a leopard skin cape in her eighties and she would dress in full Spanish national costume, or stroll through Hyde Park wearing a Louis XVI coat and three-cornered hat over a curly blonde wig. She was a keen hunter, but when she became too old to ride she still turned up to the meets dressed in full hunting gear and would follow the hunt in comfort in her carriage. For several years before her death she kept a coffin in her home so that she could lie in it now and then to test it for comfort. The ironic fate of Lord Cardigan, one of only 195 soldiers who rode out of the Valley of Death from 693 who rode in, was to die in a fall from his horse while riding on the estate.

Lovestruck general

During heavy fighting in Beirut in 1983 the Syrian Defence
Minister, General Mustafa Tlass instructed his men to stop
attacking Italian peacekeeping soldiers because of his lifelong
crush on the Italian actress Gina Lollobrigida. General Tlass told
his men, "Do whatever you want with the US, British and other
forces, but I do not want a single tear falling from the eyes of
Gina Lollobrigida." Tlass divulged that he had also had a
"thing" for Madonna, Cicciolina and Marilyn Monroe.

Dandy admirals

The British submarine commander Sir Herbert Shove generally
carried two white rats in the pockets of his uniform. Admiral
Sir Algernon Charles Fiesché Heneage, or "Pompo" as he
was known to the men under his command, was obsessive
about his personal appearance. He wore his hair set in curls
and took 240 shirts to sea with him; the dirty ones were
sent home for laundering on any available ship bound for
England.

Nothing but a pith helmet

Orde Charles Wingate was a brilliant but unorthodox British
military leader in the Second World War. His three campaigns
in Palestine, Ethiopia and as brilliant commander of the Chindits
in Burma established him as a military legend and widely
regarded as the father of modern guerrilla warfare. Winston
Churchill believed him to be "a man of genius who might well
have become also a man of destiny". He also had his share of
detractors who thought him simply barking mad. Wingate's
personal habits were described by colleagues as "a bit *outré*".
He suffered from prolonged bouts of depression he called
"nervous attacks," which he was able to endure only by cease-

lessly repeating the phrase "God is good". Wingate was often
verbally and physically abusive. He struck soldiers who made
mistakes and threw violent tantrums. On one occasion, suffering
from depression and taking medication, he tried to commit
suicide with a knife. Wingate ate large quantities of raw onions
for his health, strained tea through his socks and always carried
an alarm clock because he didn't trust watches. More baffling
was his habit of strolling around in front of his fellow soldiers
stark naked. Wingate got his kit off whenever and wherever the
mood took him. He dictated letters in the buff and once made a
lasting impression on a Jewish leader by briefing him
completely nude. Wingate hardly ever bathed, his preferred
grooming method was to scrub himself with a huge brush, often
during conversations with visitors. He died aged forty-one in an
airplane crash in Burma. No identifiable remains of Wingate
were ever found, save for his trademark pith helmet.

Pregnant with an elephant
The Duke of Wellington had more to occupy his mind at
Waterloo than the small matter of defeating Napoleon.
Wellington's ally, the famous Prussian field marshal Leberecht
von Blücher, suffered from fits of senile melancholia which led
him to experience bizarre hallucinations. Blücher once confided
to Wellington that he was pregnant and about to give birth to an
elephant, and that moreover the cad who had raped him was a
French soldier.

143

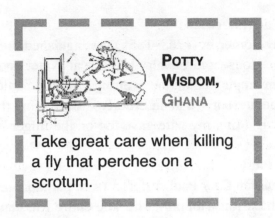

POTTY WISDOM, GHANA

Take great care when killing
a fly that perches on a
scrotum.

A cheering spectacle

The Holy Roman Emperor Henry VI motivated his troops by
having nuns stripped and smeared with honey, then decorated
with feathers and sent on horseback through the ranks of
cheering men.

The doctor Pope

The only Portuguese Pope, John XXI, was also the only doctor
ever to become pontiff. He was originally appointed physician to
the Vatican in the mid-thirteenth century, largely on the strength
of his medical treatise in which he prescribed lettuce leaves for
toothache, lettuce seed to reduce sex drive and pig dung to stop
nosebleeds. While receiving his medical advice, three popes,
Gregory X, Innocent V and Adrian V died in quick succession.
The doctor was duly elected pontiff, possibly in the hope that his
medical skills would enable him to live longer than the previous
three. Within twelve months of his election however the roof of
his new palace fell in, crushing him horribly and he died six
days later.

Bring that arm back!

Lord Fitzroy Somerset (1788–1855) distinguished himself as the leader of the Household Cavalry brigade at Waterloo, but had his right arm amputated on the evening after the battle. After it was removed he snapped at an orderly, "You, bring that arm back. There is a ring my wife gave me on the finger."

Mad Czar Paul

The mad Russian Czar Paul suffered from paradomania – an unnatural obsession with militaria. The entire Russian army, of which Paul was commander-in-chief, was forced to adopt the antiquated Prussian uniform of his hero Frederick the Great, right down to the last detail of old-fashioned gaiters and powdered pigtails. Paul became fanatical about his soldiers' uniforms right down to the last epaulette, always at the expense of military efficiency. He made them wear costumes that were so tight-fitting that they made breathing difficult and fighting practically impossible. Underneath they wore straitjackets to make them stand erect, and on their heads they wore thick, heavy wigs with iron rods inserted in them to make the hairpiece sit straight. To make his soldiers goose-step perfectly without bending their legs, he strapped steel plates to their knees. The night before a parade his men would labour until dawn to cover their wigs with grease and chalk. They all knew that even a hair out of place could mean arrest, a thrashing, or deportation.

ANIMAL NEWS And So to Sheep

Among the many remedies available to sufferers of insomnia is a book entitled *Count Sheep*. On every page, the book features hundreds of photos of sheep, arranged in columns and rows for easy enumeration. In all, the home edition features 65,000 sheep; a travel edition is available featuring only 28,000.
LA Times

"Squaw-killer" Custer

General George Custer was an unstable egomaniac who went on from being the most incompetent student in his class at West Point to become one of the US Army's worst generals. Custer was also a cowardly commander who, by massacring 103 Cheyenne, earned the nickname "squaw-killer". Every one of Custer's 211 men were scalped at Little Big Horn – save Custer himself. Perhaps fearing the worst, he had already had his famous golden locks shorn off in favour of a close crew-cut.

"No doubt he is a little mad at intervals . . ."

One of Wellington's senior commanders during the Peninsular War, Sir William Erskine, was certifiably mad and had twice been confined to lunatic asylums. Wellington heard of his appointment with stunned disbelief and wrote to the Military Secretary in London for an explanation. The Secretary replied, "No doubt he is a little mad at intervals, but in his lucid intervals he is an uncommonly clever fellow, and I trust he will have no fit during the campaign, although I must say he looked a little mad as he embarked." During one of Erskine's less lucid intervals he was found at dinner when he should have been defending a strategically important bridge. He eventually sent five men to defend it: when a fellow officer queried his decision Erskine thought better of it and sent a whole regiment, but pocketed the instruction and forgot all about it. Sir William's mental health wasn't his only problem. His eyesight was so poor that before a battle he had to ask someone to point him in the general direction of the battlefield. He eventually committed suicide by jumping out of a window in Lisbon. Found dying on the pavement, he asked bystanders, "Why on earth did I do that?"

A favourable situation
When General Alexander Haig was asked for his summary of 1 July 1916, the first day of the battle of the Somme which saw 57,470 British soldiers either dead or dying by nightfall, most of them killed during the first half hour of the attack, he replied: "The general situation was favourable."

> **Thought for the Day**
>
> After all is said and done, more is said than done.

The bounders who wouldn't fight fair
General Kitchener, while fighting the Boers in South Africa in 1900, complained bitterly that the enemy didn't fight fairly. The

bounders were always on the move or taking advantage of surrounding cover, he said, instead of standing quite still in the open where they could be shot down by British rifles and machine guns.

Bats out of hell

During the Second World War the Allies called upon their finest scientific minds to help give them a competitive edge. The Americans turned to the Harvard chemist, Dr Louis Fieser, who unveiled a brand new secret weapon he was confident would bring to an early conclusion the war with Japan – the incendiary bat. Fieser's cunning plan was to collect millions of bats and keep them cold, thereby inducing a state of hibernation. The slumbering bats would then be released over Japan, each carrying a tiny incendiary device containing one ounce of napalm. As the bats fell they would warm up, settle under the eaves of buildings and set fire to them. Fieser imagined a "surprise attack" with fires breaking out all over Tokyo at 4:00 in the morning. The plan was abandoned after trials at the Carlsbad Army Air Field in New Mexico when a number of bats, blown out of the target area by high winds, set fire to and destroyed a US army hangar and a general's car.

"Not worth a pinch of owl dung"

The bombastic Confederate General John Pope was considered one of the most incompetent leaders of the American Civil War, described by a colleague as a man "not worth a pinch of owl dung". He lost the faith of his men when he made an address praising the western armies and disparaging the efforts of the eastern forces. In typical fashion he declared his headquarters "would be in the saddle". This led to a quip that he didn't know his headquarters from his hindquarters. At Chillianwalla in 1849 the near-sighted General Pope faced his cavalry in the wrong direction and led them in a charge away from the battlefield. The charge soon became a panic until the fleeing horsemen were stopped by a Chaplain who threatened to shoot Pope if he didn't turn round.

Wind Abuse

LEGAL NEWS A grocery assistant, Tom Morgan, sued his co-worker, Randy Maresh, for $100,000 on the grounds that he was inflicting severe mental stress. Maresh was, allegedly, assaulting Morgan by farting at him. According to Morgan, Maresh would "hold it and walk funny to get to me," before evacuating himself. Maresh's attorney argued that flatulence was a form of free speech, and so covered by the First Amendment. The judge ruled that no law directly covered the subject of flatulence, and threw the case out.

Time

"Old Bald Head"

The Confederate General Richard Stoddart Ewell, or "Old Bald Head" as he was known by his troops, was a brave but flawed military leader who ate nothing but wheat boiled in milk and harboured the delusion that he was a bird, a problem that became apparent whenever he cocked his head to one side and made chirping noises. To complete the picture, Ewell was also known for his beaky nose. He served under General "Stonewall" Jackson in 1862 and was seriously wounded at Second Bull Run. Ewell returned to action with a brand new wooden leg and newly married to a lady he always referred to as "Mrs Brown". He escaped further injury, except for an incident where his wooden leg received a direct hit from a Yankee sharpshooter's bullet.

Monty at Hind Quarters

British Allied commander Field Marshal Bernard Law
Montgomery of El Alamein (1887–1976) was known to be both
arrogant and highly ambitious. Monty was on record as asserting
that he was one of the three greatest military commanders of all
time (along with Alexander the Great and Napoleon). His Chief
of Staff Sir Alan Brooke commented to King George VI at a
social function in 1944 that the problem with "Monty" was that
"every time I meet him I think he's after my job." The King
replied, "You should worry. When I meet him I always think
he's after mine." Monty's odd behaviour at the front often left
his long-suffering chiefs of staff scratching their heads. One day
in France in 1944 a young officer returned from hospital after
being wounded. Monty summoned the young man to his caravan
and ordered him to strip. The puzzled officer did as he was told.
Monty peered at him for a while, then ordered him to dress: "I
wanted to assure myself that you are fit for duty. You can go
now." In 1967 Montgomery urged the House of Lords to throw
out a bill to legalize gay sex, warning that it would be a "charter
for buggery . . . this sort of thing may be tolerated by the
French, but we're British – thank God." In 1985 the book *Monty
at Close Quarters* was published, a collection of anecdotes by
men who served under Monty during World War II. It was
known in the trade as *Monty at Hind Quarters*.

"Bulletcatcher" Kitchener

General Earl Horatio Herbert Kitchener (1850–1916),
immortalized as a poster art icon of the British army recruitment
drive for the First World War, enjoyed his reputation as the hard
man of the British Empire; he once claimed that in the heat of
battle he caught a bullet in his teeth.

Mad, bad and dangerous to know

"A disordered appendix"
Although the press baron North Northcliffe went completely
mad in his later years, his editors were still obliged to follow his
instructions because he was still the boss. Northcliffe once
cabled the editor of the *Daily Mail* complaining that there
weren't enough giraffes in the Teddy Tail comic strip and on
another occasion instructed him to publish the entire contents of
every menu on board the ocean liner *Aquitania*. Northcliffe later
became convinced that the Germans were trying to assassinate
him by poisoning his ice-cream. He once cabled King George V:
"I am turning Roman Catholic." The King cabled back,
"I cannot help it." On a trip to Europe Northcliffe became
convinced that someone was trying to kill him by poisoning his
ice-cream, and was subsequently returned to England in a strait-
jacket. His newspapers asserted that the great man was suffering
from "a disordered appendix".

Whatever takes your fancy
The Ottoman Sultan Mahomet III enjoyed watching women's
breasts being scorched off with hot irons.

Pickled mistress
The Russian Czar Peter the Great kept the head of one of his
favourite former mistresses pickled in alcohol in a bedside jar.

This way to the circus
The Roman Emperor Nero had crucified Christians covered in
tar and set alight to form avenues of glowing human torches to
show spectators the way to Christians versus Lions contests.

How to deal with sibling rivalry

Behind the battlements of their Grand Seraglio Palace, the Ottoman Sultans of Turkey perfected a traditional method of assassination. It involved strangulation with silk bowstrings, performed by deaf mutes who had their eardrums perforated and their tongues cut out to make them candidates for the job. The practice began with Mahomet the Conqueror (1431–81) who introduced a law which stated that his successors had the right to execute their own brothers to help smooth the path of succession and avoid unnecessary sibling rivalry. When Mahomet III took the throne in 1595, his father's dedicated work in the harem meant that the new Sultan had to murder his nineteen brothers all aged under eleven, and throw seven of Murad III's pregnant mistresses into the river Bosphorus. Thereafter, close male relatives were spared execution and instead incarcerated in a windowless cell called "The Cage" with only deaf mutes and sterilized concubines for company, sometimes for up to 50 years. By the time the new Sultans came to power they were more often than not completely insane. The practice was finally abolished in 1789, but by then hereditary madness was already firmly established in the Ottoman line of succession.

Queue here

There are 92,000 Americans currently on a waiting list to go to the moon.

A man's best friend?

When animal experiments first became widespread at the turn of the century, many of the tests involved reflected more on the mental state of the surgeons than the results they expected to achieve. In 1908 the American Charles Guthrie transplanted the head of a dog on to the body of another dog. The animal

survived for a day. In 1950 the Moscow surgeon Vladimir
Demichov created a two-headed dog from one large and one
much larger animal. The creature lived on for 29 days.

The prostitute emperor
The Roman Emperor Elagabalus, although he married five times
in four years, was sexually confused. He liked to dress up and
pretend he was a female prostitute, and set aside a room in his
palace where he would hide behind a curtain and solicit
passers-by. His unfortunate "clients" were expected not only to
humour him, but also to pay well for the privilege.

Gorilla centrepiece
The wealthy nineteenth-century naturalist and explorer Charles
Waterton was noted for anti-social behaviour which earned him
affectionate respect as one of England's great eccentrics, at a
time when similar behaviour by a commoner would have earned
a one-way ticket to Bedlam. Waterton loved to exhibit his prized
collection of stuffed animals around his home, but found
orthodox taxidermy too boring. He kept himself amused by
grafting parts of different animals on to each other, and once
surprised his dinner guests by displaying the partially dissected
corpse of a gorilla on his dining table.

Do as I say, not as I do
Although Edgar Allan Poe never actually spent time in an
asylum, he was said to have been certifiably insane. Poe was an
alcoholic and laudanum addict but it didn't stop him joining the
local Temperance Society and giving lectures on the evils of
drink. In 1849 he was found lying in the gutter suffering from
delirium tremens and died a few days later.

153

URBAN MYTHS
True or False – you decide

A CIGAR AFICIONADO'S CLAIM

A cigar smoker once bought several hundred expensive
cigars and had them all insured against fire. Once he had
smoked all the cigars, he tried to make a claim. His
argument was that fire had destroyed the cigars. The
company refused the claim, and a court case ensued. The
judge's decision was in favour of the aficionado – he ruled
that the insurance company had agreed to insure against
firc, so as a result it was legally responsible. The company
paid the claim. But when the man accepted the cash, the
company immediately had him arrested for arson.

A tax on beards
Peter the Great tried to pay for his almost perpetual war-making
by imposing massive taxes on beards and bee-keeping.

The American Society for Indecency to Naked Animals
In the 1960s the American Society for Indecency to Naked
Animals (sic) claimed a membership of 50,000 people who were
dedicated to forcing animals to wear clothes for the sake of
decency. The society's President Clifford Prout asserted
that his pressure group was so strong that within a few years it
would be normal to see dogs and cats wearing trousers.
In1963 they picketed the White House in an attempt to make

Jackie Kennedy clothe her horse. Mr Prout explained that the
Society's somewhat misleading name was due to an unfortunate
grammatical error which could not now be changed for financial
reasons.

Unlucky Sporus
The Emperor Nero was besotted with his beautiful second wife
Poppaea, and once wrote a song about her fabulous, long,
auburn hair. Three years after the wedding day, however, while
Poppaea was pregnant, they had a tiff during which Nero
accidentally kicked her to death. The Emperor was grief-
stricken, but found consolation soon afterwards when he spotted
a young male slave named Sporus who very much resembled his
late wife. Nero had him castrated and went through a marriage
ceremony with him.

Shooting at the moon
In Phnom Penh in 1972, two people were killed and fifty injured
when hundreds of Cambodian troops suddenly opened fire at the
moon. *The Times* reported that the soldiers had fired into the sky
to prevent an eclipse of the moon by a monster frog called
Reahou, who wanted to eat the moon and must be stopped.

Roman pastimes
The favourite pastime of the Roman Emperor Tiberius was to
sodomize young boys. If they protested, he had their legs
broken.

The catch
While Robert Maxwell was busy stealing around £500 million
from his employees' pension funds, at the same time he was
appearing in an expensive video production designed to

persuade workers that their money was safe in his hands. It was called *What's the Catch?*

POTTY WISDOM, CHINA

When one is past thirty, one can about half comprehend the weather.

Stalin's overseas murder squad

Anatolevich Sudoplatov, head of Stalin's newly-formed special overseas murder squad, offered this advice to his recruiting officers in 1946: "Go search for people who are hurt by fate or nature – the ugly, those suffering from an inferiority complex, craving power and influence but defeated by unfavourable circumstances. The sense of belonging to an influential, powerful organization will give them a feeling of superiority over the handsome and prosperous people around them and for the first time in their lives they will experience a sense of importance. It is sad and humanly shallow but we are obliged to profit from it."

MURDER AND MAYHEM

Murder and Mayhem: The Rostov Ripper

The Soviet Union always played down its crime figures, insisting that crime was largely a problem for the wicked capitalist West, although in the mid-1980s, the Tass News Agency admitted that a man would go on trial in the city of Vitebsk for the murder of thirty-three women. But in April 1992, in the new Russia, Andrei Chikatilo, a fifty-six-year-old teacher of literature, went on trial in Moscow for murdering fifty-three children – eleven boys and forty-two girls – at Rostov over a twelve-year period. Chikatilo admitted that he lured his victims into the woods, tied them to trees and stabbed them between the eyes, after which he sliced up the bodies and ate the flesh. After three months in prison in 1984 for theft of state property, he made up for lost time by killing eight people in one month. A convicted rapist was mistakenly executed for one of Chikatilo's crimes.

Ever the scientist
The childhood hobby of the Russian Czar Ivan the Terrible was throwing live dogs off the Kremlin roof "to observe their pain".

The wine and lute-string torture

The Roman Emperor Tiberius became bored with the array of
tortures in fashion at the time and decided to invent a few of his
own. His favourite was to force the victim to drink vast
quantities of wine until the bladder was at maximum pressure,
then tie up his genitalia with a lute string. Tiberius was such a
well respected torturer that many of his prisoners committed
suicide as soon as they were accused rather than bother waiting
for the trial.

A thorough job

When Caligula ran out of money he found a novel way of
raising cash – he opened his palace as a brothel, and high-
ranking members of the Senate were forced to pay 1,000 gold
pieces each for the privilege of having sex with his sisters. They
were then ordered to send their wives and daughters to work
with his sisters in the palace brothel. Caligula was finally killed
when one of his guards ran a sword through the Emperor's
genitals: another group of guards meanwhile murdered his
wife then dashed out the brains of his baby daughter against a
wall.

One way to deal with stand-up comedy

Tamurlane, a descendant of Genghis Khan, was considered the
most violent of all the Mongol leaders. He celebrated his
conquest of Sabzawar in 1383 by having 2,000 prisoners buried
alive and had 5,000 people beheaded at Zirih, using their heads
to build a pyramid. In India he massacred about 100,000
prisoners and had thousands of Christians buried alive.
Tamurlane was not known for his sense of humour: he had
anyone who told a joke put to death.

Vlad the Impaler

Although the historical "Count Dracula" Vlad Tepes had an unparalleled appetite for sadism he was considered a hero in his country. Tepes, who ruled over Walachia (now part of Romania) between 1456 and 1476, had about 20,000 of his enemies impaled on wooden stakes, and enjoyed drinking the blood of his victims. In his spare time he forced wives to eat the roasted bodies of their husbands, and parents to eat the flesh of their own children. He was also a brilliant general and was adored by his fellow countrymen because he defeated their sworn enemies, the Turks. When a large troop of Tartars strayed into his territory, he selected three of them, had them fried, then forced the others to eat them. When Turkish envoys arrived at his palace to sue for peace, he had their hats and coats nailed to their bodies.

Self-execution

Unlike Tiberius, Caligula and Claudius before him, Nero didn't enjoy watching men die because he couldn't stand the sight of spilled blood. He preferred to order his enemies to commit suicide: they usually did.

The Unholy Inquisition

During the Holy Inquisition, first unleashed by the Catholic Church in the mid-fifteenth century, a woman could be tried as a witch for simply being old enough, ugly enough, or being in possession of a cat, a wart, or red hair. Some of the ingenious tortures devised by the Dominicans to extract confessions from witches were subtle, some less so. In Germany, suspect witches were force-fed salted herring then denied water. Some had spikes forced beneath their fingernails and toenails and the soles of their feet burnt; others visited the rack, the "Spanish Boot", or were whipped, scourged, had their limbs dislocated or their bodies filled with water. Most confessed. Historians have calculated the total number of victims to have been between five and six million.

UFOLOGY
Ezekiel's Rocket

Josef F. Blumrich, a NASA space engineer who had spent most of his life designing and building aircraft and rockets – among them the giant Saturn V rocket – was irritated with Erich von Daniken's idea that what the prophet Ezekiel had seen was a UFO, and set out to refute him. Incredibly, he himself became a convert, and worked out a reconstruction of the spacecraft he thought Ezekiel had seen, including details of how it might have been operated.

Go to Mass

The full force of the Holy Inquisition at its most brutal was saved for a religious sect known as the Waldenses, who had settled in the Piedmont region of northern Italy. One of the favourite methods of torture used by the soldiers was to place small bags of gunpowder in the mouths of victims and to set fire to them. Records show that one Bartholomew Frasche had holes drilled through his heels and ropes passed through the wounds and was dragged through the streets. Daniel Rambaut had his fingers and toes amputated a joint at a time until he promised to be a good Catholic. Sara Rastignole had a sickle thrust through her lower abdomen. Martha Constantine was raped and her breasts removed. Mary Pelanchion was stripped naked, and hung head first from a bridge so that soldiers could use her for target practice. Jacopo di Rone had his nails torn off with red-hot pincers and holes bored through his hands, and strips of his flesh were cut off with a sword until he agreed to go to Mass.

No half measures
Czar Ivan IV, the Terrible, emerged from a serious illness when he was twenty-three years old. He was given to bouts of random and spectacular brutality and to tearing clumps of his hair out until his scalp bled. He also specialized in ingenious deaths for his enemies; when the archbishop of Novgorod was suspected of organizing an uprising against him, Ivan had the entire population, about 50,000 people, massacred by tossing them into a freezing river. He then had the archbishop sewn into a bearskin and hunted to death by a pack of hounds. When he conquered Withenstein he had the defeated Finnish leader roasted alive on a spit. He died, however, playing chess.

A revolutionary in a hurry
The Nantes lawyer Jean-Baptiste Carrier was a French Revolutionary in a hurry, for whom the guillotine was far too slow and inefficient. He had his victims packed into barges, towed into the river Loire, then drowned. Couples were stripped naked and tied face to face, while Carrier's henchmen stood on the river banks with axes in case anyone escaped drowning. The water became so polluted with human corpses that fishing was banned. Carrier also discovered that the guillotine was an unsatisfactory method of beheading infants. The heads of tiny children were chopped in half because their necks made too small a target for the blade: one executioner collapsed and died

from a heart attack after beheading four little sisters. Instead Carrier had 500 children rounded up in a field then shot and cudgelled to death.

Joke of the Day

Three men are waiting expectantly outside the labour ward of the city hospital. After a few minutes, a nurse comes out to tell the first man:

"Congratulations. You are the father of twins."

"Twins!" he exclaims. "How about that? I work for the Doublemint Chewing Gum Company!"

Five minutes later, a nurse comes out to tell the second man:

"Congratulations. You are the father of triplets."

"Triplets!" he says. "What an amazing coincidence! I work for the 3M Organization!"

The third man stands up ashen-faced and mutters: "I need some air. I work for 7-Up!"

Practice pageboys

The Ottoman Sultan Osman II enjoyed archery practice on live pageboys.

Purged of the will to live

Mussolini was the first twentieth-century dictator to make torture official state policy. His blackshirts invented their own technique – they would pump a prisoner full of castor oil to "purge him of the will to live".

Chilli torture

In 1975 President Julius Nyerere's Tanzanian police forced confessions from prisoners by inserting hot chilli peppers into their eyes, nostrils, ears, mouths and anuses.

The Piranha brothers

Monty Python's Flying Circus satirized the 1960s London's gangland scene with a sketch featuring Doug and Dinsdale Piranha, two brothers who terrorized victims by nailing their heads to the floor and screwing their pelvises to cake-stands. The inspiration for this famous sketch came not from the Kray Twins Ron and Reggie, but from the Richardson gang, who terrorized South London at around the same time. Although the Krays earned more notoriety, in terms of sheer sadism the Richardsons were in a league of their own. Led by Charles Richardson and his younger brother Eddie, they specialized in torture. While Charles dressed up in judge's robes, victims were tried before kangaroo courts, then had their teeth removed with pliers and electrical generators attached to their testicles with crocodile clips. The Richardsons' tour de force however was staking victims to the ground with 6-inch nails then removing their toes with bolt cutters.

 Don't worry, be happy

Be confident in who you really are and happiness will follow.

The ex-monk, Pol Pot

Pol Pot, the Cambodian whose philosophy of Rural Revolution wiped out 3 million of his fellow countrymen, was a former Buddhist monk.

Death by coffee

The Turks evolved a new method of assassination during the reign of the Ottoman Sultans in the seventeenth century: a cup of Turkish coffee was laced with chopped hair and ground glass, which was guaranteed to destroy the victim's intestines during a long and painful death.

Rough justice for tax evaders

Indian tax collectors in the nineteenth century persuaded defaulters to pay up by forcing them to drink buffalo milk laced with salt until the victim was half-dead with diarrhea.

The Battle of Arnhem 1944

After breaking out from Normandy, Montgomery put forward an ambitious plan to outflank German defences by securing bridges across the Maas, Waal and Lower Rhine. In Operation Market Garden, on 17 September, three airborne divisions – the US 101st and 82nd and the British 1st – were parachuted in between Nijmegen and Arnhem. The Americans took and held bridges over the Maas and Waal, but the British landed too far from the bridge at Arnhem to seize it with ease. They fought their way to Arnhem but were then attacked by the 9th SS Panzer, whom they repulsed in bitter fighting – so violent that the Germans were ultimately reluctant to engage them. As they held out against infinitely greater forces, an attempt by the Polish Parachute Brigade to relieve them failed, and on 25 September some 2,400 survivors withdrew by boat. The rest were finally compelled to surrender. They lost 1,130 dead; 6,450 were taken prisoner. German casualties were over 3,000.

The sexually perverse train-wrecker
The Hungarian Sylvestre Matushka had a unique sexual
perversion – he was turned on by watching large-scale human
catastrophes. As the odds against him coming across more than
a couple in a lifetime were not good, he decided to engineer a
few himself. In twelve months he derailed two trains with
explosives, killing twenty-two passengers and injuring sixteen.
He was finally arrested in 1932 while attempting a third
derailment, and jailed for life.

Dial M for Mengele
Thanks to Argentina's Peronist pro-Nazi sympathizers,
Dr Joseph Mengele and other leading Nazis were allowed to live
openly under their own names when they fled to Argentina after
Word War II. Mengele was even listed in the Buenos Aires
phone book.

Churchill as Home Secretary
When Winston Churchill was Home Secretary in 1910 he
advocated that in the interests of racial purity, mentally
incompetent people should be neutered and tramps and
vagabonds rounded up and placed in concentration camps.

Tragedy and statistics
Joseph Stalin, who killed more people in thirty years than Ivan
the Terrible and all of the other Russian Czars managed in over
400 years, reasoned his behaviour thus: "The death of a man is a
tragedy: the death of a thousand is a statistic."

The Empress Elagabalus
The Emperor Elagabalus was Rome's most celebrated trans-
sexual. After failing to find a doctor who could perform a

sex-change operation he settled for castration and "married" a hunky slave called Zoticus. He called himself the Empress and took to hanging around brothels so that he could satisfy the customers himself. Elagabalus was murdered on the lavatory and his body thrown into the Tiber.

Murderous America
One in every 1,000 Americans is a murderer.

How did you enjoy that?
Richard Wagner always composed in a stiflingly hot room perfumed with roses while wearing a silk dressing gown, which belied the fact that he was also a notorious womanizer. Wagner was also touchy about critics: he often invited friends around, treated them to a sneak preview of his work then asked them for a frank opinion. Anyone who didn't offer a glowing review would be threatened with physical violence.

Fish fight
Genghis Khan murdered his own brother in an argument over a fish.

Bodysnatchers
Although the names Burke and Hare are commonly associated with bodysnatching, they never once robbed a grave. In the flourishing market of the nineteenth century "resurrection" trade they decided to improve their business turnover by cutting out the middle man (i.e. natural death) and creating a few corpses of their own. Burke, who had served as a medical orderly on the battlefield at Waterloo, gave the English language the word "burking", meaning "to kill stealthily", originally for the purpose of selling the victim's body for anatomical research.

Together, he and Hare stalked the Edinburgh slumlands in the 1820s and accounted for at least sixteen victims. Their preferred method of assassination was suffocation: one lay across the victim's chest while they other held the mouth closed and pinched the nostrils.

In the wrong place at the wrong time
When Genghis Khan died in the middle of a siege, his followers were determined that his death be kept a secret until his son and heir Ogatai was safely in control. Khan's final victims were the bystanders who innocently spotted his funeral procession as it headed for the burial ground: they were all put to the sword.

Stabbed in the groin
After an attempted rebellion of his troops, the Roman Emperor Domitian extracted confessions by holding a blazing torch under the prisoners' genitals. Courtiers guilty of even the mildest of criticism were crucified upside down. His inevitable assassination in AD 96 was almost a carbon-copy of Caligula's death – he was stabbed in the genitals.

Ear skirts
While the French Revolutionary Jean-Paul Marat was inciting mobs to attack the jails of Paris in 1791 to purge them of counter-revolutionaries, Parisian women wore severed ears pinned to their skirts as souvenirs. In six days half the population of Paris's prisons were slaughtered.

Woolding
The French seventeenth-century pirate Jean David Nau – "Le Lolonais" to his friends – was probably the most feared of all pirates. He invented his own technique for torturing

prisoners for pleasure. He had a cord tied around their heads, which he twisted with a stick until the victim's eyes shot out: this trick was known as "woolding". Lolonais's own demise was an altogether messier affair. He was captured by Darian Indians, who slowly tore him limb from limb while he was still conscious then tossed bits of him into a fire while he watched.

The motivational techniques of Columbus
Christopher Columbus fed his dogs on the bodies of murdered Indians. Natives who were unable to deliver him with sufficient gold had their hands hacked off.

Leniency
Genghis Khan's conquests were marked by acts of breathtaking sadism; he once stormed a town called Termez and slaughtered all of the inhabitants; one old woman was about to be killed but she begged for mercy in return for a pearl, which she said she had swallowed for safekeeping. The old woman was promptly disembowelled and several pearls were discovered inside her. Khan heard about it and ordered that all of the dead should be opened up and their stomachs inspected. He was not however entirely without compassion: he once decided that a defeated foe, who turned out to be an old childhood friend, should be spared the expected bloody execution; he had him rolled in a carpet and kicked to death instead.

Pig-sticking
King Miguel of Portugal liked to toss live piglets in the air so he could catch them on the point of his sword.

Thought for the Day

The only thing more accurate than incoming enemy fire is incoming friendly fire.

The wet-trousered disciplinarian

Queen Victoria's father Edward, Duke of Kent made a career in the British army where he earned himself a reputation as a brutal disciplinarian. Like many of the officer class he believed that the only way to lick a soldier into shape was to beat him into submission; the added bonus for the perverted Duke however was that he was sexually aroused by the sight of men being whipped, which unfortunately also made him wet his trousers. At his posting in Gibraltar he thrashed his soldiers at the drop of a hat to the point of mutiny; it was said that the number of floggings in the Duke's regiment went up roughly in line with his laundry bill.

Prolific murderers

And the winner is . . .

In 2006 Jack the Ripper was named the worst Briton of the past 1,000 years. The infamous killer received twenty-four per cent of the vote in a poll for *BBC History* magazine.

Mudgett the mass murderer

America's busiest mass murderer was the former New Hampshire medical student Herman Webster Mudgett. During the Chicago Exposition in 1893 he seduced, drugged and murdered young girls in a house on 63rd Street, known as his "Torture Castle". After murdering his victims Mudgett burned and dissolved the corpses in acid or lime, saving the best bits for further experimentation in his upstairs laboratory. When police searched his home they found the remains of 200 corpses, but there must have been many, many more. He was hanged on 7 May 1896.

Thuggee membership fees

The ancient Indian killer cult Thuggee (hence the word "thug") was an exclusive club with a strictly controlled membership. In order to retain it, you were obliged to strangle a minimum of one innocent victim a year.

Britain's busiest female serial killer

Britain's all-time busiest female serial killer was Mary Anne Cotton, born in 1832 in a Durham pit village. Her chosen method of execution was arsenic poisoning. She killed at least fifteen, and probably up to twenty-one people, including three husbands, eight of her own children, four step-children and her mother. She died horribly: her bungled hanging in March 1873 took several minutes to complete.

The man who strangled 931 people

Although the precise figures will probably never be known it is likely that Chairman Mao killed more people than Stalin and Hitler combined. Discounting political leaders however, the world's most prolific murderer was a member of the Indian Thuggee cult named Behram. At his trial he was convicted of strangling 931 people over a fifty-year period, each and every one of them with the same strip of cloth.

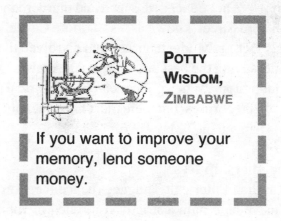

POTTY WISDOM, ZIMBABWE

If you want to improve your memory, lend someone money.

The Yorkshire Ripper and the "triangle of terror"
Peter William Sutcliffe, the "Yorkshire Ripper", sparked off the biggest murder manhunt in British history between July 1975 and November 1980 when he raped and murdered thirteen women. Most of his victims were prostitutes, mostly bludgeoned to death with a hammer or strangled in an area between Leeds, Bradford and West Yorkshire known as the "triangle of terror". Sutcliffe was discovered during a routine police check while he was having sex with a prostitute in a parked car in Sheffield. He was tried at the Old Bailey in May 1981 and is currently serving life imprisonment. In 1987 he lost an eye when he was attacked by a fellow Broadmoor psychopath.

URBAN MYTHS
True or False – you decide

HOW TO PREDICT THE GENDER OF A BABY

Through history people have claimed to be able to predict the sex of a baby before it is born. Here are a few of the methods used:

- **High or Low?** A girl is carried high – and the stomach has a round appearance, while a boy is carried low and the stomach has a wider extension.
- **A Kicker Or An Idler?** Girls kick more than boys. According to one expert this is because boys are innately lazier, even before birth.
- **Hands Up?** If the baby's hands are raised, the child is a girl; if they are down, it is a boy.
- **Which Side?** If the unborn kicks on the right side of the mother's womb, he's a boy; if on the left, she's a girl.
- **Stripey Mom**: A woman with a stripe down her middle will have a boy.
- **Fast Heartbeat**: If a baby's heart beats over 130 beats per minute it is a girl – under 130 it is a boy.
- **Sweet And Sour**: A woman who has cravings for sweets will have a boy; if she craves sour foods she's carrying a girl.
- **Hairy Legs**: If the mother's leg hair grows more rapidly than usual during the pregnancy, it will be a girl.
- **The Spinning Wedding Ring**: Tie your wedding ring to a piece of string or a lock of hair and hang it over the mother's stomach. If the ring spins counter-clockwise, it's a boy. If it spins clockwise, it's a girl.

Frederick and Rosemary West

Frederick West and his wife Rosemary formed the most
extraordinary homicidal double act in British criminal history. In
1994 police dug up their home and garden at 25 Cromwell
Street, Gloucester and discovered a succession of bodies which
had been buried from between seven and twenty-three years
previously, including those of two of their daughters. Fred West
hanged himself in his cell on New Year's Day 1995 but not
before telling police that there were twenty more undiscovered
bodies and that his wife Rosemary and his brother were among
those responsible. In December 1996 West's younger brother
John, a fifty-four-year-old retired dustman and father of four,
also hanged himself in his garage, hours before a jury had the
chance to convict him on charges of raping his own niece on
more than 300 occasions.

Amelia Dyer, the baby "farmer"

Amelia Dyer, a former Salvation Army worker from Bristol, may
have been the UK's deadliest ever female killer. In the 1870s she
worked as a midwife, supplementing her income with the illegal
Victorian trade of "baby farming", a convention whereby the
illegitimate or inconvenient babies of middle-class women would
be farmed out to working-class foster mothers for anything up to a
few years at a time. Dyer's handling fee was usually £10 per child.
In 1895 police dragged the Thames near Richmond and found the
bodies of seven infants, all parcelled, taped and weighed down
with bricks, all children who had been "farmed" by Amelia Dyer.
She never revealed how many she had killed, but her carefully
detailed accounts showed that she had handled scores of children
over a period of twenty years, none of whom could be traced. The
jury took five minutes to declare her "Guilty – not insane", and she
was hanged at Newgate prison on 10 June 1896.

That's entertainment

Dwarf entertainment
Dwarfs, for anyone who could afford to keep them, were the eighteenth-century equivalent of TV; if you were royalty you had one in every room. King George I had a court dwarf called Christian Ulrich Jorry, who entertained at supper parties, a gift from a German nobleman. Queen Victoria was also much amused by dwarfs. She showed an "infantile delight" in General Tom Thumb – the dwarf Charles Stratton – who was invited back to the palace for several royal command performances.

Jim Morrison's cock
Jim Morrison of The Doors was found guilty of exposure after asking his audience one evening, "Do you want to see my cock?"

A beautiful voice
In 1994 Thai businessman Chan Ka Sek walked into a Bangkok karaoke bar with his two bodyguards and spent the next three hours at the microphone, treating fellow customers to *Candle in the Wind* four times. When an irate customer complained that Sek was hogging the microphone, one of the bodyguards shot him dead. Sek confessed, "We were carried away by the beauty of my voice."

The non-singing duo
Eighties duo Milli Vanilli were voted worst band of all time, in a survey held in 2006. The US duo lip-synched to all their songs: it wasn't until they won a Grammy that the public found out they never sang a note.

Barry Manila

In the Philippines Barry Manilow is worshipped almost as a god. In 1983, 50,000 Filipinos paid to see him perform five nights running, and his albums are widely bootlegged.

Miss Piggy: banned in Turkey

Because the Koran teaches that pigs are unclean, Miss Piggy is always edited out of Turkish television re-runs of *The Muppet Show*.

TV suicide

On 15 July, 1974 Christine Chubbock, thirty-year-old hostess of a Florida morning talk-show, interrupted her reading of the news broadcast and said: "In keeping with Channel 40's policy of bringing you the latest in blood and guts and in living colour, you are going to see another first . . . attempted suicide." She then produced a .38 revolver and shot herself in the head. It emerged later that she had scripted her suicide so as not to disrupt the TV schedule.

The singing nun

Proof that the devil really does have all the best tunes came in the form of The Singing Nun, aka Sister Luc-Gabrielle, a Belgian nun with an acoustic guitar, who was tragically never quite able to repeat the success of her unexpected smash hit single of 1963 *Dominique*. She did however come up with a million-selling album featuring such classics as *Mets ton joli jupon* ("Put on your pretty skirt") and *J'ai trouvé le Signeur* ("I have found the Lord"), shortly before her popularity was inexplicably superseded by Beatlemania. Her new career flopped and facing bankruptcy she took her own life by carbon monoxide poisoning in a double suicide pact with her lesbian lover.

Death by harmonica
The Mexican entertainer Ramon Barrero played "the world's smallest harmonica" until, mid-performance in 1994, he inhaled a D-minor and accidentally choked to death.

Not a constitutional right
In 1991 the lead singer of Milwaukee rock band the Toilet Rockers was convicted of disorderly conduct after exercising what he claimed was his "constitutional right" to defecate onstage and fling his turds at the audience.

A Crunchie wrapped in chamois leather
Black Sabbath's lead singer Ozzy Osbourne really did bite off the head of a bat, but it wasn't deliberate. He thought that the dead bat, thrown onstage by a fan, was a rubber toy. Osbourne was immediately rushed to hospital for a course of tetanus jabs which left him unable to walk for days. He said, "It was like eating a Crunchie wrapped in chamois leather."

Gentlemen's gallery
The whipping of semi-naked female prisoners at London's Brideswell prison in the eighteenth century was so popular that a special gallery was constructed for spectators.

Barnum Blaxploitation
The American showman Phineas T. Barnum exploited dozens of freaks throughout his career but none more shamelessly than Joyce Heth, a poor old blind and semi-paralyzed black woman who Barnum advertised as "nurse to General George Washington . . . now at the astonishing age of 161 years". In fact she was only 80 years and Barnum had acquired her from a sideshow in Philadelphia. When Joyce Heth died in 1836 he

found another way of making money from the poor woman – he hired a leading pathologist to perform an autopsy on her in front of a paying audience.

Finished in Finland
Donald Duck was originally banned in Finland because he doesn't wear underpants.

Package tour to an execution
In 1889 Thomas Cook's travel agency organized a package tour to watch the executions by guillotine of Messrs Allorto and Sellier. He filled 300 seats on a chartered fleet of horse-buses.

More of everything
The Sicilian Frank Lentini was probably the world's biggest crowd-pulling sideshow freak. The so-called "King of Freaks" was the result of non-separating triplets, which left him with three legs, two sets of genitals and four feet.

Poker-faced
Illegal gamblers in Manila often have corpses sitting in on their card games. The Filipino police have a habit of busting gambling dens and demanding bribes to allow the game to continue, but because most of them are devoutly Catholic they would never raid a wake or a funeral. The gamblers usually buy the bodies from the unclaimed corpse section of the local mortuary.

Anti-groupie ring
In ancient Rome members of the showbiz fraternity were expected to wear rings through holes pierced in their foreskins to discourage them from taking advantage of female groupies.

Rigged rodeos

Although the traditional North American rodeo is sold as harmless, red-blooded all-American entertainment, it is almost as inhumane as bull-fighting. The animals used, far from being wild, outlaw stock which need to be subdued by heroic cowboys, are generally ordinary domestic livestock. They are deliberately goaded into a frenzy by raking them with spurs, constricting the genitals with leather straps and the application of electric prods to their rectums.

Two years better spent

The average Briton will spend two years of his or her life watching TV advertisements.

TV hazard

Every year 7,000 Britons end up in hospital as victims of TV-related accidents. The 1992 casualty list included a woman who tripped and crashed head first through the screen, a man who landed a punch at his TV during a boxing match, a teenager who dislocated her knee while copying the dancers on *Top of the Pops*, a rottweiller owner who became so excited during the programme that his dog attacked him, and a boy who fainted while watching a particularly bloody scene in *Casualty* and woke up in his local accident unit.

Rat "sport"

Rat killing was one of the most popular spectator sports for the Victorian gentleman. For one shilling he could watch and place bets on dozens of dogs as they ripped their way through hundreds of live rats in a large pit. The winning dog, i.e. the one who destroyed the largest number of rats, received a special collar and a cash prize for the owner. The record was held by a dog who killed 500 rats in less than six minutes. The dogs usually suffered appalling injuries as a result of savage rat bites, usually to the mouth and muzzle.

Ladies' day at the Surgeon's Hall
In the eighteenth century Surgeon's Hall in London was regularly decorated with the dead bodies of executed murderers for public viewing. Not surprisingly, naked corpses attracted voyeurs: *The Times* reported with distaste that women had queued to see the naked corpse of a reputedly well-endowed killer who had robbed and murdered a servant girl then enjoyed a three-in-a-bed romp with the corpse and his girlfriend.

Gala hangings
The term "gala day" derives from the gruesome eighteenth-century custom of declaring public holidays during notable executions at Tyburn (now Marble Arch) in London, to entertain the mob. These occasions were originally known as "gallows days". In total, about 60,000 people were put to death at Tyburn.

The Jim Rose Alternative Circus
The Seattle-based Jim Rose Alternative Circus boasts the world's most tasteless speciality acts. Their star turn is Matt Cowley, who entertains people by sticking 47 feet of tubing up his nose and into his gut; he then pumps a mixture of beer, chocolate and ketchup into his stomach. The resulting green mixture of "bile beer" is then pumped back out again and offered to a member of the audience for consumption. Another Alternative Circus favourite is the transvestite Mr Lifto, who perforates his foreskin with a coat hanger then suspends weights from it.

ANIMAL NEWS Batty Blood Bank

Vampire bats in Texas are being forced to change their diet. The South American, blood-drinking bats at the Houston Zoological Gardens in Texas have had their supply of beef blood ($1.20/gallon) cut off because of the meat shortage. Curator Richard Quick explained that the meat packing firm that used to provide the bats' liquid diet had recently been forced to close down. Until the crisis is over the bats are being fed on *human* blood discarded by local hospitals.

Sunday Mirror

Bedlam

Watching the insane at the Royal Bethlem (Bedlam) Hospital in the eighteenth century was the latter-day equivalent of a day out at London Zoo. Spectators flocked to buy tickets from the Hospital so they could watch the mentally ill cavort. Hospital records for 1779 noted that some visitors were abusing the system, and it was decided that the words "and three friends" should be printed on the invitations to limit the numbers to four per ticket. At the Hospice de Charenton lunatic asylum in northern France the inmates were made to wear fancy dress costume and perform for the amusement of paying customers.

Protestant fun

During anti-Popery demonstrations in the seventeenth and eighteenth centuries British Protestants entertained themselves by putting live cats inside effigies of the Pope, which were then set ablaze. The tortured animals would give out screams which, to all-round amusement, appeared to come from the dummy

Pope's mouth. In France it was once a Midsummer's Day tradition to toss live cats on to a public bonfire, or to torture cats at fairgrounds for general public amusement.

Pig organ

When King Louis XI of France, noted for his sick sense of humour and bizarre whims, once demanded to be entertained by "a consort of swine voices", opportunity knocked for the Abbot of Baigne – France's only entertainer on the novelty pig organ. The abbot laid a range of pigs out side by side, and when he struck the organ keys small spikes would prick the pigs causing them to squeal "in such an order and consonance as highly delighted the king and all his company".

Your eatin' heart

In 2004 Armin Meiwes, a 42-year-old computer expert from Germany, was sentenced to just eight and a half years for killing and eating a man he met over the internet when his lawyer success-fully argued that the victim had been a consenting dinner date. Meiwes, who fried and ate his victim's penis, said he planned to list his "recipes" in his forthcoming autobiography and was looking forward to seeing his story made into a film starring High Grant and Brad Pitt. Meanwhile German filmmaker Rosa von Praunheim began work on his movie based on the convicted cannibal with the working title *Your Heart in My Brain*. It begins with Meiwes being confronted in prison by his victim's head.

Royalty

The sartorially eccentric Richard II
The court of King Richard II (1377–1399) was renowned for decadence and sartorial eccentricity. The king himself was known for his fantastic gemstone-covered ballgown and, a dead giveaway for effeminacy in the fourteenth century, took a regular bath. He had an open affair with Robert de Vere, Earl of Oxford. When de Vere died the King had a breakdown and became completely inactive, and was deposed and murdered.

Killjoy monk
King Henry III of France was known as the King of Sodom and wore spectacular ballgowns while chasing pretty French boys around his court. Henry's effeminate followers, a gang of young male courtiers known as Les Mignons, slavishly copied him in every detail, painted their faces and wore their hair long and piled high on their heads. The royal party was cut short when he was stabbed to death by an outraged monk, Jacques Clément.

What a lice boy
In 1983 Diana, Princess of Wales went on a walkabout in South Australia, mingling freely with the crowds of people who had turned out to see her and her husband Charles on their royal tour. Along the way she met a small boy and playfully tousled his hair.

"Why aren't you at school today?" Diana beamed.

"I was sent home," replied the boy, "because I've got head lice."

POTTY WISDOM, SPAIN

A woman's advice is never worth having, yet no one but a fool refuses to follow it.

Cuckold's revenge

When England's King John found that his wife Isabella had taken a lover, he had him killed and his corpse strung up over Isabella's side of the bed.

That's entertainment

The Russian Grand Duke Constantine, a grandson of Catherine the Great, amused himself by kicking Hussars to death and firing live rats from a cannon.

Fair game?

The Russian Empress Anne loved hunting, but couldn't be bothered with the thrill of a long chase, or for that matter any chase at all, and most of the time didn't even get out of her carriage. A special hunting area was prepared in the park at Peterhof which was so thick with imported bears, wild boars, stags and other animals that all she had to do was poke her gun out of her carriage window to be sure of hitting something. Nothing however was left to chance: to ensure that she went home with plenty of trophies, the animals were driven past the muzzle of her gun at point-blank range. Every now and then the Empress would fancy a spot of hunting but was too idle to get out of bed. For these occasions the palace aviary was always fully stocked so that she could have a few flocks to shoot at from her bedroom window.

Stormin' Norman
King Henry I, the third Norman king of England, was blessed with allegedly phenomenal sexual stamina and set an undefeated record for an English king by fathering at least twenty-one illegitimate children.

The martyr queen
Queen Victoria ate too quickly, mixed whisky with her claret, and consequently was a martyr to her flatulence.

France's most infamous debauchee
The Duke of Orléans, regent to the boy-king Louis X, was one of France's most infamous debauchees. He held orgies at his home most evenings, had naked prostitutes served up nightly to his dinner guests on silver salvers and at one time kept one hundred mistresses, every one of them renowned for their ugliness: when his mother chided him for his choice of women he replied, "Mother, all cats are grey in the dark." He allegedly slept with his favourite eldest daughter, the none too fragrant Duchess de Berry, who regularly drank herself senseless and would roll in her own vomit on the carpet and eventually, according to her death certificate, ate herself to death. The Duke was chiefly infamous however for his drinking binges. He was already a senile and purple-faced old man in his early 40s, although he was still capable of knocking back seven bottles of wine a night, and his friends marvelled that he was alive at all. When he arrived in London, people who had

never seen him before placed bets that he would be dead within three months. In 1721 he took a new mistress who was nearly thirty years younger than him, against the advice of his doctors. The effect on his health was predictably disastrous: he was sitting by the fireplace of his drawing room at Versailles one day when he had a massive stroke. When a doctor tried to bleed him, a lady courtier shouted, "No! You'll kill him . . . he has just lain with a whore.' Two hours later the Duke was dead, aged forty-nine. Although everyone knew that the drink and wild living had killed him, royal etiquette required that there should be an official post mortem: unfortunately while it was being carried out the Duke's favourite dog snatched his master's heart and ate it.

Mausoleum Day

King George VII's birthday, 14 December, is cheerfully known to the royal family as Mausoleum Day because it was the anniversary of the death by cancer of Prince Albert and the death of Albert's third child Princess Alice some seventeen years later.

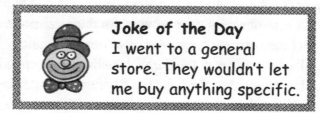

Joke of the Day
I went to a general store. They wouldn't let me buy anything specific.

Bring back hanging

King William I abolished capital punishment in England, but his motives weren't entirely charitable: he preferred to castrate, mutilate and blind people instead so that they were walking testaments to his authority.

Farting Roland

King Henry II kept a court jester named Roland who was required to fart for the amusement of his guests at the annual Christmas Day banquet.

True love

Queen Eleanor, wife of Edward I, saved her husband's life by sucking the pus out of a septic knife wound.

Curried head of Saracen

Although the exploits King Richard I, the Lion-Hearted, in the Third Crusade made him the hero of countless legends, Richard saw little of England (less than three years) and even less of his Queen Berengia. There are a number of apocryphal stories about his alleged male lovers, including his romantic attachment to his adversary the Muslim leader Saladin (who, in fact, he never actually met) and the gay minstrel Blondel (who almost certainly never existed). Richard fathered no heirs. King Richard did however once dine on curried head of Saracen.

No smoking

The Ottoman Sultan Murad IV was an early and passionate supporter of the anti-smoking lobby. He decreed the death penalty for anyone who was caught smoking tobacco and wherever he travelled around Turkey his stopping-off points were usually marked by spot executions of smokers. Even on the battlefield nicotine addicts were not safe from the Sultan. He had his own soldiers beheaded, or hanged and quartered, or would sometimes crush their hands and feet and leave them helpless in no man's land.

URBAN MYTHS
True or False – you decide

THE GIANT PYTHON

In late 2003, several news agencies broadcast a story about villagers in Indonesia capturing a 49-foot-long python, which weighed a staggering 983 pounds and had a diameter of 2.8 feet.

It was also reported that this mammoth reptile ate three or four dogs a month. The snake was said to have been caught on the island of Sumatra by members of the Kubu tribe. They apparently worshipped the extraordinary snake as something between a monarch and a deity and were reluctant to allow scientists to examine it.

If true, this would have been an astonishing snake indeed. The previous *longest* snake ever found was a mere 32.75 feet (10 metres) (a snake shot in Indonesia in 1912). The *heaviest* living snake is 403 pounds, a Burmese Python which lives at the Serpent Safari Park in Gurnee, Illinois.

A bloodless coup

When the King of Siam wanted to have some of his relatives murdered he was reminded of an inconvenient Siamese tradition which forbade the spilling of royal blood on the ground: he had them pounded to death with a mortar in a large pestle instead.

Don't do that again!
King Phillip II of Spain's son and heir Don Carlos had young girls whipped, had animals roasted alive while he watched and killed six men for fun. Dissatisfied with a pair of new boots, he had them cut into pieces and force fed to the cobbler. One evening when some water was inadvertently emptied from a house balcony and splashed near him, he had the occupants executed.

Strange statistician
King Edward VII faithfully recorded the height and weight of everyone who ever visited his home at Sandringham.

Thought for the Day

To be sure of hitting the target, shoot first, and call whatever you hit the target.

Fair's fair
In 1741 the Comte de Charolais, a cousin of France's King Louis XV, ordered his coachman to run over any monks he encountered on the road and shot a man he saw working on a roof, just for the hell of it. The king pardoned his naughty cousin but warned, "Let it be understood I will similarly pardon anyone who shoots you."

Ring sting
The Indian Prince the Maharajah of Jaipur declared a 15-mile
exclusion zone around his capital where he alone was allowed to
hunt. He had poachers tortured by pushing ground hot chillies
into their rectums.

A good picture
Russia's Czar Peter the Great had an awesome libido which he
sated on anyone who happened to be passing, irrespective of
sex or age. He paid the Saxon artist Danhauer to paint nude
portraits of his favourite pageboys, and once startled the visiting
Duke of Holstein by grabbing him by the ears and shoving his
tongue down his throat. One of the Czar's lovers, Abraham
Hannibal, was known at court as "the negro of Peter the Great".
He had originally been bought in a Turkish slave market and
given to Peter as a gift. Pushkin reported that their relationship
was so intimate that Peter once removed a tapeworm from
Abraham's anus with his own hands. "The anecdote is rather
dirty," noted Pushkin, "but it gives a good picture of Peter's
habits."

A stickler for royal etiquette
King George V was a renowned stickler for royal etiquette; he
wore his crown every day while he was signing State papers,
even if no one was looking, to remind himself "of the
importance of it all".

Bestiality and sodomy in Ptolemaic Egypt
The Ptolemaic dynasty of Egyptian pharoahs were considered
highly debauched; the not-easily-shocked explorer Sir Richard
Burton was amazed by the "bestiality and the sodomy which
formed the delight of the Egyptians". King Ptolemy IV was

considered the most depraved of them all. He married his sister Arsinoe in 217 BC then took a homosexual lover, an Alexandrian Greek named Sisibius, who started a wild and unsubstantiated rumour that caused the king to have his mother Berenice and his brother Magus respectively poisoned and scalded to death. The king's predilection for sex with wild animals may have had some part in his premature death aged forty-one.

Rufus the Sodomite

King William II, "Rufus" (c.1056–1100), the second of William the Conqueror's three surviving sons, was a squat, portly man with a foul temper which frequently made him red-faced with anger, leading to the nickname of Rufus, which would serve to distinguish his reign in history. He never married and had no offspring; it is recorded that his monks were shocked by the king's "foul practices of Sodom".

Death by red-hot poker

King Edward II (1307–1327) at the age of twenty-three made an arranged marriage to twelve-year-old Isabella of France – an age gap thought to be not particularly disgusting by the standards of the day. Edward's "favourite" Piers Gaveston turned up for the wedding wearing a purple pearl-studded ballgown: the bride's French relatives stalked out in protest. The marriage, stressed from the beginning by Edward's close proximity to Gaveston, erupted into open warfare when the young king gave his favourite most of his wife's best jewellery. Queen Isabella had Edward's lover hanged, but had something altogether more interesting in mind for her husband. She arranged for him to be incarcerated in Berkeley Castle then killed by a method thought appropriate in the circumstances – he was held down while a red-hot poker was inserted into his rectum.

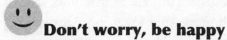 **Don't worry, be happy**
If you try to make every day a significant day, you are on
your way to a happy life.

Henry V boiled in a cauldron
When King Henry V died of dysentery just outside Paris his body
was boiled in a cauldron and dismembered before it was shipped
home. His cask was filled with incense – a wise precaution
because it was two months before he could be interred.

Henry the Foolish
King Henry VI suffered from mental illness for much of his
reign, probably a legacy from his insane grandfather Charles VI,
"the Foolish", of France. In 1453 Henry had a complete mental
breakdown which lasted seventeen months, during which time
he couldn't recognize his own wife.

Edward the Eater
King Edward IV was a compulsive eater and drinker who grew
grossly obese. He liked to force himself to vomit between
courses so that he could gorge on more food.

My coffin for a horse trough!
King Richard III is the only English king since the Battle of
Hastings to have no known grave. During the dissolution of the
monasteries, his grave was rifled and his remains tossed
into the River Soar at Leicester. His coffin was used as a horse
trough.

A welcoming salute

Towards the end of the Ottoman Empire, Turkey's Sultans were
keen to soak up Western culture, although the visit to
Constantinople by the French Empress Eugénie showed that the
Turks still had much to learn, especially when it came to royal
receptions. As the Empress's Imperial yacht *L'Aigle* approached
the Bosphorus, a salute was fired by thirty Turkish cannon.
Unfortunately the gunners had not been told to fire blank rounds
at their guests, and so Eugénie ducked as cannon balls rained
down around her yacht. Her visit was made even more
memorable by the Sultan's parting gift, a Turkish carpet
fashioned from human hair, which made such an impression that
it caused one of her ladies-in-waiting to faint.

Dead flowers from the graves of deceased royals

Queen Victoria collected dead flowers taken from the graves of
deceased royals. She began her collection with some that grew
on her late husband Albert's last resting place and it just sort of
took off from there.

Known by his hump

King William III of Orange (1689–1702) was known as one of
England's ugliest kings. Courtiers couldn't help noticing either
that he was immune to the charms of his young and attractive
wife and co-ruler Queen Mary; it was soon whispered that King
Billy was sleeping with a Dutch pageboy, Arnold Joost van
Keppel, who was mysteriously elevated to Earl of Albemarle.
Queen Mary's indifference towards her husband has been
interpreted as proof that she was also a lesbian, although it is
more likely that she simply may have found her husband
physically repulsive. They died heirless. William fretted that his
subjects didn't love him. He was however highly flattered one

day when he went out walking dressed in farmer's clothes and bumped into a doctor along the way who recognized the king immediately. William smiled and enquired how this had been possible. "I know you," the doctor replied, "by your hump."

POTTY WISDOM, NIGERIA

Talk is cheap – until you hire a lawyer to do it for you.

The honeymoon rooms

Czar Ferdinand I of Bulgaria (1908–1918) was second cousin to Queen Victoria. Although six feet tall and heavily bearded, Ferdinand wore women's jewellery, powdered his face and slept in a pink nightgown trimmed with Valenciennes lace and spent his days chasing butterflies or seducing his male chauffeurs. He married twice to keep up appearances and produced an heir, Prince Boris. The second marriage was one of convenience, a fact made brutally apparent to his new wife Princess Eleonore von Reuss-Köstritz on their wedding night. When Ferdinand discovered that they had been assigned a double room, he flew into a furious rage and had it swapped for two singles.

Compulsory bowlers

Afghanistan's King Amanullah was so impressed by his first visit to London after the First World War that he went straight

home and passed a law compelling his male subjects to wear
bowler hats.

The Tulip Age

The Ottoman Sultan Ahmed III had such an obsession with
tulips that the period of his reign became known in Turkish
history as the Tulip Age. It began as a harmless hobby when
Ahmed imported 1,200 different rare bulbs from Mongolia for
his gardens. Each April the Sultan held a fantastic tulip fête,
always on a moonlit night. Tulips in multi-coloured vases and
jugs of coloured water were displayed on miles of shelving in
the palace gardens, while turtles carrying candles on their backs
wandered around the tulip beds. Guests were forbidden to wear
clothes that didn't colour co-ordinate with the Sultan's tulips.
Ahmed valued his tulips more than he valued a human life. His
gardening fetish became such a massive drain on Turkey's
economy that he was assassinated in a palace coup.

A birthday treat

Due to an unfortunate oversight King Henry VII's wife Queen
Katherine lay above ground, neglected and covered only by a
loose cloth in an open wooden cask for several hundred years in
Westminster Abbey for all to see. Samuel Pepys had a birthday
treat when he went to visit the corpse on 23 February 1668.
"I had the upper part of her body in my hands, and I did kiss her
mouth, reflecting upon it that I did kiss a Queene, and this was
my birthday." By the time Pepys stole his kiss she had been
dead for over 230 years.

God save our king (from his anal fistulas)

The British National Anthem was originally written as "Dieu
Sauvez le Roi" by French nuns at the cloister of Saint-Cyr to

celebrate King Louis XIV's successful recovery from an
operation on his anal fistulas.

A Love-Hat Relationship

A by-law passed in Cotton Valley, Louisiana, makes it
an offence to play tennis while wearing a hat that
might startle a timid person.
Tennis Magazine

Bad-tempered Henry . . .

King Henry VIII's syphilis may have been the reason behind his
difficulty in siring an heir, and his bad-tempered behaviour.
During his thirty-eight-year reign he had about 72,000 people
put to death.

. . . and his sickly son

King Henry VIII's sickly son reigned for just six years as
Edward VI. His death, aged fifteen, was officially explained as
consumption, or more correctly tuberculosis. The symptoms
however fitted the pattern of syphilis, not TB; he died bald and
without fingernails.

The bearded queen

Queen Elizabeth I, who boasted that she had a bath once a
month "whether she need it or no", also "swore like a man" – a
trait she inherited from her father Henry VIII who was famous
for his salty language. In her later years it was widely rumoured
that she had grown a beard.

The exploding queen

When Queen Elizabeth I died of pneumonia she lay in state for
several weeks and her coffin was watched over at night by relays

of ladies-in-waiting. Elizabeth had left orders that she was not to
be disembowelled or embalmed, and gradual decomposition
would have led to to a build-up of gases in her body. According to
an eye-witness Elizabeth Southwell, one night Elizabeth's body
burst open "with such a crack that it slit the coffin open".

The richest rent boy
Rex fuit Elizabeth: nunc est regina Jacobus (Elizabeth was
King, now James is Queen) was the witty Latin quip doing the
rounds in 1603 when King James I succeeded the Virgin Queen.
Although he fathered seven children, James' preference was for
the young men chosen as his attendants, especially George
Villiers, who found his way into James' bedroom as the King's
Cup Bearer then went on to become one of the richest nobles in
England – the most successful rent boy of all time.

"Such an institution"
King James I was even less enthusiastic about Parliament than
his son Charles I, who began his reign a short 5 feet 7 inches tall
and, thanks to Oliver Cromwell, ended it even shorter. James
once said: "I am surprised that my ancestors should have
allowed such an institution to come into existence."

Good llama
Queen Henrietta, wife of the Belgian King Leopold II, kept a pet
llama which she taught to spit in the face of anyone who stroked it.

Bad valet
Serbia's Prince George, eldest son and heir of King Peter I, was
struck off the line of succession in 1909 after kicking his valet
to death.

The children of Palhava

King John V of Portugal, the inappropriately self-styled Most
Faithful King, successfully combined his twin passions for
Catholicism and sex by sleeping with nuns. The king enjoyed
open sexual relations with members of the Odivelas Convent
which resulted in the birth of at least three illegitimate sons,
known as "the children of Palhava" after the palace in Lisbon
where they grew up.

Now wash your hands

The eighteenth-century Prussian King Frederick William I was
considered by his contemporaries to have been most eccentric, not
because he was a demented, vicious psychopath who would fly into
uncontrollable rages and thrash the living daylights out of anyone
who crossed him and once had to be restrained from murdering his
own son, but because he washed his hands regularly.

Thirty bastards

King Philip IV of Spain, although evidently insane for most of
his reign, fathered about thirty bastards.

The electric throne

When Emperor Menelik II of Ethiopia heard about America's
exciting new means of executing criminals, the electric chair, he
decided to order one. When the chair arrived however the
Emperor found there was just one snag: he couldn't get it
working because Ethiopia didn't have any electricity. He had it
converted into a new throne instead.

"My Lords and Peacocks . . ."

When England's "mad" King George III first showed signs of
mental illness, it was hushed up by his courtiers, who rallied

around him by pretending to be mad themselves. The cat was finally let out of the bag in 1811 when he began his address to the House of Commons, "My Lords and Peacocks . . ."

Whimsical

The certifiably insane Raja of Akalkot reigned over the Indian state of Porbandor in the mid-nineteenth century. His problem was brought to the attention of the ruling British one day when, on a whim, he lopped off the ears and nose of a courtier .

"And this is my uncle . . ."

Everywhere he went, Germany's Kaiser Wilhelm II carried with him a collection of photographs of all his dead Hohenzollern relatives dressed in their funeral attire.

The tight-fisted queen

Spain's Queen Maria Christina threw lavish fancy dress balls and encouraged her guests to dance and make merry until the early hours, but afterwards always sent them a bill for the food and drink they had consumed.

The glass-bottomed king

The mad French King Charles VI became convinced that his legs and his buttocks were made of glass and refused to travel by coach in case they shattered. He eventually became so unstable that his wife Queen Isabeau decided that it was too risky to share a bed with him, and ordered one of her servants, Odette de Champdivers, to wear her clothing and take her place. The king slept with Odette regularly, never once noticing the difference.

Pleased to meet you
Kaiser Wilhelm II had numerous diamond and sapphire rings, which he always wore with the stones facing inwards so that his handshake hurt people.

First attempt
The French Empress Eugénie, wife of Napoleon III, once attempted suicide by breaking the heads off phosphorus matches and drinking them dissolved in milk.

The surgeon czar
Czar Peter the Great was a keen amateur surgeon and anatomist. Once on a trip to Holland, and just after a heavy meal, the Czar witnessed with fascination the anatomical dissection of a human cadaver. When two of his nauseous attendants made it clear that they didn't quite share his enthusiasm for the sight of the inner workings of the body laid bare, Peter forced them to bite into the muscles of the corpse. Although the Czar was not a particularly competent surgeon no one ever dared to turn him down when he offered to wield the knife. When the Czarina Martha Apraxina, widow of his half-brother Theodore III, died of indigestion, Peter personally opened up her corpse just to find out if the rumour that she was still a virgin at the age of forty-nine was true. The Czar also once removed twenty pounds of water from the dropsical wife of a rich Russian merchant named Borst. Peter was extremely proud of his handiwork, but was furious when the woman selfishly died shortly afterwards. He ordered an autopsy to prove that he hadn't been responsible for the death. Not very surprisingly, the autopsy revealed that Peter was entirely blameless.

Regal requirements

When Persia's ruling monarch Reza Shah had an overnight stay
in a remote village, all of the dogs within a one-mile radius were
put down in case they barked and disturbed his sleep.

George the Tiger Slayer

King George V once shot thirty-nine tigers in a single day.

Sultan Scribe

Turkey's Sultan Abdul Aziz developed a "thing" about black ink
and ordered every government document in existence re-written
in red. The order only took about twenty years to complete.

Another mad monarch

King Christian VII of Denmark (1749–1808) became king
shortly before his seventeenth birthday, by which time he was
already showing the first signs of serious mental illness. He
spent his evenings stalking the streets of Copenhagen with a
gang of equerries, brandishing a spiked wooden club, occasionally destroying brothels. At home Christian played at mock
executions and had a rack made for himself, on which he lay
while his boyfriend Conrad Holcke beat him until he bled. He
celebrated his betrothal to King George III's fifteen-year-old
sister Princess Caroline Matilda by hanging her portrait in the
royal lavatory. Although completely insane, Christian was
awarded honorary degrees by both Oxford and Cambridge
Universities.

HEROES

Squadron Leader Douglas Bader, British Second World War fighter ace

Despite having lost both his legs in a pre-War plane crash, Douglas Bader went on to become a celebrated fighter ace during the Second World War. He was not averse to getting some fun out of his disability. Occasionally, he would come across someone who complained of a stiff knee or a twisted ankle. "Have it off, old boy, have it off!" was his immediate response, as he picked up his right leg and waved it encouragingly at the startled sufferer. While staying with friends during his convalescence, Bader came into conflict with the resident terrier, a testy character with very fixed ideas about the order of things in its household. One evening at dinner, Bader's foot got a little too close to the spot under the table where the terrier was accustomed to lie at mealtimes, and a warning growl was heard. Bader moved his foot temptingly close. There was a louder growl, then the sound of teeth snapping into metal . . . then a yelp of surprise and the terrier shot out from underneath the table with its tail between its legs and the laughter of the assembled guests ringing in its ears.

Rude King Charles

When King Charles II and his court spent the summer of 1665 in Oxford to escape the Plague, the locals were outraged by their "rude" behaviour, and noted that "at their departure their excrement was left in every corner, in chimneys, coalhouses and cellars". Charles was known as "Old Rowley" after a great old racehorse that had gone on to become a famous stud stallion. The king was allegedly the first royal personage ever to use a condom, although there are many dukes, earls and barons today who can trace their lineage directly back to the king's failure to wear one. He had at least thirteen mistresses, of whom Nell Gwynne, the Covent Garden orange-seller and actress, was the best known.

Buried bowels

The deposed Stuart king James II had his body buried at the priory church of the English Benedectine monks in Paris, his head and brains deposited in the Scots College, Paris and most of his bowels buried at the parish church of St Germain.

The king's loose box

King Edward VII, Queen Elizabeth II's great-grandfather Edward the Caresser, slept with about three different women a week for nearly half a century. Although considered a demon for "proper form", when it came to females neither rank nor social status mattered to him as he was equally happy in the arms of princesses or prostitutes. At his coronation in 1902 a special area set aside at Westminster Abbey for his various mistresses was nicknamed "the king's loose box".

The foursquare queen

Queen Anne suffered from gout, and although she was very short she was so bloated she had to be carried throughout her coronation in a large chair. All of Anne's seventeen children died before she did. Only one, William Duke of Gloucester, made it through infancy. He expired at the age of eleven "from excessive dancing on his birthday". When Anne died (her coffin was said to have been as wide as it was long) the stock exchange index went up by 3 per cent.

URBAN MYTHS
True or False – you decide

THE MAGNETIC MAN

A couple were eating at their local restaurant – as they sat down the waitress came to set their table. The husband began to play with his knife as they talked. He realized that the knife had begun to stick to his hand although he was not holding it. He tried to put the knife back on the table but the spoon also attached itself to his hand and to the knife.

He told his wife so she picked up her own cutlery, but they did not stick to her. However, when he tested them, they stuck to him. The waitress told them that she had never seen this happen before. However, she had heard that due to its location, the restaurant had a strange magnetic pull from deep down in the Earth's core. It seemed that this magnetic pull could also affect some people. The couple were worried by this and left the restaurant. Once he was away from the restaurant, the man's magnetic attraction to metal faded.

Several months after this incident, he was in a different restaurant, without his wife, when the same thing happened once again. Again he showed the waitress and talked to her about the magnetic pull of the earth he had experienced before. Again he left the restaurant, but this time as he walked out the door, he collapsed. Passers-by tried to resuscitate him but he was pronounced dead at the scene.

The post-mortem showed symptoms similar to a cardiac arrest, but with some puzzling anomalies, which in some respects looked to the doctors closer to the burns one might receive from a lightning strike – their verdict was "unknown causes". The magnetic pull of the earth affects some people more than others but can be intensely dangerous if it affects you.

MURDER AND MAYHEM

Murderer Suicides

One third of all murderers commit suicide. But this is because most murders are committed within the family, in a state of jealousy or rage, and the killer is overwhelmed with remorse or despair. Unfortunately, few serial killers commit suicide – although it has been argued that the incredible carelessness that often leads to their capture is a kind of psychological suicide.

The wisdom of discretion
King George II's wife Queen Caroline decided that her own children ought to be protected against smallpox with the new but highly unpredictable vaccine, but insisted on using human guinea pigs first. She had experimental inoculations on six

condemned prisoners at Newgate prison. The men agreed to undergo the operation on condition that they would be pardoned if they survived it. Five of the prisoners recovered and walked free. The sixth kept very quiet about the fact that he'd already had smallpox and was immune, and also escaped the gallows.

Visiting Buckingham Palace

When George III bought it, Buckingham Palace cost £21,000. The annual cost to Scotland Yard of protecting the Royal family today is £30 million. Costs escalated in 1982 after the Irishman Michael Fagan was allowed to wander into the Queen's bedroom unchallenged and then sit on her bed chatting to her for half an hour, and a group of German tourists were found camping in her garden. The first unscheduled visitor to Buckingham Palace was seventeen-year-old Edward Jones, who admitted regular break-ins between 1840–41. The boy claimed to have spent several nights in the palace and had actually sat on the throne and spent time in the royal kitchens. Jones was finally found curled up asleep under Queen Victoria's sofa. He was rewarded for his persistence with two years on a treadmill.

POTTY WISDOM, SPAIN

Do not blow in a bear's ear.

Mad King George

In the last ten years of his reign King George III spent much of his time conversing with long dead friends and indecently exposing himself to his servants. Although he was the most dramatic manifestation of "the royal disease", almost the entire royal line of Hanover suffered from porphyria, a rare hereditary metabolic disorder which causes its victims to suffer various symptoms including mental derangement. Most historians now accept that the disease has even deeper roots in the bloodline of British monarchy, and that it was endemic in the Stuarts, and passed to the Hanoverians by the Electress Sophia, granddaughter of James I and mother of George I.

The cherry brandy king

King George IV was regularly plastered on cherry brandy, which he quaffed "in quantities not to be believed". His appalling hangovers were legendary; he used to try to cure them by opening up one of his veins. Although his wishful thinking wife spent a lot of time sticking pins in wax effigies of him and throwing them on the fire, he expired from cirrhosis of the liver.

The fat king

Although King George IV owned one of the most corpulent backsides ever to occupy the British throne, he had the poet Leigh Hunt jailed for two years for daring to call him fat.

The lock library

King George IV had a unique system for recording the number of women he slept with. He would ask each lover for a lock of hair, which he then placed in an envelope and labelled. When he died his brothers went through his personal belongings and found seven thousand envelopes containing enough hair to stuff a sofa and hundreds of women's gloves.

A happy marriage
King George IV's wife Queen Caroline danced in public semi-naked, tried to seduce senior British politicians and had a string of foreign lovers. She was short, fat, ugly, and, because she didn't care much for personal hygiene, stank. George IV slept with her once on their wedding night and thereafter never again: as he was blind drunk throughout and spent half the night under the grate where she left him, she was amazed when she found herself pregnant. Caroline was tried for adultery, and locked out of her own coronation at Westminster Abbey. She remained, however, far more popular than her husband.

Thought for the Day

Therapy is expensive.
Popping plastic bubblewrap
is cheap.

A shameless spendthrift and a vain, overblown sot
King George IV was considered a shameless spendthrift and a vain, overblown sot, but the real black sheep of the family was his younger brother Ernie. The one-eyed Duke of Cumberland was shunned by his brothers and sisters and feared by his own

mother. He was suspected of having made his sister Sophia pregnant and of murdering his valet.

No refunds

King William IV, nicknamed "Pineapple head" because of his oddly-shaped dome and florid complexion, was a prolific and dedicated womanizer. In ten years he fathered ten illegitimate children by the Irish actress Dorothea Jordan alone. According to a popular story of the day, when William tried to cut back the allowance he was paying her, the actress handed him a piece of paper, which at the time was attached to all playbills: it simply read "No money refunded after the rising of the curtain."

The palace without a bathroom

When Victoria inherited Buckingham Palace in 1837 it didn't even have a bathroom. Her predecessors, the Georgian royals, believed it was "sweat, damn it, that kept a man clean".

Hungry guests

Meal times with Victoria were particularly hard on her guests, especially lower-ranking visitors. Royal etiquette demanded that the Queen was always served first, and she would always start eating as soon as the food arrived. As soon as she had finished and put down her knife and fork the plate of everyone else present had to be removed immediately, thus guaranteeing that at some of her larger banquets at least half of her guests would starve. One day a brave and hungry guest insisted that the footman return his still-untouched plate to the table. Queen Victoria noticed, made enquiries about the custom and ended it.

UFOLOGY
Northern Lights

In June 1954, the Stratoliner of the British Overseas Airways Corporation was three miles out of New York, on its way to London, when Captain James H. Howard noticed a large elongated object and six smaller objects about thee miles off on their left side.

As the plane approached Goose Bay, Canada, for refuelling, the large UFO seemed to change shape and the smaller ones converged on it. Then they seemed to disappear inside it, and the big one shrank.

Howard contacted the Ground Control and the US Air Force sent a Saber Fighter to the scene. Captain Howard did not see what happened, because he had to leave Goose Bay for London.

Howard, his co-pilot, and several passengers all confirmed the sighting of the UFO. But in 1968, the United States Air Force dismissed the sighting as "an optical mirage phenomenon".

Cruel queen

When her unmarried lady-in-waiting Flora Hastings fell ill with a swollen stomach, Queen Victoria needed little convincing that the girl was unashamedly pregnant. She wrote in her diary, "We have no doubt that she is – to use plain words – with child!" and set about vilifying the girl's name. The truth emerged a few months later when Flora died in agony from a tumour on her liver.

A blood-shot glass eye

When Victoria's son Albert carelessly shot his own brother-in-law Prince Christian in the face, Christian had to have an eye removed. He went on to collect a number of glass eyes which he was fond of producing at dinner-parties and explaining the history of each at length, and became a renowned "glass-eye bore". His favourite was a blood-shot one which he wore when he had a cold.

Joke of the Day

A little pig walks into a bar, orders a drink and asks where the toilet is. "Just along the corridor," says the bartender.

Then a second little pig walks into the bar, orders a drink and asks where the toilet is.

"Just along the corridor," says the bartender.

Then a third little pig walks into the bar and orders a drink. The bartender says: "I suppose you want to use the toilet too?"

"No, I'm the little pig that goes wee wee wee wee all the way home."

The importance of not being Ernest

Prince Albert's father Ernest worked hard at building himself a reputation as the most enthusiastic debauchee in the dukedom of Saxe-Coburg – a position rivalled only by Albert's sex-mad brother Ernest Junior. The Prince Consort, Queen Victoria's husband, mindful that both sides of the royal family had more than a fair share of oddballs and degenerates, was genuinely

worried that some of it might rub off on their son Edward.
Albert subjected him to a regime of military strictness and
regularly had Edward's bumps felt by a phrenologist for signs of
mental instability.

Victoria, Duke of Clarence

Edward VII's eldest son the Duke of Clarence was just one of
many on a long list of prominent Victorians suspected of being
Jack the Ripper. "Eddie" was a regular at a notorious
homosexual brothel off Tottenham Court Road called The
Hundred Guineas Club, which required members to use
women's names: a strong traditionalist to the end, he called
himself Victoria in honour of his grandmother.

Kleptomaniac Queen

Whereas King George V was content to collect stamps, his wife
Queen Mary was the only known royal kleptomaniac. She was a
prolific collector, especially of ornaments, family portraits and
miniatures, and during her lifetime she amassed a huge and
eccentric private collection. What made hers different from other
royal collections were the methods she employed to put it
together. On her frequent visits to London's antique dealers and
occasionally on visits to the homes of wealthy friends, the queen
was prone to taking what she wanted without paying for it, often
slipping small items into her handbag. Buckingham Palace
became aware of Queen Mary's problem when some of her
victims complained about the thefts, and the queen's ladies-in-
waiting were quietly instructed to keep a close eye on her. From
then on, whatever Queen Mary stole was usually retrieved by an
aide and mailed back to the original owner with a covering letter
explaining that there had been a "mistake". When stories about
Queen Mary's compulsive stealing leaked out, the palace

explained it as "her natural keenness to save anything worth-while for the nation".

10,000 birds shot in four days

King George V was an obsessive game shooter whose idea of a good time was to blaze away until he was ankle-deep in spent cartridges. Even his entourage were appalled by the number of birds he killed. On one of his "massacre shoots" at Sandringham he and six others killed 10,000 birds in four days. This didn't stop George from regularly claiming that he was an animal lover. To prove it, he had a pet parrot whose privileged life in the royal household was legendary. The parrot was regularly allowed to roam over, and soil, the breakfast table: George would slide a mustard pot over the offending faeces and continue his meal.

George the Homophobic

King George V, unlike his ancestors William II, Richard I, Edward II, Richard II, James I and William III, was vociferously homophobic. He said, "I thought chaps like that shot themselves" and once warned, "I won't knight buggers."

Abroad is awful, I've been there

King George V was also a xenophobe, albeit a somewhat confused one, as his real surname was Saxe-Coburg-Gotha. He once proclaimed, "Abroad is awful. I know. I have been", and wasn't coy about his dislike of foreigners, although whether in his case this meant the British isn't entirely clear.

The Hitlerian Restoration

King Edward VIII, whom Hitler planned to kidnap and restore to the British throne, once boasted that "every drop of blood in my veins is German."

Philip Schleswig-Holstein-Sonderburg-Glücksburg-Beck

The Duke of Edinburgh, whose real surname Schleswig-Holstein-Sonderburg-Glücksburg-Beck was found to be a bit too obviously Germanic for even the royal family's liking, had three brothers-in-law who fought for Hitler, including an enthusiastic and high-ranking Nazi who was a close personal friend of Herman Goering. None of them got an invitation to his wedding.

ANIMAL NEWS Cow Wreckers

When BEA helicopter pilot Captain Dick Hensen set down in a field in Maldon, Essex, he paid little attention to a nearby herd of cows. However, when he returned from making a phone call a few minutes later he was horrified to see that the cows had licked most of the paint off the machine. One had even gouged a hole in the perspex cockpit windshield with a questing horn. The helicopter was so badly damaged it had to be taken out of service.
Sunday Express

An honorary member of the SS

Princess Michael of Kent's father was a member of Hitler's SS, although, according to an official palace explanation, only an "honorary" one.

Twice-buried royals

Every English monarch, from Henry I in 1135 until at least the beginning of the nineteenth century, has had two separate funeral ceremonies: one for their corpse, the second for the burial of their eviscerated entrails.

Chosen by God
An opinion poll taken in 1963 showed that a third of the population of Great Britain believed that Queen Elizabeth II was chosen by God.

The mad sultan
The mad Ottoman Sultan Abdul Aziz, when he discovered that one of his servants shared his second name, passed a law which made it illegal for anyone else to be named "Aziz". This was roughly comparable to banning the name "Smith" in England.

Pickled penis and other curiosities
Czar Peter the Great's pride and joy was his Museum of Curiosities, created to satisfy his interest in freaks of nature. The items he collected included a man without genitals, a child with two heads, a five-footed sheep, a deformed foetus, the organs of a hermaphrodite, "the hand of a man who died by excessive drinking with all its blood stagnated in the veins" and the corpses of Siamese twins. Each became a specimen in Peter's museum, individually pickled in huge alcohol-filled jars. The museum caretaker, a hideously deformed dwarf, must have realized that one day he too would be stuffed and put on display. One of Peter's prize curiosities was a pickled phallus, donated by the Prussian King Frederick William: it had caught Peter's eye on his trip to Berlin and the Prussian King was only too delighted to get rid of it. Peter thought it would be fun to get his wife Catherine to kiss it: she accepted his invitation, but only after he hinted that he might decide to cut her head off if she declined.

Battle trophies
When Egypt's king Menephta defeated the Libyans in 1300 BC he took home with him, as battle trophies, the penises of all his slain enemies.

Cannibals

Birth control
Aborigines in western Australia in the nineteenth century controlled the size of their tribe by eating every tenth baby born.

The Mad Butcher of Kingsbury Run
Between 1935 and 1938 in Cleveland, Ohio, the Mad Butcher of Kingsbury Run slaughtered at least twelve people, mostly vagrants, by chopping the bodies into small pieces then leaving them in piles in alleys and on wasteland. The body parts were often mixed, and few of the heads were ever recovered. The killer was never identified.

Pizza deliverance
In 1984 Argentinian police found a set of bones belonging to a missing nineteen-year-old, Carlos Sanchez, beneath a Buenes Aires building which was used by devil worshippers. The occupants explained that they had phoned an order for pizzas, but after an interminable delay had decided to eat the delivery boy instead.

Cure for a limp
Some south American cannibals believed you could cure a limp by eating someone else's good leg.

Zombie sex slaves

The Milwaukee cannibal Jeffrey Dahmer, who admitted at his
trial in February 1992 to killing seventeen people, performed
crude lobotomies on some of his victims in the hope of creating
zombie sex slaves. Police raiding his apartment found severed
heads in the fridge, skulls in his filing cabinet and body parts in
a kettle, but were puzzled by the discovery of a human heart in
the deep freezer. Dahmer explained, "I was saving it for later."
Two years later he was beaten to death with a broomstick by a
fellow inmate at the Columbia Correctional Institute.

Class-conscious cuisine

During China's cultural revolution in the 1960s and 1970s,
members of Chairman Mao's Red Guards ate the flesh of their
enemies to show their leader that they were fully class-
conscious.

Leg pâté

In Wisconsin, USA, in 1989 John Weber was convicted for the
murder of a seventeen-year-old schoolgirl, Carla Lenz. During
the trial he confessed that he'd made a pâté from his victim's leg
and eaten it himself.

Boring beef

In 1818 the Maori chief Touai was shipped over to England
from New Zealand and paraded around London's polite society
for his curiosity value. The chief survived the culture shock
surprisingly well, and was able to live in London successfully
for several years. Eventually however he became desperately
homesick. He missed his family and his friends, of course, but
what he missed most of all, he confessed to his hosts, was the
taste of human flesh. Beef, said Touai, was a major bore. Where

he came from the idea of a good Sunday roast involved the
participation of a black man, preferably middle-aged. He
explained that most Maoris preferred the taste of black flesh,
although if they were really hungry they could, at a push,
manage to swallow the odd white missionary.

Real-life psycho
Ed Gein, a middle-aged man from Wisconsin, was the
inspiration for the films *Psycho* and *Silence of the Lambs*. Gein
was both a cannibal and a necrophiliac. He began by digging up
female corpses to satisfy his perversions, but then graduated to
murder as a means of obtaining bodies. A police raid on Gein's
well-stocked fridge in 1957 helped account for fifteen bodies.
There they discovered human skin bracelets, a human drumskin,
two lips on a string, four noses in a cup and dozens of human
organs. Gein later admitted that he enjoyed draping himself in
the skin of his dead victims.

Self-satisfied
In 1945 a German soldier who had been accidentally left behind
in the German retreat was discovered by the Allies locked in an
abandoned railroad truck in Belgium. He had survived by eating
portions of his left leg and drinking his own blood.

Captain Cooked
Captain James Cook, who had often written in his journals about
the cannibalistic habits of Fijiians, Samoans and New Zealand
tribesmen, probably ended up as an Hawaiian buffet. All that
Cook's men could find of him after he had been killed and
dismembered at a heianu ceremony at Keala Kekua were a few
bones and some salted flesh.

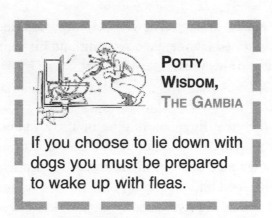

POTTY WISDOM, THE GAMBIA

If you choose to lie down with dogs you must be prepared to wake up with fleas.

Serves seventy-five
A man weighing 150 lbs (68 kg) would provide enough meat to provide a meal for seventy-five cannibals in one sitting.

"But I'm feeling much better today . . ."
The Nirhor tribe in India were endo-cannibals, i.e. people who only ate friends and relatives. The very thought of eating a stranger however made them nauseous. Whenever a Nirhor tribesman fell sick, his closest friends would kill and eat him before his meat was spoiled by disease. Even if the victim protested that he might be getting better they would kill and eat him anyway. It was a no-win situation: any Nirhor tribesman lucky enough to reach a great age would be sacrificed and eaten by way of celebration.

The king is dead, long live the king!
The Djoukous tribe of central Sudan strangled their kings after a rule of seven years before removing the royal brain, heart and kidneys for his successor to eat. In the Niger Delta it was customary for the local ruler to mark his accession to power by

entering the palace through a newly-cut door, stepping over the blood of a sacrificed couple, then retiring into his inner sanctum to make a meal of his predecessor's heart.

Child stew

Throughout the great Egyptian famine of 1201, many survived by slaughtering and eating children. A Cairo doctor named Abdi al-Latif left a detailed diary of the famine. Children were regularly kidnapped only to end up on someone's dining table and were often sold ready-roasted or boiled. Latif described how a woman was caught red-handed and was dragged before the authorities with a roasted child still hanging around her neck. Grave-robbers ate, and sold, the bodies they dug up. People who had been caught eating human flesh often tried to excuse themselves by claiming that they were only eating the remains of a close relative. At first the authorities made a determined effort to stamp out the practice by burning the culprits, but in time the Egyptians grew indifferent to cannibalism. The mania for eating children eventually spread to the rich, by which time it had become a fashion, rather than a necessity. Often two or three children at a time were thrown into a single cook-pot: on one occasion the authorities found ten assorted heads marinating in a selection of choice herbs and spices.

Bottoms up

The cannibal Cubeo tribe of Brazil were skilled in creating the world's most grisly cocktail: they exhumed a partially cremated corpse, burned the bones to ashes, mixed it with the local brew then drank it.

URBAN MYTHS
True or False – you decide

CHICKEN MAYO SANDWICH

A woman orders a chicken sandwich with no mayonnaise in a cafe. When she bites into it, there is some kind of sauce coming out of it, which looks like mayonnaise. The kitchen staff insist to her that there was no mayonnaise in the sandwich. She gets her money back nonetheless, takes a bagel instead, and leaves the restaurant. When the kitchen staff inspect the sandwich, they realize that the piece of chicken flesh contained an infected wound. When the woman bit into it, she bit through this wound, and released a squirt of a pus-like substance. Needless to say, the restaurant staff don't rush to tell anyone about their discovery, but later on one of the waiters tells someone at a party, and the story is passed around, until eventually the woman who ate the sandwich is told the story by her cleaner.

Food preparation
The African Bafum-Bansaw tribe gave their victims an enema before they ate them by forcing boiling palm oil into their bowels, because it made the flesh more tender.

Cabin boy cassoulet
In 1838 the American author Edgar Allan Poe wrote one of his most famous tales *The Narrative of Arthur Gordon Pym*, a story about three men cast adrift in a boat, who survived by

killing and eating their companion, a cabin boy named Richard
Parker. In 1884, thirty-five years after Poe's death, a yacht
called the *Mignonette* sank in a storm en route to Australia
from England. Four of the crew put to sea in an open boat,
and three were rescued twenty-four days later. They had
survived by killing and eating the fourth member, a cabin
boy named Richard Parker. They eventually returned home
to a heroes' welcome and received only six months'
imprisonment.

Don't worry, be happy
There will always be something good you can accomplish,
however small.

A treat for the ladies
Fijian cannibals while dining always saved the victims' brains as
a treat for the ladies.

Chinese cannibalism
When the Chinese famine of 206 BC killed half the population,
human flesh became the staple diet. The taste for human flesh
however seems to have lingered on long after the famine.
During the T'ang dynasty in the late ninth and tenth centuries
cannibalism was permitted by law and human flesh was sold
publicly in street markets.

A thoughtful note
Grandfather Albert Fish went to the electric chair at Sing Sing
prison in 1936 after killing and eating at least fifteen children.
His final victim was a ten-year-old girl. Fish wrote to her

mother, six years after she'd vanished: "Grace sat on my lap and kissed me. I made up my mind to eat her."

Bone marrow and brains

Neanderthal man was probably a cannibal by instinct. Many prehistoric skulls discovered with their bottoms bashed out may have indicated a quick way of turning a skull into a drinking vessel, but the more likely explanation was that it was done to tease out the brains. Archeologists say that the unusually large number of cracked skulls and broken bones at Stone Age sites points to the fact that our ancestors were quite partial to human brain and loved to suck on a bit of juicy bone marrow whenever it was available.

The food trade

Many Africans captured and sold for slavery in the eighteenth century believed that their white captors were cannibals and that white men bought them for the purpose of either eating them themselves or selling them to be eaten by others.

Airline food

When a Uruguayan plane on a flight to Chile in 1972 crashed in the Andes, its surviving passengers were marooned in the mountains for ten weeks. Of the forty-five passengers only sixteen were found alive: they had survived by eating the bodies of the other twenty-nine passengers who had died in the crash.

Eating the enemy

Chinese warriors often ate their enemies in the belief that human flesh, especially foreign flesh, was a great stimulant for a man's courage. The idea that you could acquire the bravery and other desirable qualities of your enemy by eating him has a long history. Maori cannibals did most of their dining alfresco on the battlefield and even carried portable steam ovens with them so they could butcher and eat their enemies on the spot. The cannibal Apiaca tribe of Brazil, who were still having people for dinner as late as 1848, roasted and ate the bodies of enemies taken in battle. A captured child of an enemy would be raised by an Apiaca family as their own, until the age of twelve to fourteen, when the foster father would creep up behind the child and bash his or her skull in. The children were then eaten during all-night feasts.

A trifle of Custer's heart

The Sioux Chief Rain-in-the-Face admitted that after the Battle of Little Big Horn in 1877 he had cut out the heart of General Custer and eaten a slice of it. He said he didn't much like the taste of human flesh – he just wanted to get his own back.

The cannibal cookbook

The anthropologist Paul Shankman once compiled a world-wide cannibal cookbook which listed the various ways mankind has chosen to cook his fellow man. It includes pot-boiling, spit-roasting, steam-baking, cookery on pre-heated rocks, in earth ovens, smoking, drying, powdering, stuffing, and eating raw. The most unsavoury preparation in Shankman's cookbook involved burying the body, then exhuming it and eating the putrefying flesh. The maggots were scraped off, wrapped in banana leaves and eaten separately as an entrée.

Cannibal comrades

During the retreat of Napoleon's Grand Army from Moscow, dead soldiers were eaten both by their French comrades and by scavenging Russian peasants. A similar fate befell the corpses of some British soldiers in the disastrous retreat from Kabul in 1842 during the First Afghan War.

Appeasing Kali
The Bindewars of India and Central Asia regularly ate their sick and elderly in the belief that it would appease Kali, the goddess of plagues, epidemics and cholera.

Manwurst
During the Allied blockade of Germany during the First World War, Germans routinely used human flesh as sausage meat.

Fritz the Cannibal
Fritz Haarmann, a meat dealer in post-First World War Germany, was Europe's most prolific homicidal cannibal. In the 1920s the Vampire of Hanover picked up young male refugees at the local railway station, and lured them back to his Jewish ghetto apartment where he sexually assaulted them and killed them by biting their throats. He then sold their flesh as horse meat in an open market in Hanover, eating what he couldn't sell. He was apprehended in 1924 after some young boys fishing in the river discovered several human skulls. Haarmann was only ever convicted of the murders of twenty-seven young men aged between thirteen and twenty, although police estimated that he probably killed as many as 600 in a single year. He was beheaded in Hanover prison on 15 April 1925.

Donner kebab
One item of American Old West folklore as yet untouched by Hollywood occurred in 1846 when eighty-seven men, women and children set out on a two thousand mile trek looking for a new life in California in a wagon train led by the Illinois farmer

George Donner and his family. The expedition was badly planned and ill-prepared with insufficient provisions to survive the harsh winter. Of the original party only forty-seven made it to the end of the trail, having survived by eating their dead companions. The decision to resort to cannibalism under such dire circumstances might have been excused as a grisly but understandable tale of a man chewing what he had to chew, except that some of the survivors struck a less than penitent attitude about their deed. One of them, Lewis Keseberg, cheerfully admitted a preference for human liver and brain soup, and paid an emotional tribute to George Donner's wife Tamsen, declaring, "She was the healthiest woman I ever ate." Years later Keseberg became wealthy by opening a steakhouse.

Trust me, I'm a doctor

Barbers and surgeons

There was no recognized professional difference between a barber and a surgeon until 1745. Barbers were allowed to perform surgical operations simply because their scissors and razors made them obvious candidates for the job. They were bound by just one code of practice which banned them from shaving, washing or brushing a man's teeth on a Sunday. They were however free to blood-let, lance boils, or amputate tumours on any day they liked. In Henry V's army at Agincourt surgeons and barbers squabbled on the battlefield over the right to perform amputations.

Copper-clad corpses

In 1891 a French surgeon Dr Varlot developed a method of
preserving corpses by covering them with a thin layer of metal –
in effect, he was electroplating the dead. Dr Varlot's innovative
technique involved making the body conductive by exposing it
to silver nitrate, followed by immersion in a galvanic bath of
copper sulphate, producing a one millimetre thick coating of
copper – "a brilliant red copper finish of exceptional strength
and durability". Why Dr Varlet wanted to do this at all,
however, is not known.

Two corpses before breakfast

Every morning without fail Sir Astley Cooper, surgeon to
George IV and the Duke of Wellington, rose between five and
six o'clock and dissected two corpses before breakfast. If Sir
Astley couldn't get hold of a fresh human cadaver, London Zoo
would occasionally chip in with a dead elephant.

Doctors are bad for your health

Statistically, doctors are very bad for your health, because
whenever they go on strike the death rate falls. During a strike
by hospital doctors in Israel, admissions to hospitals fell by 85
per cent and the national death rate halved. When doctors in
Bogota, Columbia went on strike for two months in 1976 the
mortality rate dropped by 3 per cent. A similar strike in Los
Angeles in the same year resulted in 60 per cent fewer
admissions and an 18 per cent fall in the death rate. In every
case, as soon as the striking doctors returned to work, the death
rate always returned to normal.

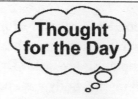

**Thought
for the Day**

Always remember, you're
unique. Just like
everyone else.

The man with the hole in his stomach

In 1822 the US army surgeon William Beaumont treated Alexis
Martin for a gunshot wound in the abdomen which had left him
with such a gaping hole that people could see right inside his
stomach. Martin lived, but the wound refused to heal and the
hole had to be plugged with wads of cloth to prevent the
contents of his stomach from leaking out. He became a medical
celebrity and allowed Beaumont to do experiments on him for
years afterwards.

Necessity is the mother of invention

For hundreds of years doctors listened to a heartbeat by simply
pressing one of their ears against the patient's chest. In 1816
however a doctor in Paris was confronted by a girl who had
such enormous breasts that he couldn't get anywhere near her
without compromising the dignity of both parties: he cleverly
rolled up a sheet of paper so that he could listen from a
respectable distance, thus inventing the stethoscope.

Tough cookie

Austria's Empress Maria Theresa was a notoriously hard woman
who had sixteen children. She was working on her government

papers when she went into labour with her fifteenth child,
Marie Antoinette: the Empress called for her dentist and had a
bad tooth pulled because she wouldn't notice the extra pain.
As soon as the baby was delivered she went back to her paper-
work.

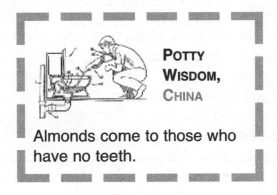

POTTY WISDOM, CHINA

Almonds come to those who
have no teeth.

The Chinese Patient

Lord Dawson of Penn, the eminent royal physician who
famously composed the lines "the king's life is drawing
peacefully to its close" shortly before slipping a hypodermic
syringe full of morphine into King George V's jugular vein to
make absolutely sure that his prose wasn't premature, served as
royal doctor to four sovereigns: Edward VII, George V, Edward
VIII and George VI. Although Lord Dawson was the best paid
doctor in the country it didn't necessarily mean that he was the
best at his job. It was widely rumoured that he once treated a
man for jaundice for six weeks until he realized that his patient
was Chinese.

Well, it's either measles or smallpox
In ancient Rome about 5,000 people a day died from measles. It
remained a major menace for hundreds of years: measles is
similar in many ways to smallpox and doctors weren't able to
distinguish between the two until the sixteenth century.

Shock treatment
Before the discovery of anaesthetics in the nineteenth century
patients undergoing surgery stood slightly more chance of dying
from shock during treatment than they did from their original
ailment.

Nazi medical experiments
The means could never justify the end, but the medical
experiments carried out in Hitler's concentration camps did
result in just one discovery which had a lasting benefit to
mankind. The Nazi Dr Dring, who committed suicide rather
than face a war trial, researched typhoid vaccines using camp
internees in exactly the same way that any other medical
researcher would use rats – exposing them to infection, then
testing their responses to different types of anti-sera. The results
of the tests were later published and became the basis for
successful German and Allied anti-typhus vaccines.

Healthy herpes
Nineteenth-century doctors were confident that herpes was a
sure sign of excellent health.

Bad example
Catherine the Great tried to set an example when she became the
very first person in Russia to receive the smallpox vaccine. It
backfired, because her subjects were convinced that she was

insane and attempting to commit suicide: the idea of infecting yourself with a deadly disease in order to protect yourself from that same disease was a sure sign of mental illness. Decades later, the Catholic Kings of Spain were still banning inoculation against smallpox on theological grounds, thus condemning generations of their own family to death in the process.

You can turn a pig's ear into a new nose
A 1991 Reuters report from Peking revealed that a Chinese farmer whose nose had been completely bitten off by a huge rat had had a brand new, working replacement nose built from a pig's ear.

Plastic surgery the devil's work?
Plastic surgery was invented about 2,000 years ago to save face for Hindu adulterers who, in accordance with the law of the day, were sentenced to have their noses ripped off. At first surgeons did their best to cover up the ragged hole by sewing on a lump of skin from the cheek or the forehead. The next great leap forward in plastic surgery took place in 1597 when the Italian Gasparo Tagliacozzi sewed the patient's forearm to his nose: not the most convenient of arrangements as the patient had to walk around with his arm welded to his nose until the transplant had taken, but it worked. Plastic surgery then took ten steps backward when the Church decided that the operations were the devil's work: Tagliacozzi's corpse was promptly dug up from his churchyard grave for good measure and re-interred in unconsecrated ground.

That should work
Popular nineteenth-century cures for whooping cough included drinking water from the skull of a dead bishop, or sheep droppings boiled in milk, or passing the patient under the belly of a donkey nine times.

Medical leeches

Although there are about 650 varieties of blood-sucking leech, sixteen of them living and breeding happily in Britain, the king of the medicinal leeches is *Hirudo medicinalis*, one-and-a-half inches long on an empty stomach, six inches when fully topped up with human blood. In the 1980s leeches once again became fashionable and were used to clean up clots of blood formed during plastic surgery. St Bartholomew's Hospital in London gets through about 96,000 leeches a year.

No sex, please, I'm dead

Due to the uncertainties of medical science in the Middle Ages it was fairly commonplace for people to be prematurely declared dead, and so a "safe" three-day waiting period, observed before the funeral took place, became the norm. It was not unknown for corpses to revive themselves within three days but, as a Canterbury monk casually observed, recoveries after seven days were quite rare. If you were lucky enough to recover however, once you had received Extreme Unction from your priest there were certain conditions attached. Anyone who carried on living after receiving the final sacrament was not allowed to have sex, or to walk barefoot, or to eat meat.

From elderly German women to skinheads

Dr Klaus Maertens designed the Dr Martens boot in the 1940s as a "comfort aid" for elderly German women with foot trouble.

Eat Marmite for your scrotal dermatitis

Marmite was originally prescribed in the Middle East as a cure for beri beri. A 1951 British army medical report confirmed that Marmite was an effective treatment for scrotal dermatitis.

Inhale the breath of two new-born calves . . .

In 1797 the Prussian King Frederick William's bloated body
was worn out by a lifetime of debauchery and for the last time
his court was filled with charlatans and quack physicians each
hoping to make a quick profit out of the king's condition. He
was told to inhale the breath of two new-born calves, to sleep
each night between two children aged between eight and ten,
and to listen to the sound of wind instruments, but in no circumstances was he to hear the sound of a violin. New-born calves,
children and wind instruments notwithstanding, Frederick
William expired from heart disease aged fifty-three.

In the medicine cabinet

Crocodile dung, pigs' teeth, asses' hooves, frog sperm, eunuch
fat, fly specks, dried vipers, oil of ants, oil of wolves,
earthworms, spiders, human excrement, sweat, semen, hair, the
saliva of a fasting man, nail clippings, the sexual organs of
various animals, feathers, fur, raw silk, spiders' webs, cast-off
snakeskins, jaw bones from the skulls of executed criminals,
moss from the skull of a victim of violent death: all of these
substances have been used by doctors for treating illness.

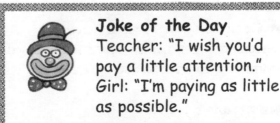

Joke of the Day
Teacher: "I wish you'd
pay a little attention."
Girl: "I'm paying as little
as possible."

Dr Disaster

Britain's worst ever "doctor" Muhammed Saeed, a bogus
Bradford GP, was granted a licence after arriving from Pakistan
and allowed to work for the National Health Service for thirty
years before he was finally rumbled. "Dr" Saeed was jailed
for five years in 1992 after variously prescribing to his 3,000
patients shampoo to be taken internally, creosote for a tooth
complaint, sleeping pills to be taken three times a day, cough
mixture to be rubbed into the skin, and suppositories to be taken
orally.

Ancient headache cure

A drastic remedy for a headache, "trepanation", was devised by
Stone Age man in the belief that head pain was caused by evil
spirits lurking inside the cranium. The prehistoric equivalent of
aspirin required at least five surgeons to administer it: four to
hold down the patient while the fifth slowly drilled a hole through
the patient's head with a sharpened flint. The evil spirits could
then escape through the hole, thus relieving any discomfort.
Some skulls were trepanned more than once: the record is held
by an Inca migraine sufferer whose skull was perforated seven
times.

Toothworms

The ancient Greeks thought that toothache was caused by
malevolent worms which lived inside the teeth.

Do not try this at home

Blood-letting, once the most profitable source of income for
surgeons, became less so with the invention of a DIY blood-
letting kit which allowed the patient to open a vein in the
privacy of his or her own home. In the nineteenth century Queen

Caroline of Bavaria tried it, opened up a main artery in her arm by mistake, and bled to death.

Cowboy surgeons
A United States Senate investigation in 1974 found that "cowboy" surgeons were responsible for more fatalities than the annual death toll during the wars in Korea and Vietnam.

A sure cure
The classic cure for brewer's droop was to burn together the livers of a frog and a hedgehog, place the ashes in a bag and carry the bag about your person.

Twentieth-century trepanation
A twentieth-century trepanation movement was founded by a Dutchman Dr Bart Huges, who in the 1960s figured out that a person's peace of mind was related to the amount of blood swilling around in the brain. He promptly cut a hole in his own head with an electrical drill to achieve "a permanent high", then wrote a book about it called *Bore Hole*. The medical and legal authorities were so impressed by his discovery that they rewarded him with a spell in a Dutch lunatic asylum. Dr Huges did in fact manage to attract two converts to his cause, the London couple Joey Mellen and Amanda Fielding. After failing to find a member of the medical profession to do it for them, they finally managed to drill holes in their own heads with the help of an electric drill and generous quantities of LSD after several abortive attempts with a hand-worked corkscrew and a saw.

URBAN MYTHS
True or False – you decide

THE $0.00 CHARGE

In 1990 a man living near Chicago was sent a bill for his unused credit card which said that he owed $0.00. He threw the bill away. But in the following months he was sent further bills for $0.00. Eventually the credit card company phoned to say that they were going to cancel his card unless he paid the bill. When he explained that the bill was for $0.00, they put it down to computer error and told him not to worry about it.

Soon afterwards he went shopping but when he tried to pay in the first shop, he found his card had been cancelled. The credit card company again said that they would take care of it. They sent him yet another bill demanding payment for $0.00 the following day.

Assuming this was just another error he ignored it, expecting that the company would sort it out. However he still couldn't spend on his card and next month he got yet another bill for $0.00 giving him 10 days to pay his account – it stated that otherwise the company would take legal action to recover the debt.

He decided the only solution was to go along with the company's mad logic, and sent a cheque for $0.00. He was happy to receive a letter from the credit card company saying that his account was now clear. However later that day his bank manager called, sounding stressed. He asked

why the man had written a check for $0.00. Apparently the
$0.00 check had crashed their check processing software.
Now they couldn't process any of their customers' checks
because the system had completely failed. This had never
happened before because no one had ever written a $0.00
check! He promised his bank manager never to do this
again.

The final straw came when the credit card company sent
a computer-generated letter saying that his check for $0.00
had bounced and that he had ten days to clear the account.
He wrote back closing the account and vowed never to get
another credit card as long as he lived.

Waiting times slashed
On 20 January 1984, David Carver, of Torquay, Devon was
operated on for the removal of a hare-lip, thus completing his
thirty-first year on an NHS waiting list.

First take your dog . . .
The most popular cure for leprosy in the Middle Ages was to
bathe in the blood of a dog. If a dog wasn't available, a two-
year-old infant would do.

Stage-door epileptics
In ancient Rome, where human blood was prescribed as a cure
for epilepsy, epileptics hung around near the exit gates of the
public arenas so they could drink the blood of slain gladiators as
they were dragged out. Elizabethan medical text books
recommended an alternative remedy – powdered human skull
dissolved in red wine.

Quick hands and an iron stomach

Before the discovery of anesthetics, when the two key qualifications for a good surgeon were quick hands and an iron stomach, it was a close call who suffered the most, surgeon or patient: at least the patient could look forward to playing with his gangrene. Most surgeons were humane men who didn't harbour any delusions about the appalling pain they inflicted on their patients. The most accomplished English surgeon of his day Sir Astley Cooper once burst into tears when a child patient smiled confidently at him just as he was about to operate. Queen Caroline's personal surgeon William Chiselden threw up before every operation, and always armed his assistant with a watch to try to keep the duration of his operations down to under three minutes. Although many operations took about an hour, Napoleon's famous chief surgeon Dominique Lorrey could amputate a leg in under fifteen seconds. The nineteenth-century Scottish surgeon and part-time bodysnatcher Robert Lister was described as "the finest surgeon in Europe". Lister's personal best for a leg amputation was twenty-eight seconds, although while achieving this record he accidentally cut two of his assistant's fingers off and the patient's left testicle.

Hastening his end

When Charles II had a fit while shaving in 1685, he was lucky to be treated with the finest medical advice of the day. He was attended by fourteen physicians who first drew blood, forced him to vomit violently then gave him a strong laxative. They shaved his head, applied blistering agents to his scalp, put special plasters made from pigeon droppings on to the soles of his feet, fed him Bezoar stones (usually found in the gall bladder of a goat) and made him drink forty drops of extract from a dead man's skull. He died two days later.

Great balls of hair!

The heaviest object ever found in a human stomach was a
5-lb 3-oz ball of hair, extracted from a woman in the South
Devon and East Cornwall Hospital in 1985.

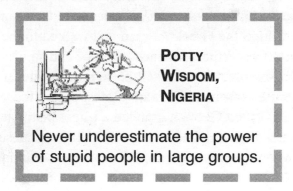

POTTY
WISDOM,
NIGERIA

Never underestimate the power
of stupid people in large groups.

Hare-brained

Nearly half of all children born in Great Britain in the eighteenth
century didn't make it through infancy – a statistic which is less
surprising in the light of some of the contemporary ideas about
childcare. Any child who survived the shock of birth stood a good
chance of reaching its first birthday if it also had the digestive
system of an ox. The best selling infant cure-all of the day
"Godfrey's Cordial" was made mostly from opium and was almost
as deadly as arsenic. Children were regularly wormed with strong
purgatives – a favourite was made from tepid milk mixed with
equal quantities of fine sugar and rat's dung. Vitamin deficiency
was rife and rickets were commonplace, but no two childcare
experts could agree on how to cure them: a favourite remedy was
woodlice in white wine, another was livers of young frogs and
ravens. Small children with teething problems either had their
gums lanced or were given strong alcohol and fed hare's brain.

HEROES

Special Boat Service Mediterranean Raiders
Formed in 1941 as an irregular hit-and-run force, the British Special Boat Squadron (SBS) had an almost unrivalled élan. This was perfectly captured in an incident where a junior SBS officer, Andy Clark, landed on a German-occupied island in the Greek Aegean and walked to the Wehrmacht officers' mess, opened the door and said to the astonished assembly, "It would all be so much easier if you would just raise your hands." Clark almost pulled the stunt off, but one quick-witted German grabbed a Luger pistol and started shooting. Luckily, Clark had brought his Glaswegian sergeant with him, who promptly subdued the room with submachine gun fire.

To the king's health
The "mad" King George III's treatment was in accordance with the standard treatment: "restraint, frequent but moderate bleedings, purges (forced vomiting or emetics), a low diet, salivations, and afterwards the cold bath". The king's condition turned out to be a goldmine for the medical profession: he was visited by a succession of quacks who hoped to make their fortune by finding a cure for his affliction. The most notorious of these was the Reverend Dr Francis Willis, who diagnosed the king's illness as arising from "severe exercise, weighty business, severe abstemiousness and too little rest". George III had occasional remissions from his condition, and in 1789 official medals were struck to celebrate his "recovery". Dr Willis meanwhile had some of his own struck for advertising purposes. On one side of the medallion there was a head and shoulders view of the physician, while the other bore the legend "Britons rejoice, your king's restored – 1789".

Close study

John Hunter, the unrivalled expert of eighteenth-century
anatomy, may have been either the bravest or the most foolhardy
surgeon who ever lived. In order to study venereal disease he
deliberately injected himself with pus from a gonorrhea patient
who, unknown to Hunter, also had syphilis. The experiment cost
him his life. Like many of his fellow anatomists, Hunter
collected the corpses of executed criminals for dissection. His
prize exhibit was the body of a 7-ft 8-in Irishman, Charles
Byrne, which he had acquired in spite of stiff competition from
a number of local anatomists who were keen to lay their hands
on the Irish "giant". Byrne meanwhile lived with a dread fear
that he might end up in a museum, and made special
arrangements to be buried at sea in a lead coffin. When he
finally died of tuberculosis, however, Hunter bribed officials to
fill the coffin with rocks and gave them £500 for the corpse.
Hunter was intensely proud of his latest plaything. He propped
the corpse up beside him on his coach while doing his rounds,
then took it home and boiled it in a large vat to separate the
flesh from the bones.

Another law-abiding Hunter

John Hunter's brother William was also an anatomist who
specialized in the collection of female corpses in various states
of pregnancy. In total he dissected between 300 and 400. As
pregnant women were never, ever executed, none of his
specimens could have been acquired legally.

Legal News: Dwarf-bowling and Dwarf-tossing
In 1990, New York State was forced to pass laws to criminalize participation in two new and popular sports: Dwarf-bowling and Dwarf-tossing. In the former, a vertically challenged individual wearing a helmet is strapped to a skateboard and propelled towards an arrangement of pins. In the latter a similar individual, this time harnessed, is thrown at a padded target. It is not known if all concerned were willing participants.
LA Times

A radiation cure for acne

When radiation was first discovered in the nineteenth century it was immediately pronounced to be as harmless and beneficial as sunshine, and so began a medical craze for radiation treatment of the most trivial ailments. For a period of around forty years into the early part of this century large numbers of people were needlessly exposed to lethal doses of radiation for such minor problems as ringworm and acne: women were treated for post-natal depression by having their ovaries irradiated.

Back from the dead

In 1819 the Glasgow surgeon Dr James Jeffrey attended a public demonstration of galvanism – the study of the effects of electrical currents passed through the human body – by a fellow lecturer Andrew Ure. The body was that of a collier, Matthew Clydesdale, who had been hanged for murder and, in accordance with the law of the day, his warm corpse handed over to medical students. Before a packed audience of students and members of the public, Clydesdale was seated in a chair and his hands were attached to a battery. As the current was switched on, the horrified spectators saw the man's chest suddenly heave and the body stand upright. Dr Jeffrey coolly saved the day by expertly slitting the man's throat with a scalpel. Although Jeffrey had technically committed murder, he was never charged because the man had already been executed and was therefore legally dead.

Vivisection too good for him

If not for a much-publicized test case in 1731, human vivisection may have flourished legally during the eighteenth century. When William Chiselden was appointed surgeon to Queen Caroline one of his first tasks was to find a cure for her profound deafness. He attempted to secure a human guinea pig in the form of a convicted criminal named Rey: the deal was that Rey would go free, and in return Chiselden would be allowed to do unspeakable things to Rey's ears, i.e. deafen him then bore holes in his ears to find out if perforation would be of value to the royal earhole. There was a huge outcry by right-wing Hanoverians, but not on humanitarian grounds. They argued that vivisection was too good for Rey and he shouldn't be allowed to cheat the gallows: in any case, Rey might escape while he was in Chiselden's custody. The authorities bowed to the pressure and Chiselden was ordered to confine his experiments to the dead. The surgeon may yet have had his own way: he eventually helped establish the Company of Surgeons, whose headquarters were suspiciously located next door to Newgate Prison.

Strictly women only

Midwifery was once the sole privilege of women and men were forbidden to attend births. A Hamburg doctor named Wertt who wanted to learn more about obstetrics managed to observe several childbirths by dressing as a woman. When his real identity was exposed he was burned at the stake.

A bundle of faggots
In ancient Greece the preferred method of hastening childbirth
was either to lift the pregnant woman and repeatedly drop her on
to a couch, or to strap the woman to a couch, turn it upright,
then pound it repeatedly onto a bundle of faggots.

Beat it out of them
A book called *Anatomy of Melancholy*, written by Robert Burton,
became the authoritative work on the subject of mental illness
when it was published in 1621. He taught that madness was often
caused by the retention of bodily excretions: the best cure was to
tie patients to a wall and literally beat the crap out of them.

Cures for madness
The standard text on the subject of madness for most of the
nineteenth century was written by the top French physician Jean
Esquirol. Mental illness, said Esquirol, was caused by living in a
new home, squeezing a pimple, old age, childbirth, the menstrual
cycle, a blow on the head, constipation, shrinkage of hemorrhoids,
misuse of mercury, disappointment in love, political upheavals,
shock, thwarted ambition, excessive study, masturbation, prostitution, religion and bloodletting. Confusingly, bloodletting was at
that time also considered to be one of the best cures for madness.

Expectorate your way to mental health
Until the twentieth century most English doctors were taught
that much mental illness was a result of large quantities of
phlegm. The standard course of treatment was to force the
patient to be violently sick three or four times a day.

Dirty linen

Verminous palace
Although the Winter Palace of St Petersburg during the reign of
Czar Nicholas l was considered to be one of the biggest and
most opulent royal residences in the world, it was perpetually
alive with vermin. This was mostly due to the Czar's reluctance
to get rid of the herd of cows he always kept on the top floor to
ensure a regular supply of milk for his family.

Lice shirt
The average number of body lice found on an infested human is
around one hundred. The record number of lice found on a
single shirt is 10,000, plus 10,000 eggs.

Tape Worm tales
In 1784 an Austrian doctor sparked off an international race for the
world's biggest tapeworm when he found a 2-ft specimen inside
one of his patients. Paris countered with a tapeworm measuring
120-ft and weighing over 2 lbs, but the day was finally won by a
Russian peasant who proudly claimed a 238-ft tapeworm for his
country. There were plenty of quacks who were quick to exploit
this new found public fear of worms. Advertising copywriters
selling patent worm powders had a field day with torrid stories
about people whose lives were wrecked by tapeworms.
Promotional material for a product called "Exterminator" claimed:
"Mr Stiles of the Lock and Key of West Smithfield was practically
eaten by a worm 8-ft long, and might still have been alive if only
he had taken the "Exterminator" . . .

A nice, warm bath
In rural Ethiopia it is still the norm to bathe in the warm,
running stream of a urinating cow.

In the stew
Personal hygiene was considered such a novelty right up until
the nineteenth century that public baths had a bad reputation.
People who habitually bathed were regarded as ill, or sexual
perverts, or both. So notorious were the "stews" or public baths
of late medieval Europe, that "stew" came to be used as another
word for brothel. Henry VIII shut down Britain's public baths in
1546 in an attempt to avert a syphilis epidemic.

The king who smelled like carrion
The French King Henri IV was renowned, unusually for the
time, for being a stickler for changing his shirts regularly, but
still went around "smelling like carrion". When his fiancée
Marie de Médicis met him for the first time the stench almost
made her faint.

Honour your parents
Children on the island of Tonga used to catch and eat their
parents' head and body lice as a sign of filial duty and affection.

Filthy rich
The poor in seventeenth-century Britain rarely had more than one
change of clothes, which made it all the more important that they
wash once a week. The rich however, who had large reserves of
linen and could therefore keep going for weeks, even months
without washing, turned personal filthiness into a sign of affluence.
Thus, personal cleanliness became inversely proportional to your
station in life : the higher up the social scale you were, the more you

stank. At the very bottom were families of miners who had to wash their pit-blackened clothes and bodies every single night.

Bathtub installed in White House!
Bathing indoors was considered a distinctly un-American activity well into the nineteenth century. When the White House had its first bathtub installed in 1851 it sparked a public uproar.

ANIMAL NEWS Pigs Might Fly II

Farmer Ted Jewell arrived at the slaughter-house in Eastleigh, Hants, yesterday, only to find that the back of his lorry was completely empty. The eleven-stone pig he had loaded at the start of the journey had completely vanished. He said, "A pig jumping over a five-foot tailboard then down six feet on to the road is almost as daft as a pig flying. But that's all that could have happened."
The People

Lice breaker
Body lice can carry many diseases, including plague. South American Indians are prone to a plague infection of the tonsils thanks to their habit of cracking lice between their teeth.

Bath year
Even after soap was first produced on a commercial scale in England in 1824, most people were content to wash their hands and face and seldom allowed soap or water near their armpits, feet or genitals for years on end.

**Thought
for the Day**

If we quit voting, would they
all go away?

Lice-saver
Natives of Malabar who suffered from head lice would call for
the local holy man, who would voluntarily take the lice and put
them on his own head for nourishment.

Only among very close friends
In seventeenth-century France it was considered bad form to
take lice, fleas or other parasites and crack them between one's
finger nails in company "except in the most intimate circles".

Don't wash behind your ears
A book of hygiene and manners published in 1671 advised
children to avoid bathing wherever possible: "Washing with
water is bad for sight, causes toothache and catarrh, makes the
face pale, and renders it more susceptible to cold in winter and
sun in summer."

Vive la différence
Some time during the sixteenth century France became a nation
of hydrophobics who believed that water was a health hazard.
The French held that human skin was permeable, and that hot
water was especially dangerous because it opened the pores
exposing the inner body to dirty air. Water, they were told, also

weakened internal organs and ligaments. Old habits die hard.
Even today the French continue to harbour a suspicion that
water is bad for the skin, which may be why they take fewer
baths and showers than almost anyone else in Europe. In a
European league table of personal filthiness, the Spanish come
top, closely followed by the French, with the Italians, who take
more baths and showers, and use more soap than anyone else, at
the bottom. The average French adult uses 4.2 bars of soap a
year – about half the amount consumed by the average Briton,
and only one in every five French men take a bath daily. The
French, and the Spanish, are far more likely to spend money on
perfumes to mask the smell of stale sweat. In Spain, even very
small children are more likely to be doused with eau de cologne
rather than be forced to bathe. The French also have the most
casual attitude to dental hygiene in Europe: on average they
brush their teeth only once every three days. Although
Scandinavians are now considered to be more conscientious
about personal hygiene than most other nationalities, this wasn't
always so; a thousand years ago the Arab historian Ahmed ibn
Fadlan described them as "the filthiest race that God ever
created. They do not wipe themselves after going to stool, nor
wash themselves after a nocturnal pollution."

Macho lice
In some Mediterranean communities, an infestation of lice is
considered a sign of virility.

The Rotten Sneakers Contest
The US town of Montpellier in Vermont holds the world's only
known annual Rotten Sneakers Contest. Previous competition
winners include eight-year-old Robert Scruton who wore his
world-beating Nikes for two years in preparation.

Diagnosis by smell
Osphresiology – the science of diagnosis by smell – was an eighteenth-century fad which briefly took the medical world by storm. Doctors claimed to be able to reach a diagnosis of the patient's ailment by smelling their sweat, stools and urine.

 Don't worry, be happy
Health is the greatest gift, contentment the greatest wealth, faithfulness the best relationship.
Buddha, c. 400 BC

A new you
Nine-tenths of ordinary household dust is dead human skin. Every seven years you can literally claim to be a new you because your outer covering will have completely replaced itself: the old you is in the Hoover bag. You will shed about 40 lbs of dead skin in a lifetime.

Pinworm tropics
In many of the world's tropical areas virtually the entire population is infested with pinworm.

Urine collection
Apart from Howard Hughes' pathological fear of germs which obliged him to spend the last years of his life clad in Kleenex tissues, he also suffered from chronic constipation and once spent twenty-eight hours on the toilet. He also had an obsession about his own urine, which he had sealed in glass jars, numbered, dated and catalogued by his aides.

And now for my next trick . . .
A salmonella germ can pass through twenty-eight sheets of toilet paper.

POTTY WISDOM, JAPAN

Drink and sing: an inch before us is black night.

Leave the landings
Apart from tanks, helicopters and submarines, Leonardo da Vinci also turned his inventive mind to the latterday problems of hygiene. When he made his plans for Ten New Towns to "distribute the masses of humanity" he advocated the use of spiral staircases in all of his houses. This, he explained, was to discourage people from urinating and defecating on the landing.

Bedwetting Britain
Britain has an estimated three-quarters of a million bedwetters.

Stop that, you're depressing me
The repeated injections of saliva produced by a hungry body louse produces a slight toxic effect that makes the human host feel depressed, or "lousy".

250

URBAN MYTHS
True or False – you decide

AMERICAN EXPRESS ISSUE A SPECIAL BLACK CARD

The Platinum American Express card is not the highest card that can be issued. A very small number of customers are issued with a special "black card". There is no credit limit on this card, and customers regularly make transactions of tens of millions – buying such items as airplanes, companies. It is also rumoured that these cards have been used for large purchases of gold and other major international asset exchanges. Anything at all can be bought with a black card.

Only the extremely wealthy qualify for this card. You cannot apply for a black Amex card but have to be invited by the company to have one. The company will not confirm that this card exists, and customers are given the card on condition of maintaining secrecy wherever possible.

The great unwashed
Louis XIV took only three baths in his lifetime, each of them under protest. Samuel Pepys is reputed to have never once had a bath in his lifetime.

U-nclean
Eighteenth-century English nobility, when faced with new-fangled standards of personal hygiene, clung to the belief that washing was decidedly non-U. One prominent lady aristocrat

who accepted an invitation to a society dinner sat down to eat with noticeably filthy hands. When someone remarked upon the grubbiness of her fingers, she replied, "Madam, you should see my feet."

Murder and Mayhem: Uses for Human Skin

Necrophile Ed Gein, on whom Thomas Harris based "Buffalo Bill" in *Silence of the Lambs*, used the skin of corpses to make himself waistcoats. This was not the first use of human skin for practical purposes. Concentration camp guard Irma Grese is said to have made lampshades of human skin. The skin of a victim of the guillotine was used to bind the second edition of Rousseau's *Social Contract* – the book that, more than any other, was responsible for the French Revolution. The skin of William Corder, who murdered Maria Marten in the Red Barn in 1827, was used for book binding in the following year.

Miserly John Overs gets his comeuppance

The miser John Overs, who made his million by operating a ferry across the Thames from Southwark to the City, lived so frugally that the rats in his house left of their own accord. His meanness led to his death. In an attempt to cut down on his bills, Overs pretended to be dead for a day, believing that his house servants would fast until after the funeral and thus reduce his food bill. The plan back-fired when his servants celebrated instead by throwing open the doors to the pantry. When Overs rose from his death bed to complain they thought he was a ghost and clubbed him to death with an oar.

Health-giving bath

Although the famous waters of Bath in the seventeenth and eighteenth centuries were famed for their health-restoring quali-ties, they almost certainly killed more people than they cured. The waters were hardly ever cleaned or emptied, and the healthy and the sick, the diseased and the unspeakably dirty were able to frolic in, and drink, a vast soup comprising mostly floating ulcers, sweat, dirt and dandruff.

Bedbug Bedlam

Of the seventy-five species of bedbug, only two feed on humans. A bedbug can live in your bed for up to four years and can go for eighteen months without a meal.

Sleep tight

A typical household pillow is home to about 2,000 house dust mites, which in turn excrete about twenty pellets of faeces each a day. It is estimated that a six-year-old pillow will have approximately one tenth of its weight comprising old human skin, dead and living mites and mite dung. Breathing in their fecal pellets, or coming into contact with them, is a major cause of allergies and asthma.

Scapegoat

During the Black Death the most popular way of keeping down the stench in houses was to keep a goat in your house: the odour of the goat overpowered the stench of death. Goatless families preferred to wear vinegar soaked rags over their nostrils.

Flay away
The common housefly transmits thirty different diseases harmful to human beings.

Here, there, bacteria
There are about 10,000 bacteria in every litre of town air, and 100,000 bacteria in one litre of drinking water.

One-handed
The amputation of the right hand is seen in the Middle East as the ultimate social stigma, because Muslims never eat with their left hand: they use it exclusively to wipe their backsides.

The retreat of the lice
Body lice are highly sensitive to changes in temperature – they will vacate anyone with a fever and quickly leave a dead person. It was reported that when the slain body of Thomas Becket lay in Westminster Abbey, a column of lice evacuated the corpse "like a retreating army".

Executions

Dead man's portrait
James Scott, the Duke of Monmouth and first-born illegitimate son of Charles II, was victim of Tower Hill's messiest execution on 15 July 1685. The handsome and popular Duke complained loudly that the axeman's blade appeared to be rather blunt, but

no one took much notice. In the event it was the fifth blow which finally severed his head from his shoulders just before he had a chance to say "I told you so." The crowd were so appalled that the axeman narrowly escaped a lynching.
It was belatedly decided that the Duke, being a rather historically important person, should have his portrait painted for posterity. His head was duly sewn back on, the joins covered up, and his portrait painted. He now hangs in the National Portrait Gallery.

In the soup
Before his electrocution in New Jersey, murderer Charles Fithina told his wardens, "I want to make a complaint . . . the soup I had for supper tonight was too hot."

Britain's bloodiest Lord Chief Justice
Sir George "Bloody" Jeffreys of Wem (1648–1689) was Britain's most sadistic Lord Chief Justice ever. He passed 331 death sentences and had hundreds more deported – usually a fate worse than hanging. One of his most notorious sentences was conferred on Lady Alice de Lisle, whom he ordered to be roasted alive. The Church were outraged by the sentence and demanded clemency: Lady Alice had her sentence commuted on appeal and got away with a beheading. Jeffreys never allowed a word of self defence and always drove the prosecution through at high speed. The cause of this behaviour was his painful bladder-stone: he was compelled to urinate hourly and had to get through the trials as fast as possible to reach the lavatory.

UFOLOGY
Northern Lights, Dr X and the Mystery of the Red Triangles

Jacques Vallée cites the case of a French doctor who wished to remain anonymous, preferring to be called "Dr X". Dr X was awakened in the middle of the night by his child, who was pointing at a flashing light in the sky. He opened the window and observed two disc-shaped UFOs. Then the two came together and blended into one. This disc then turned to a vertical position, so its blinding light illuminated the front of the house. Suddenly there was a loud bang, and it vanished.

The doctor now found that a leg injury had suddenly healed, and so had an old war wound. Subsequently, he lost weight, and a red triangle formed around his navel. The same triangle formed on the child. Vallée notes that, as a consequence of the experience, both the doctor and his wife have developed an almost mystical attitude of accept-ance towards life and death. Strange coincidences occurred, the doctor and his wife became telepathic, and on one occasion he experienced levitation.

Nebraska's nuttiest judge

In 1998 Nebraska's Judicial Qualification Commission recommended that Omaha Judge Richard "Deacon" Jones be removed from public office. Charges against him included signing official court papers with names "A. Hitler" and "Snow White"; setting eccentric bail amounts, including "13 cents" and "a zillion pengos", personally and indiscreetly supervising a young male probationer's urine test and setting off a firework in the office of a judge with whom he had an argument.

Piecemeal beheading

The most badly executed beheading in history was that endured in 1626 by the French Count Henri de Chalais, condemned to death for his part in a royal assassination plot. When it was time for Chalais to be publicly beheaded with a sword, the regular executioner could not be found and an inexperienced replacement was drafted in at the last minute. The Count's head was hacked off by the stand-in on the twenty-ninth stroke; he was still breathing at the twentieth.

Fit for pigs

When California's notorious San Quentin gas chamber was installed in the 1930s it was tested on live pigs. The city authorities were so proud of their "humane" new system that, in a desperately miscalculated exercise in public relations, they invited newspaper reporters to witness their first disposal of a human being. The reporters were appalled by what they saw: one described it as "more savage than being hanged, drawn and quartered".

257

Joke of the Day
A termite walks into a
bar and asks: "Is the bar
tender here?"

What a way to go

In thirteenth- and fourteenth-century England, high treason
against a king was considered to be the worst possible crime:
accordingly, hanging was considered much too mild a deterrent
for traitors. After Simon de Montfort was killed at Evesham in
1265 his limbs were hacked off and sent to various parts of the
kingdom, while his head and testicles were parcelled up and sent
to the wife of one of his enemies. The rebel William Wallace
got the full treatment in 1305: he was dragged through the
streets of London behind a horse, then hanged, but taken down
from the scaffold while he was still alive. Then his entrails were
cut out and burned, and he was quartered and decapitated. His
arms and legs were sent to Scotland, while his head was
mounted on London Bridge.

What do the USA and Iran have in common?

The USA shares a distinction with Iran as being one of the only
countries to execute the insane and the mentally ill. After being
reprieved four times on the day of his execution, Robert Alton
Harris went to the gas-chamber in 1992 even though his
prosecutors knew that he had been brain-damaged from birth by
his mother's alcohol abuse. His final request was that everyone
on San Quentin's death row be treated to ice cream. In January
1992 the mentally retarded Ricky Ray Rector was killed by

lethal injection. His executioners struggled for an hour to find the vein, and Rector tried to help them.

A bit harsh?

Thanks to the Waltham Black Act, the most notorious piece of legislation on the subject of capital punishment ever, the number of offences punishable by death in England by the early nineteenth century was greater than anywhere else in the world. Added to the already impressive list of offences for which one could be hanged were the heinous crimes of "associating with gypsies", "writing on Westminster bridge", "impersonating a pensioner of Greenwich Hospital", "writing a threatening letter", "appearing on a highway with a sooty face", "damaging a fish-pond", or "cutting down a tree". In 1800 a ten-year-old boy was hanged for "secreting notes in a post office", and in 1801 a thirteen-year-old boy was hanged for stealing a spoon.

The added cruelty of crucifixion

Although the Gospels' description of Christ's death is the most famous account of crucifixion, it was a commonplace method of execution widely used throughout the Middle East. As if the lingering death by suffocation on the cross wasn't enough, it was usually augmented by whatever torture took the executioner's – or the mob's – fancy, including broken legs, stoning or flaying the victim's skin. The Romans in particular liked to amuse themselves by nailing the victim up in different positions: upside down was a big favourite.

Donated to science while still alive

In 1740 a seventeen-year-old rapist named William Duel was hanged, and emerged from a deep coma to find that his body had been donated to science and a surgeon's knife was busily slicing into his vitals. Duel survived and his death sentence was subsequently commuted to transportation for life.

Justice?

America's most horribly bungled execution by electric chair was also one of the first. In 1893 William Taylor was condemned for killing a fellow inmate in Auburn Prison. As the first electric charge surged through his body, his legs went into spasm and tore the chair apart by his ankle strappings. The charge was switched off while hasty repairs were made to the chair. The switch was thrown again, but this time there was no current because the generator had burned out. Taylor was taken out of the chair and drugged to dry to deaden any pain he may have felt. By the time the power had been restored Taylor was already dead. The law however had to be carried out, so the dead man was once more strapped to the chair and the current was passed through him for another 30 seconds. A warden announced, "Gentlemen, justice has been done."

Prolonged execution

The execution of the failed French regicide Robert-François Damiens was the most prolonged recorded in history. On 2 March 1757 Damiens was stripped and chained down on a wooden scaffold, where his right hand was to be burned off. A fire was lit, but it kept going out, so one of the executioners improvised by gouging out lumps of flesh from various parts of Damiens' body with red-hot pincers while boiling oil and melted wax, resin and lead were poured into the wounds. Between his screams Damiens was heard to cry out "My God, take pity on me" and "Jesus, help me!" The executioners then took long leather straps and wound them up the length of his arms and his legs. Each strap was attached to a rope, which in turn was affixed to four horses, which were then whipped, each pulling in a different direction. Damiens was a very muscular man and the horses selected to tear him limb from limb were not quite up to the task. For more than an hour the horses were urged on while Damiens screamed in agony. As dusk fell, an attending surgeon suggested that they might want to speed things up by cutting Damiens' sinews, and the executioners began hacking at his joints with knives. The horses were again whipped and after several pulls, ripped one arm and a leg from Damiens' body. As the second arm was pulled out, Damiens' lower jaw was seen to move, as though to speak. He died at 10.30 pm, five-and-a-half hours after the execution had started.

A lucky escape

Two men have survived three hangings apiece. The murderer Joseph Samuels was reprieved in 1803 after the rope broke twice on the first and second attempts and the trapdoor failed to open on the third. A trapdoor mechanism also saved the life of convicted murderer John Lee in 1884. Even though it worked every time it was tested, it failed to open three times in the space of seven minutes. Lee was let off with life imprisonment.

Back from the dead

In 1903 a young American, Frederick van Wormer, was sent to the electric chair for the murder of his uncle. Van Wormer was duly electrocuted and pronounced dead. In the autopsy room, as he was about to go under the scalpel, his eye was seen to flicker and he moved a hand. The prison doctor confirmed that two full charges of current had failed to kill the prisoner. Van Wormer was carried back to the chair and several more currents were passed through him until his death was beyond dispute.

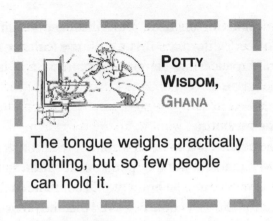

POTTY WISDOM, GHANA

The tongue weighs practically nothing, but so few people can hold it.

Saved by acupuncture!

When Albert Fish was sent to the electric chair at Sing Sing prison in 1936, the first electric charge failed, allegedly short-circuited by dozens of needles the old man had inserted in his own body. Doctors discovered a total of twenty-nine needles in his genitals.

Another botched execution

The electrocution of John Evans in Alabama state prison in 1983 required three surges of 1,900 volts of electricity each over a period of fourteen minutes to finish him off. Eye-witnesses saw Evans struggling for breath as smoke began to pour from the electrodes on his head and one of his legs. The autopsy revealed that he had endured fourth and second degree burns while he was still alive.

Showtime

Although there hasn't been a public execution in the United States since 1937, the gassing of Robert Alton Harris in 1992 was the next best thing. Harris was puzzled to find that forty-eight people, including eighteen journalists and a film crew were allowed in to see California's first execution for twenty-five years. Several broadcasting companies expressed an interest in screening the gassing.

Life after the guillotine

The guillotine held a morbid fascination for the French medical profession, who marvelled at the speed of execution and speculated whether or not the brain would continue to function after decapitation. Some people believed that the razor-sharp blade struck the victim so cleanly that they had lost their heads before they knew anything about it, a theory fuelled by dozens of stories about victims who continued to protest after they had lost their heads. Eye witnesses recorded that when the head of Jean Paul Marat's assassin Charlotte Corday was held up and slapped by the executioner, it showed unmistakable signs of anger. Subsequently French doctors were allowed to carry out various macabre experiments on severed heads, including pinching the cheeks, sticking things up the nostrils, holding lighted candles near to the eyeballs, and even shouting the victim's name very loudly in the ear of the severed head. In 1880 the murderer Menesclou had the blood of a living dog pumped into his head. It was recorded that the head responded with a look of "shocked amazement". Much more recent research by Russian doctors actually gives some substance to these stories: they have found that if for any reason the brain is suddenly cut off from its oxygen supply, it uses an emergency system which effectively keeps the victim conscious for several minutes.

Insane

The state of Louisiana abandoned electric chair executions in 1991 because of the pain inflicted on the victim by burns,

preferring to execute their criminals by lethal injection on a
surgical trolley. In 1992 they pressed for legislation which
would allow them to medicate insane criminals so that they can
experience the terror of facing death by execution.

Nothing but revenge

Britain's last official executioner Albert Pierrepoint terminated
the lives of 450 murderers and traitors during his twenty-five-
year career, but he wasn't altogether happy in his work. After
resigning he wrote: "I do not now believe that any one of the
hundreds of executions I have carried out has in any way acted
as a deterrent against future murder. Capital punishment, in my
view, achieved nothing except revenge."

Thoughtful executioners

In 1983 inmates on Death Row in Bangkok Gaol complained
that the sub-machine gun used for dawn executions was too
noisy and was making them lose sleep. The considerate
governor obliged by purchasing a silencer.

Improvements in hanging

In the eighteenth century "hanging" in Britain consisted of being
slowly strangled at the end of a rope. The hangman often had to
speed the process up by hanging on to the victim's legs.
Recoveries from execution by hanging were not infrequent. The
hangman William Marwood made the system slightly less
offensive in 1871 when he perfected the long drop, by which the
victim fell from six to ten feet thus dramatically reducing the
suffering endured by those hanged. The drop caused fracture
dislocation of the neck's vertebrae, severing the spinal cord and
medulla, and so causing instant death.

Half hanged

A woman freshly hanged in1724 in Musselburgh, Scotland became the centre of a grisly dispute between her family and a bunch of enthusiastic anatomists. Her relatives were determined to give her a decent Christian burial: a party of medical students meanwhile had other plans for the corpse and were equally determined to get their hands on it. A bloody fight broke out over the body, which settled the argument by suddenly sitting upright. She lived on for another thirty years with a new nickname – "Half Hangit Maggie Dickson".

Hitler's favourite form of execution

When Hitler came to power in 1933 one of the first things he did was re-introduce an old favourite method of capital punishment – the axe.

A reprieve two minutes too late

In eighteenth-century London criminals condemned to the gallows were traditionally allowed to stop off at the Church of St Giles in the Field for a last pint on their way to execution. One man, a teetotaller, refused the offer of a drink because he wanted to press on and get it over with, thereby missing a reprieve which arrived two minutes after he was hanged.

If at first . . .

In 1752 in London a nineteen-year-old traitor, only minutes after his execution, sat up on the dissecting table. A quick-thinking surgeon responded by clubbing him to death with a mallet.

Death by molten lead
The Roman Emperor Constantine employed an alternative to the most common death sentence of the day, crucifixion: he had molten lead poured down the throats of the accused.

Death by the thousand cuts
China has the world's most refined and most revolting systems for the disposal of criminals, including strangulation, decollation and the infamous Ling-chi, or "Death by the Thousand Cuts". The precise technique of Ling-chi varied from region to region, but by and large a basic routine was observed: the executioner was presented with a basket covered with a cloth. Inside the basket was a collection of knives, each knife inscribed with the name of a body part. The executioner selected a knife at random, and proceeded to cut off the listed body part. Desperate relatives of the condemned man would often bribe the executioner to find the knife labelled "heart" as quickly as possible.

Fast and painless?
When thirty-four-year-old American rubbish van driver Billy White was executed in April 1992 by lethal injection in Huntsville prison, it took medical attendants forty minutes to locate a vein and another nine minutes for him to die.

Decapitation by sword
The official method of execution in the Arab states of Saudi Arabia, Yemen, Qatar and the United Arab Emirates is decapitation by sword.

At last
Before he was finally executed in Florida in 1988, William Darden survived six death warrants on last-minute appeals.

266

Macabre candlestick holders
English executioners did a roaring trade in selling portions of their victims as souvenirs. The most saleable mementoes were severed hands, to be turned into candlestick holders.

Thought for the Day

Teamwork is essential – it gives the enemy someone else to shoot at.

"In his lifetime he never looked so well"
London Bridge became the prime site for displaying the severed heads of villains who had lost them to the executioner's axe because it was the only route in to the city from the south, and served as an early reminder to visitors that they were expected to behave themselves. The heads were first "parboiled", an embalming technique which involved boiling the head in a large kettle containing salt and cumin seed – the latter used to keep hungry seabirds at bay. It was reported that the head of John Fisher, executed by Henry VIII for refusing to acknowledge his ascendancy over the Pope as head of the English Church, actually got better-looking after it was parboiled and spiked on the Bridge. An eye witness commented that "in his lifetime he never looked so well". The rejuvenated head caused such a stir that after a fortnight the executioner was ordered to take it down and throw it into the River Thames.

URBAN MYTHS
True or False – you decide

"PAID IN FULL"

It is rumoured that you can settle any debt if your creditor accepts a check made out for a fraction of the amount owed, with the words "Paid in Full" written on it. Once they have cashed such a check, they cannot pursue you for any unpaid balance.

One man ran up credit card debts over $250,000. He lived a lavish lifestyle, staying at expensive hotels and gambling at resorts around the world. He was able to get away with this because several of his creditors inadvertently accepted checks for far less than he owed, with "Paid in Full" written on the back. This created a legal contract whereby they had acknowledged the check as final payment of his debts.

The companies did not test the case in court because they were scared of setting a precedent. Not many people know about this loophole, but if there was a court case, it would become more widely reported and abused as a result.

Friendly firing squad

When Romanian President Nicolae Ceaucescu and his wife Elena were summarily executed by a firing squad on Christmas Day 1989, the soldiers fired so wildly that several were injured by "friendly fire".

Bargain execution
Albert Pierrepoint's fee for executing Ruth Ellis, the last woman to be hanged in Britain, was fifteen guineas – £15.75.

"Have a nice death"
A born-again Christian from Texas, Judge Charles J. Hearn, demonstrated his newfound faith by adding a smiley face to his signature. Some of his critics pointed out that this was not very appropriate behaviour for a judge, especially a judge signing a death warrant. The defence lawyer for a man sentenced to death by Judge Hearn in 1993 complained, "It's like he's saying 'have a nice death.'"

Beyond belief

A bit late now
In 1992 tenants of an apartment block in a strictly orthodox Jewish area near Tel Aviv, Israel stood by and watched as a fire gutted their homes. They later explained that they had delayed phoning the fire brigade for half an hour while they went to see their rabbi to ask him if it was OK to use a telephone on the Sabbath.

Charneldelier
A church in the Czech town of Sedlec has a chandelier made entirely of human bones.

Poor Martin
Martin Luther suffered from chronic constipation.

Pope Joan

The Vatican's Chair of St Peter, the ancient red marble throne on which popes were ceremoniously inaugurated, had a hole in the seat which made it resemble an elaborate commode. According to legend, the seat allowed a physical examination of new popes to establish their gender. It was alleged that in the ninth century the Christian Church had accidentally elected a woman who ruled for two years as Pope John. Her secret was discovered only after she gave birth to a child during a procession.

Fasting

During the feast of Ramadan, Muslims are not allowed to swallow even their own saliva.

Zion City

In 1888 John Alexander Dowie, Christian zealot, faith healer and founder of the Apostolic Church, purchased ten square miles of land in Illinois on the shores of Lake Michigan where he founded the fundamentalist community of Zion City, home to about 5,000 of his followers. The rigidly puritanical Dowie's creation was an entirely self-supporting community with new factories built for the manufacture of lace, confectionery and furniture, but short on entertainment, bereft of theatres, cinemas or dance halls. From his church pulpit Dowie, absolute ruler of Zion City, dispensed the law, preached religious intolerance and railed against various earthly sins, including sex, oysters, pork and life assurance, citing little known Old Testament injunctions against shellfish and randy insurance salesmen. Dowie believed that druggists and physicians were instruments of the devil. When his own daughter was severely burned after accidentally knocking over an oil lamp, he banished one of his followers for trying to put Vaseline on her burns. Many others who came to his faith cure sessions also died of their illnesses without any medical attention. In 1895 he was charged with manslaughter and neglect by the city of Chicago and convicted, but the higher courts ruled that the conviction was unconstitutional. In 1901 Dowie declared that he was the prophet Elijah and took to wearing biblical clothes and embarked on an expensive and ultimately ruinous campaign to spread the word of the Apostolic Church to the rest of America. With his financial problems mounting he turned to a close friend and disciple, the millionaire preacher Wilbur Glenn Voliva, whose $10 million fortune had been made from the manufacture of chocolate biscuits. When Voliva studied Dowie's accounts he found a discrepancy of about $2 million. Voliva denounced his old friend as a fraudulent polygamist, banished him from the community and established himself as the new leader of Zion. Fifty-nine-year-old Dowie, paralyzed by a crippling stroke and evidently insane, died two years later.

Flat earthery

Wilbur Glenn Voliva, the second chief administrator of Zion City, home of the Apostolic Church in Illinois, ruled the 16,000 inhabitants with an iron hand, banning cigarettes and alcohol and imposing a 10 p.m. curfew. Women were forbidden to cut their hair, expose their necks or straddle a horse, wear lipstick or "immodest clothing" including swimming costumes and high heels. No one was allowed to whistle, sing or even hum on Sundays, or drive a vehicle over 5 mph. Voliva's extraordinary laws were policed by his Praetorian Guard, who wore special uniforms with the word "PATIENCE" written on their helmets and wore small bibles on the belts instead of truncheons. Some offenders were summarily fined on the spot; the unlucky ones were delivered to Voliva himself and given a one-hour lecture on their sins. Voliva's theories on how to run a community were one thing, his grasp of astrophysics were quite another. In 1922 Voliva became the first religious broadcaster to found a radio station, the 5,000 watt WCBD, to preach "flat earthery" to people as far away as New Zealand. Voliva's regular broadcasts taught that the earth was saucer-shaped, that the north pole was positioned at the centre and the south pole was a crust of ice running around the outer rim. The rest of the universe, the sun, the stars and the moon were fastened to the sky and were much closer than the astronomers – "poor, ignorant conceited fools" – had always claimed. "The idea of a sun millions of miles in diameter and ninety-one million miles away is silly," Voliva explained. "The sun is only thirty-two miles across and is not more than three thousand miles from the earth. It stands to reason that it must be so. God made the sun to light the earth and therefore must have placed it close to the task it was designed to do." The sun's apparent cycle of rising and setting, he continued, was merely an optical illusion. Voliva had frequently predicted the world's imminent destruction, but always found new calculations for future Armageddons. When he died in 1934, aged seventy-two, his offer of a $5,000 reward to anyone who could prove the earth was not flat remained uncollected.

Robert Browning and Elizabeth Barrettt
Elizabeth Barrett's enduring testimony to her great love for her husband:
How do I love thee? Let me count the ways.
I love thee to the depth and breadth and height
My soul can reach, when feeling out of sight
For the ends of Being and ideal Grace.
I love thee to the level of everyday's
Most quiet need, by sun and candle-light.

I love thee freely, as men strive for Right;
I love thee purely, as they turn from Praise.
I love thee with the passion put to use
In my old griefs, and with my childhood's faith.
I love thee with a love I seemed to lose
With my lost saints! – I love thee with the breath,
Smiles, tears, of all my life! – and, if God choose,
I shall but love thee better after death.

Sex with the gods

Until the death of Hirohito, emperors ascending the Japanese
throne had to perform a ritual during which they pretend to have
sexual intercourse with the gods.

I am not a woman

The Roman Catholic church adopted celibacy as a code for the
priesthood in 1123. Three hundred and fifty years later Pope
Innocent VIII became known as "the Honest" because he admitted
that he had fathered several bastards. He only owned up to disprove
a rumour going around Rome at the time that he was a woman.

Never mind the parsons

For hundreds of years until the end of the nineteenth century
parsons were affectionately known as "bollocks" or "bollacks".
This little known fact formed the basis of a successful legal
defence in 1978 when the Sex Pistols used it to save their debut
album *Never Mind the Bollocks, Here's the Sex Pistols* from a
nationwide ban.

Mad Mayr

An eighteenth-century German religious fanatic named Mayr,
who by his close association with Prussia's vacuous King
Frederick William II became one of the most powerful men in the
country, attempted to demonstrate his deep faith by eating a whole
Bible. Mayr lived, although instead of achieving a higher level of
consciousness he was only able to achieve a higher level of
indigestion. One day Mayr was preaching a sermon from the
pulpit when he decided to liven things up by producing two loaded
pistols and firing them into the packed congregation, luckily
wounding only one of the assembled worshippers. Not a moment
too soon, Mayr was certified insane and locked in an asylum.

Kissing the Bible

In English courtrooms, the custom of kissing a Bible when
taking a judicial oath often led to syphilitic infection.

"Get thee to a nunnery"

Because of their deservedly bad press, the term "nunnery" in
Elizabethan times also meant brothel: when Hamlet told Ophelia
"Get thee to a nunnery", it wasn't an invitation to join a
convent.

Women should be punished during childbirth

When anesthetics first became available in the nineteenth century,
the Christian Church opposed the use of them in obstetrics,
because childbirth was supposed to hurt: pain was God's way of
punishing women for Eve's sin in the Garden of Eden.

Christian castrati

The early Christian church encouraged men to castrate
themselves to ensure that they would go to heaven.

274

The word of the parrot
Italy's most exclusive cult was founded by an Italian nun, Sister
Florence Christina. She left her convent in Bologna in 1989 to
reveal to the world that she was receiving God's word on a
regular basis via her ten-year-old pet parrot.

A conundrum
The medieval Christian church was faced with a problem
whenever a pregnant woman died, because unbaptized babies
were not allowed burial in Christian cemeteries. The foetus
would often be cut from the mother's corpse and buried outside
the cemetery in unconsecrated ground.

Effluvia tinctures
Many early Christian monks and nuns believed that the body
fluids of the deceased, especially those of saints or clergymen,
had special medicinal and curative properties. Among the
effluvia of a corpse that would be used to make tinctures, oils
and balms were blood, saliva, ear wax, urine, faeces and sperm.

Saint Nicholas and Black Peter

The most famous of all the Christian saints, St Nicholas, patron saint of children, was born so insufferably pious that he refused to suckle milk from the breast of his mother on official fast days. One of his chief claims to fame was that one day he came across three boys who had been chopped up and pickled by a wicked innkeeper. St Nick prayed over the pickle tub and the boys made a complete and remarkable recovery. His image as Santa Claus is more recent and owes more to a series of early Coca-Cola advertisements than it does to the Calendar of Saints; in some parts of the world however he still rides a white horse wearing purple robes accompanied by his helper, Black Peter.

Japanese 201st Air Group: Kamikaze

On 25 October 1944 a Japanese Zero aircraft screamed out of the sky above Leyte Gulf, in the Philippines. Sailors in the American fleet below watched in paralyzed horror as the Zero, guns blazing, dived straight at the carrier *USS Santee*, blowing an enormous hole in the flight deck. The Japanese suicide pilots had made their first attack. Dubbed "Kamikaze", or Divine Wind in reference to the typhoon which saved Japan from invasion in the thirteenth century, the volunteer suicide pilots were a last desperate gamble to halt the US tide in the Pacific Theatre. The pilots, who were treated as gods in Japan, drew for inspiration on the *Bushido* code of the old Samurai warrior class, especially its vaunting of the "good death" in battle. Flying aircraft loaded with 550-lb bombs the Kamikaze achieved spectacular successes, particularly after the introduction of the *kikusui* ("floating chrysanthemum"), which consisted of mass attacks by suicide bombers. During the battle of Okinawa, *kikusui* were responsible for the sinking

of forty-four US vessels. Thereafter, to American relief,
Japan simply ran out of aircraft to continue the Kamikaze
attacks.

The American Nostradamus
Edgar Cayce (1877–1945) was variously known as the
"American Nostradamus" and "the sleeping prophet" because of
his habit of going into a trance to predict the future or heal the
sick. Although Cayce's track record on the predictions front was
generally so erratic that he was obliged to keep up his day job
selling photographic supplies, he had one notable success just
before the 1929 Wall Street Crash when he advised a client
against investing in the stock market because he saw "a
downward movement of long duration". Cayce is also said to
have foreseen the First and Second World Wars, the
independence of India, the formation of the state of Israel and
the assassination of President Kennedy. He also predicted the
fall of communism in China, that California would fall into the
sea in 1969 and that Christ would return after a Third World
War in 1999. In the year 2000, Cayce predicted, the Earth's axis
would shift and mankind would be destroyed by flooding and
earthquakes. Cayce's followers, the Association for Research
and Enlightenment, keep this memory alive from their base at
his former home in Virginia.

A harmless crank?
The eighteenth-century prophet Richard Brothers was born in
Newfoundland but went to England to join the navy in 1771. In
1786 he married Elizabeth Hassall, but returned to his ship
directly after the wedding and upon arriving home several years
later, found his wife living with another man, the father of her
several children. Somewhat dispirited, Brothers decided to leave

the country but was stopped en route and commanded by God to turn back. It was around this time that he became interested in "prophetical writings" and interpreting various dreams which were coming to him with increasing frequency. He took his own surname as a sign that he was descended from King David through James, "one of the brothers of Jesus" and accordingly styled himself "the Prince of the Hebrews and nephew of the Almighty". Brothers wrote a couple of pamphlets, *A Revealed Knowledge of the Prophesies and Times: Book the First* and *Book the Second*, published in 1794 which publicized his claim as a prophet that the millennium would begin on 19 November 1795 and pronounced that he was to lead the return of the Jews to the Holy Land and undertake the rebuilding of Jerusalem. The British government, who had hitherto regarded Brothers as a harmless crank, viewed his writings with deep suspicion and had him arrested and declared insane and placed him in a private asylum. Despite his continued prophetic output his eleven-year incarceration reduced his devotees to a handful. Brothers's remaining followers petitioned for his release in 1806, after which he lived with friends until his death in 1824.

The Panacea Society's box
In 1814 Joanna Southcott, a sixty-four-year-old spinster and part-time fortune teller from London, caused a minor sensation when she claimed she was pregnant by the Holy Spirit. A small army of followers camped outside her front door to wait for the impending miracle, but the new messiah failed to arrive on the predicted date and Miss Southcott died ten days later. Her devotees, undismayed by the failure of the prophecy, concluded that the child had gone to heaven and would return later. A post-mortem however revealed that Miss Southcott was not with child and that the appearance of pregnancy was probably the result of flatulence. She nevertheless

acquired a cult following in The Panacea Society, a small sect based in Bedford. In the early 1900s cult leader Helen Exeter announced that the messiah would return in 1914, but didn't live to see her forecast fail as she was drowned early that year. The Society now pin their hopes on a locked and sealed box, about the size of a small coffin and sealed with copper nails, once belonging to Southcott, which they believe will reveal the date of Christ's return. The box however can only be opened in the presence of twenty-four bishops of the Church of England, a logistical improbability, but hope springs eternal; in 1999 The Panacea Society took out a series of newspaper advertisements in the UK national press demanding that the bishops assemble to open the box, however their demand went unheeded.

How long is your toothbrush?
Hindus have rules which dictate the length of a man's tooth-brush. The correct length for an average Hindu is 10 inches. It is shorter for the lower castes, but longer for a Brahmin.

 Don't worry, be happy
If you have a place to live and someone to love you are blessed.

Soprano supply
In order to keep the papal choir of the Sistine Chapel happy with a steady supply of sopranos, the Catholic Church was still castrating choir boys until 1878.

Cult count
The US has about 3,000 religious cults: Britain has around 600.

ANIMAL NEWS Pigs Eat Plane

"This is a very unusual case . . . pigs eating an aeroplane," remarked the prosecuting council at a recent case at Devizes Crown Court in Wiltshire. In the dock was Wilfred Grist, swineherd at Craymarsh Farm, Seend, which is owned by Mr Sam Cottle. Grist was accused of deliberately letting 968 pigs out of their sty with malicious intent.

The pigs celebrated their new-found freedom by eating most of the fabric off an Auster aeroplane parked nearby. They went on to lunch on two and a half tons of hay, a straw rick, half a ton of cattle food and thirty asbestos sheets. They also uprooted three acres of pasture, damaged four farm gates and killed ten of their own number in fights. In his defence, Grist claimed that Cottle had hit him. Then, he said, the farmer and his brother had forced him into a car saying that they were going to throw him into a slurry pit. Mr Cottle did not deny the accusation, although he added that he had soon changed his mind . . . He decided that it would be much better to drop Mr Grist into the giant animal-food mixer instead.
Daily Mirror

Philip the messiah

A group of villagers in the New Hebrides islands in the Pacific Ocean believe that the Duke of Edinburgh is their messiah and that he will one day cure all known diseases and grant them eternal youth. Prince Philip's small band of followers expect that on his return he will restore paradise on earth and resume his rightful place among them, wearing of course the traditional penis gourd. They also believe that Philip secretly runs the Commonwealth and has been able thus far to get away with the tricky business of concealing his true identity from the Queen.

The Russian castrates

In 1757 a Russian mystic named André Ivanov formed a sect called Skoptzy – literally, "castrates". The fundamental belief of the cult was the virtue of castration, taking as their tenet Matthew 19:12: "and there be eunuchs which have made themselves eunuchs for the kingdom of heaven's sake." Ivanov declared that testicles were the "keys of hell" and their amputation conferred upon the initiate "the right to mount the spotted horse of the apocalypse". He had himself and his thirteen disciples castrated, an operation carried out with a red-hot iron. The Skoptzy also wore complementary stigmata – cruciform cuts and burns of the shoulders, under the arms, on the belly, pelvis and thighs. Ivanov was arrested and banished to Siberia, where he eventually died, but the authorities failed to halt the spread of the Skoptzy cult. Kondrati Selivanov, one of the original disciples, was declared "the new Christ descended among men" and under his leadership the new sect grew in size and power. By 1770, Selivanov was finding a wider audience and could be found preaching his doctrine in St Petersburg, where he eventually became the protégé of Baroness Krudener, the mistress of the Czar. The Baroness considered Selivanov to be a saint. In 1859 three young noblemen died as the result of their initiatory rites and public outcry over these deaths led to massive popular opposition to the Skoptzy, forcing many of them to flee abroad. As late as 1900 there were still an estimated 5,000 male members of the sect in Russia.

Joke of the Day
Two weevils come to town from the country. One works hard and becomes very rich. The other becomes the lesser of two weevils.

Sacred springs

Since the Stone Age mankind the world over has been taught that fresh water rivers, springs and water holes were sacred and that interference with them would bring divine retribution. This wasn't because latter-day priests believed that water was a power greater than ourselves, but it was a rather effective way of stopping your brethren from defecating in your water supply.

Busy saint

The feast day of St Fiacre, the patron saint of hemorrhoid sufferers, is on 30 August. He combines the job with looking after gardeners and non-specific venereal disease sufferers.

The Pope who swallowed a fly

Pope Adrian IV, also known as Nicholas Breakspear, the only English Pope, choked to death after accidentally swallowing a fly.

Acne requiem

In Biblical times even a bad case of teenage acne was likely to get you branded as a leper and shunned by society. As you would also, to all intents and purposes, be written off as a dead man, you would even have had a requiem mass sung for you, as was the custom for all living lepers.

Grave-robbing Jim Morrison-worshippers

The First Church of The Doors is probably the world's most marginal religious cult. They worship Jim Morrison (lead singer of The Doors until he died, bloated from his heroin addiction, in a bath) as a God. In 1990 two members of the cult were caught attempting to rob his grave.

The winklepicker plague

Depending which official Church explanation you believed, the Black Death was caused by wearing winklepicker shoes, going to the theatre or hanging around with witches. The only point on which English and Spanish Catholics were in complete agreement was that the disease was God's retribution for something or other, and so the penance of flagellation might divert it. The Pope ordered a mass display of public flogging, and thousands of people wandered around Europe whipping themselves. Another popular theory was that the disease was caused by Jews who were poisoning water supplies. Just in case, tens of thousands of Jews were rounded up and burned or hanged.

The queer old dean

Dr William Archibald Spooner gave his name to the mangling of consonants that produces "spoonerisms" – first recorded in 1900 and defined in the Oxford English Dictionary as "an accidental transposition of the initial sounds, or other parts, of two or more words", as in the time he referred to Queen Victoria as "the queer old Dean". Spooner did not acquire the confusing speech mannerism that made him famous until he was well into middle age. According to legend, he stood up one day in the college chapel to announce a hymn, "Kinkering Kongs Their Titles Take . . ." and it sort of took off from there. As many alleged spoonerisms are now known to be apocryphal, the final word on the subject should rest with the great man himself. A couple of years before his death in 1930 at age eighty-six, Spooner told an interviewer that he could authenticate only one of his famous gaffes – the very first one attributed to him while announcing the hymn "Kinkering Kongs . . ."

Stuffed ark

In the mid-1950s a Dutchman, John Roeleveld, from Erbeck in the Netherlands answered a call from God to collect, stuff and mount two of every known animal species in preparation for Armageddon. When police raided his home in response to complaints by neighbours in 1992 they found a warren of concrete bunkers crammed with thousands of stuffed animals going back forty years. Many of the specimens were antiques, but most had been stuffed by Roeleveld himself. There were also thousands of eggshells, bones and insects preserved in formaldehyde. Roeleveld explained that God had promised him that his collection would rise up and live again after judgment day, and that the vast collection of junk littering his garden, including thousands of items of scrap metal and broken furniture, would also be made new.

Follow me

In 1994 a Seventh Day Adventist minister persuaded nine people sharing a canoe with him to follow Jesus Christ's example and walk with him across the waters into the middle of Lake Victoria, Tanzania. They all drowned.

URBAN MYTHS
True or False – you decide

THE COLANDER LIE DETECTOR

Bucks County Police Officers adopted an ingenious approach to getting stubborn suspect to confess. They made a few changes to the Xerox machine to turn it into a mock lie detector.

They placed a typewritten card saying *"He's lying"* into the copier. To persuade the suspect this was a bona fide device, they placed a colander over his head, and wired the metal to wires which disappeared into the photocopier.

Whenever the detectives suspected that the suspect was lying, they would press the copy button for a "read-out". Each time they would receive a piece of paper saying *"He's lying."* Apparently the suspect became convinced that the machine was real and finally cracked and confessed to his crimes. However the judge threw the case out of court when he heard how the confession had been obtained, so the Police Department was subsequently forced to go back to more traditional methods of interrogation.

Tree-climbing preacher
In May 1883, an English lay preacher named Henderson was rescued after being found stuck fast in a tree nearing Reading, in Berkshire. Apparently the Reverend Henderson liked to climb trees as if they were natural pulpits to rehearse his sermons. Six

months later Henderson was found dead in a tree in dense and remote woodland near Hag Thorn. It is believed that he starved to death. The body was badly decomposed and could only be identified by his overalls.

Cardboard congregation

Father Denham, the misanthropic vicar of Warleggan in Cornwall until his death in 1953, surrounded his vicarage with barbed wire and demanded that anyone who wanted to visit him should make an appointment – late-comers were simply refused entrance. He was also extremely miserly – his home contained no furniture and he lived on a diet of nettles and porridge. Eventually, when his parishioners gave up his sermons completely, he filled his pews with cardboard effigies.

Aztec antics

Although the Aztecs are generally considered to have been civilized, long before the Spanish arrived on the scene their everyday existence was a constant onslaught of barbaric religious brutality. They practised human sacrifice, mostly for religious ceremonial reasons and partly as a means of population control, on an unprecedented scale. The Aztecs butchered and ate well-fed slaves in elaborate ceremonies, and slaughtered captives to provide food for their animals. In one week in 1486, to commemorate the dedication of the temple of Huitzilopichli, about 70,000 captives were marched to the temple in a two-mile-long procession and killed. Their elaborate forms of sacrifice, which might include drowning, decapitation, burning or burial alive, were often performed by priests who wore the flayed skin of a sacrificed female.

LEGAL NEWS

Greet the Devil
City officials of Toccoa, Georgia, have ruled that no public money is to be used as funding for Yoga classes on the grounds that this discipline is a form of Devil worship.
LA Times

POTTY WISDOM, ZAMBIA

It is too late to fatten the cow on market day.

No rest for the wicked
During the fourteenth-century Holy Inquisition the church took to digging up the bodies of non-believers it wished to disgrace and publicly mutilating their corpses. The remains of the famous heretic John Wycliffe were raised more than forty years after his death, then burned and tossed in a stream to punish him for his opinions. Sometimes corpses went through mock trials. When Pope Formosus was declared a heretic he was dug up, dressed, condemned by a papal synod then thrown in the Tiber.

King Tomlinson
The Revd Homer A. Tomlinson, born in Indiana in 1892, was the son of the Revd A. J. Tomlinson, leader of the Church of God of prophecy, a little known Pentecostal sect commonly

known as the Holy Rollers. At twenty-four Homer Tomlinson
went to New York to work in an advertising agency but returned
to the ministry of his father's church after being "almost hit by
lightning". Revd Tomlinson junior had a flair for self-publicity,
first demonstrated in 1940 when he performed the world's first
parachute wedding ceremony at the New York City World's
Fair, when the bride and groom, the minister, the best man, maid
of honour and four musicians were all suspended from
parachutes. When he failed to succeed his father to the leadership in 1943 he went off to form a splinter group of his own. In
1952, claiming to have been "hailed almost as a new Messiah"
during extensive travels abroad, Tomlinson returned to the US to
run for president as the candidate of the Theocratic Party. He
advocated the union of church and state, the abolition of taxes,
the return of tithing and the creation of two new cabinet posts:
Secretary of Righteousness and Secretary of the Holy Bible.
Tomlinson was to run for the presidency again in 1960 and in
1964, but after two more failed campaigns topped his political
efforts by declaring himself to be King of the World. The Bible
anticipated the appearance of a global sovereign, he said, and he
was sure that the scriptures referred to him. He travelled
extensively, although probably not the million air miles he
claimed, to spread the news of his monarchy, briefly visiting
101 countries for a series of local coronation ceremonies, mostly
performed at the local airport. During these coronations
Tomlinson wore blue silk robes, held an inflatable plastic globe
as a symbol of his authority, and while seated on a folding chair
had a gold-painted iron crown placed on his head. Tomlinson
made extensive claims for the benefits to mankind of his reign
as King of the World. He had fended off revolutions, averted a
war between Israel and the Arabs, ended droughts and launched
a period of world peace and harmony. His 1958 coronation in

Moscow's Red Square, for example, had "melted the iron curtain". The Soviet press, unimpressed by the fact that a king had appeared in their midst and wrought instant international peace, simply referred to Tomlinson as "an American actor". Tomlinson claimed a worldwide following of somewhere between 50 million and 100 million people. A more realistic estimate would have put the number at under 3,000.

Thought for the Day

The enemy attacks on two occasions. When he's ready and when you're not.

The Reverend Stalin
Joseph Stalin trained for five years as a priest.

The Voice of the Interplanetary Parliament
In 1954 Shropshire taxi driver George King was visited by aliens who informed him that Jesus was alive and well and living on the planet Venus and that futhermore he had been selected by the Hidden Masters to become the Voice of the Interplanetary Parliament. King's mission on earth was to represent spirituality in its battle with materialism. In his quest he would be assisted by the Hidden Masters, who would occasionally lend support by visiting humanity in their flying saucers. King changed his name to Sir George King, OSP, PhD,

ThD, DD, Metropolitan Archbishop of the Aetherius Churches, Prince Grand Master of the Mystical Order of St Peter, HRH Prince De George King De Santori, and Founder President of the Aetherius Society. He subsequently retired to live in Los Angeles with his wife, Lady Monique King, Bishop of the American Division.

Looking good

Myriad merkins
About 2,000 merkins, or pubic hair wigs, are sold annually worldwide. They originally became popular when the regular treatment for venereal disease involved shaving off all the pubic hair.

Spare ear
The famous French racing driver Jean Behra (1921–1959) wore a plastic right ear after losing one in a racing crash in 1955. He always carried a spare false ear in his pocket just in case.

Pomaded and adorned
In the sixteenth century it was fashionable for aristocratic ladies to let their pubic hair grow as long as possible so it could be pomaded and adorned with bows and ribbon.

Braquette bragging
In fourteenth-century Europe, high-ranking noblemen were permitted to display their genitals below a short tunic. Those who were not impressively endowed could wear a leather falsie called a *braquette*.

Pretty at a few paces

Although Napoleon's Josephine was the subject of many highly
flattering portraits, she was not a great beauty. Josephine was six
years Napoleon's senior and, according to a contemporary, the
Duchesse d'Abrantes, "her teeth were frightfully bad, but when
her mouth was shut she had the appearance, especially at a few
paces distant, of a young and pretty woman."

Virgin's blood moisturizer

The seventeenth-century Hungarian lesbian Countess Elizabeth
de B'athory scorned the more traditional moisturizers and anti-
wrinkle creams, preferring to bathe in warm virgin's blood. To
maintain a regular supply she slaughtered more than 650 girls.

Queen Pug-face

All of the the kings of the ruling house of Hanover were noted
not only for their ugliness but also for the plainness of their
wives and mistresses. The attentions of George I were shared by
two middle-aged ladies who, because of their somewhat
contrasting figures, were known as "The Elephant and the
Maypole". Queen Caroline of Ansbach, wife of George II, chose
his mistresses for him taking care to select only women who
were even uglier than she was. George III's wife, Queen
Charlotte of Mecklenburg-Stretz, was so physically repulsive it
was suggested at the time that the King's bouts of madness were
brought on by the trauma of having sex with her. When she
arrived in England to take her throne, Londoners greeted her
with cries of "pug-face". When Charlotte requested a translation,
she was told that it meant "God Bless Her Majesty". George
IV's mistress Maria Fitzherbert is described as having a long
pointed nose and a mouth misshapen by badly fitting false teeth.
He was revolted by the sight of Caroline of Brunswick, the bride

his father had selected for him, the moment he clapped eyes on
her. On his wedding day he went through the marriage
ceremony "looking like death", and at one point tried to run off
but was restrained by his father. William IV, after proposing but
being turned down by eight different women, found a bride at
last in Princess Adelaide Saxe-Coburg-Meinengen, who was
described by a contemporary as "frightful . . . very ugly with a
horrid complexion".

Booty beauty
Excrement was once widely used as a beauty treatment, and in
some parts of the world still is. Hare dung was a cure for
sagging breasts; camel dung was rubbed into the scalp to make
the hair wavy. Ass or hen dung was used to cure skin blemishes,
swellings, or burns.

Bearded lady
The longest recorded female beard belonged to Janice Deveree
of Kentucky, who in 1842 sported a 14-inch goatee.

Horse urine for hair loss
Dog urine was promoted as the Tudor equivalent of Grecian
2000. Horse urine rubbed into the scalp reduced hair loss; a pint
of cow urine a day promoted healthy skin. The drinking of
human urine was recommended to improve virility.

The toothless Queen
When Queen Elizabeth I finally lost all of her teeth she took to
stuffing layers of cloth under her lips to fill out her face.

Age-old nose-jobs
The first nose-jobs were performed 2,000 years ago by amateur Hindu surgeons with often gruesome results. Cutting off noses was a common punishment for theft.

Make-up punishable by death
During the reign of Elizabeth I the Church proclaimed that any woman found guilty of "leading a subject of her majesty into marriage" by wearing cosmetics, make-up or high-heeled shoes should be burned as a witch. This was an unusual ruling, given that the Queen herself was a prolific cosmetics abuser, especially in her later years. According to the fashion of the day unmarried women wore their breasts exposed – a habit Elizabeth favoured well into her sixties. Her breasts were heavily powdered and covered in ceruse, the popular lead-based whitener which scarred and poisoned the women of northern Europe for centuries, and her veins were highlighted with blue dye.

Arsenic wafers
Eighteenth-century French women used to eat arsenic wafers to make their skin fashionably pallid.

More than skin deep
Many modern skin creams and beauty treatments contain extracts of cows' brains, sheeps' spleens, spinal cord and stomach lining, and foetal cells from calves. Some up-market perfumes contain ambergris – a product of the sperm whale – and civet, which is extracted from the sex glands of the civet cat.

Packaging, hype and profit
The raw material cost of a modern beauty treatment selling at £35 is about 20p: the rest is packaging, hype and profit.

Toothing

Early British dentures were mounted sets of human teeth
extracted from corpses. "Toothing" in the early nineteenth
century was big business, and the teeth of the dead became
valuable commodities. Many bodysnatchers took to "toothing"
as a lucrative way to spend their spare time. In 1808 two of
England's most notorious bodysnatchers, the prize-fighter and
gangleader Ben Crouch and his side-kick Daniel Butler went on
a "busman's holiday" to the Peninsular War to collect teeth from
corpses on the battlefield. Teeth from the dead of the American
Civil War were shipped to England to be worn by the rich and
the fashionable.

Whitener

In 1911 an American mail order con netted hundreds of
thousands of dollars with the promise of a miracle treatment that
could turn blacks into whites.

The hair of the rat

The Chinese believed that they could prevent hair loss by eating
rat flesh.

Fair-complexioned

Until Edward Jenner found a cure for it by deliberately infecting
a small boy with the fluid from cowpox blisters then exposing
him to infectious victims – not one of the most ethical
experiments in medical history – smallpox was the biggest killer
mankind had ever known. The description "fair" didn't normally
apply, as it does today, to people with blonde hair. It was used
to describe a complexion unscarred by smallpox – virtually
everyone else was hideously marked by the pustular rash.

Pierced gums
At the end of the seventeenth century it was the fashion for women to have their gums pierced with hooks to keep their dentures in place.

Smallpox masks
In the smallpox-ravaged seventeenth century "complexion milks" were all the rage. The favourite was a mixture of dung, minced veal and goat hair mixed with lemon juice, milk or cucumber water. Not surprisingly they didn't improve complexions which remains scarred, sallow and spotty. Most women who could afford them took to wearing masks out of doors.

Powdered pig bone powder
Sixteenth-century face powder was made of crushed pig bones.

"Liquid sunshine" radium water
In the 1920s beauty parlours all over the US installed X-ray equipment to remove unwanted facial and body hair. Radiation was touted as a cure-all for every imaginable disease: products available included radioactive toothpaste for whiter teeth and better digestion, radioactive face creams to lighten the skin, even radium-laced chocolate bars. A brisk trade in radioactive patent medicines thrived well into the 1930s. One of the most popular preparations was radium water, promoted in the United States as a general tonic and known as "liquid sunshine". It was responsible for the deaths of several thousand people. In 1932 Frederick Godfrey the "well-known British Hair Specialist" was advertising a radioactive hair tonic, and as late as 1953 a company in Denver was promoting a radium-based contraceptive jelly.

The death of Marat

The most ruthless French revolutionary Jean Paul Marat had to
spend most of his time in the bath to obtain relief from a number
of painful and disfiguring skin diseases picked up during the
years he spent hiding in cellars and sewers. He also met his
death in his bath-tub when Charlotte Corday severed the aorta
near his heart with a sharpened table knife.

"What's that?"

In a highly competitive field, Joseph Biggar, the nineteenth-
century parliamentarian who invented "obstruction" and brought
about the Commons guillotine, was said to have been the ugliest
Tory MP ever. Biggar was described as having a hunchback, a
"grating voice", a "face like a gargoyle", bony hands and
abnormally large feet. He also took to wearing in the Commons
a bizarre foul-smelling waistcoat fashioned from an unknown
species of animal skin. When Biggar rose to make his maiden
speech, a startled Benjamin Disraeli turned to a colleague and
said, "What's that?"

The ugliest woman in history

The ugliest woman in history is said to have been one Julia
Pastrana, a Mexican who lived in the mid-1800s. She was
ruthlessly exploited by her manager, who married her to ensure
that he had sole rights of ownership, then turned her into an
international freak-show exhibit. When she became pregnant he
made a small fortune by selling tickets to the birth. The
deformed child died stillborn and the mother died soon
afterwards. For her husband the grief of losing his family
came a poor second to the shock of losing his livelihood. He
had mother and child embalmed, placed in a class case, and
shunted off on a lucrative world tour.

The pig-faced lady

The origin of the sexist "paper bag" joke was probably the unfortunate Miss Tannakin Skinker, who lived in northern Germany in the early to mid-seventeenth century. She was born to wealthy parents, and had a perfectly normal body, but hog-like features which earned her the unflattering nickname "the pig-faced lady". The girl's deformity was kept a secret by her parents for years, but eventually news of her condition leaked out and a flood of voyeurs flocked to the family home. Against all odds her family tried to increase her eligibility rating by their daughter in the finest and most expensive clothing and throwing in a dowry of about £40,000. One young man, undaunted by dressing the stories circulated by people who had seen the girl, commented, "Put her head in a blacke bagge and what difference between her and another woman?" As soon as her veil was lifted however he went the same away as all the other enterprising suitors and ran away in horror. Miss Tannakin lived out her days as a single woman.

The bad-teeth regiment

Soldiers of the Cheshire regiment in the First World War had such bad teeth they were supplied with small mincers to help them eat their food.

Socrates, a drunkard and a brute

Physiognomy is the ancient science of judging a person's character by their appearance. A Greek physiognomist once deduced from the uncannily pig-like features of the philosopher Socrates that he was a drunkard and a brute. When Socrates's followers violently objected to this, the great man intervened and announced that the reading was, in fact, quite correct.

Kissing cousins

You have close cousins of the gonorrhea bacteria living in your mouth and throat.

POTTY WISDOM, DENMARK

To tell the truth is dangerous; to listen to it is annoying.

A pint a day

The average human anus expels about one pint of methane gas per day.

The castration "cure" for baldness

There is no known cure for male pattern baldness which will leave you with your testes intact. As baldness relies upon the male testicular hormone testosterone, castration is the only answer. The side effects of castration however include loss of body hair, a falsetto voice, a tendency to obesity, insomnia, a weak bladder and poor eyesight.

Parasite paradise

Parasites can live in virtually every organ or tissue in your body, but some species target specific parts. Guinea worms live beneath your skin, roundworms go for your lungs or muscle tissue, while flukes head for your bloodstream, your liver, your intestine or your lungs. Tapeworms flourish most happily in your intestines or even your brain. Your body can easily accommodate a tapeworm up to ten metres long: the good news is that they can't breed inside you, or at least not without exiting then re-entering your body.

Don't lick the hand that feeds you
Hydatid cysts are formed by the larval stage of the tapeworm. It commonly exists in dogs, but a dog can pass it on to a human with a simple lick of the hand. Once this cyst is inside your body it can and often does swell to the size of a football.

Planet Bacteria
You have roughly about the same number of bacteria and other organisms on your skin and hair as there are people on earth.

Skin sock
The average pair of socks traps about 200 milligrams of dead skin a day.

Hairy hussies
English women grow four times as much underarm hair as Chinese and Japanese women.

Skin sky
Every day you shed about 10,000 million skin scales into the atmosphere.

Not quite exercise
Picking your nose consumes only 20 calories an hour.

MURDER AND MAYHEM

Murder and Mayhem: Serial Murder

When the problem of serial murder was first publicized in the
United States, various experts estimated that the number of
victims amounted to between 3,000 and 5,000 a year. In the late
1980s, a more careful estimate by the National Center for the
Analysis of Violent Crime (NCAVC) revealed that the actual
figure was probably between 300 and 500 a year – frightening
enough, but hardly on the same scale as the earlier "expert"
estimate.

Lousy
There are three types of lice which are partial to your company,
pediculus humanus (the head louse), *pediculus humanus
corporis* (the body louse) and *phthirus pubis* (the pubic louse, or
"crab"). The body louse likes to live in your clothes and will
only venture out on to your skin when it is hungry, and then like
all lice, it feeds by sucking your blood. Apart from during
sexual intercourse, you can catch pubic lice from lavatory seats,
bed linen or moulting pubic hairs.

URBAN MYTHS
True or False – you decide

CHARLIE CHAPLIN ONCE LOST A CHAPLIN LOOK-ALIKE CONTEST

At the peak of Charlie Chaplin's fame in 1915, Charlie Chaplin look-alike contests were a common form of entertainment. Entrants would dress in the famous man's trademark suit and moustache and execute a few Chaplinesque moves for the judges.

Apparently Chaplin himself once entered one of these competitions and lost. The myth is that the contest was held in Monte Carlo in Europe, and Chaplin came third (there are various accounts of who won the competition, including the suggestion that it was won by Chaplin's brother Sid). There is some truth in this common myth – Chaplin did indeed do badly in a Chaplin look-alike contest. However the real competition he entered was in San Francisco, and rather than coming third, Chaplin actually failed even to make the finals.

Teeming armpits
Your armpits and groin carry the largest population of bacteria: on average, a grown man will have about one million in each armpit. This figure is known to be accurate because it is based on surgically removed skin, frozen then sectioned.

Variety floorshow
Children carry a much greater variety of bacteria than adults, mostly because they come into contact with the floor more often.

Athlete's foot amputations
At any one time you could be walking around with anything up to 155 different types of yeast colonies on your skin. One of the most populous strains *Pityrosporum ovale* lives in and around your nose, with a population density of anything up to half a million per square centimetre. Athlete's foot is caused by a fungus – a more evolved form of yeast. In the US airforce severe cases of athlete's foot were treated by amputating toes.

Ubiquitous herpes
More than 90 per cent of the population are carriers of the herpes virus.

Damnable dandruff
Dandruff sufferers tend to have a higher yeast population than other people, as do people who are taking steroids, because the drug suppresses the body's natural immune defences and encourages yeast and fungal growths on your body.

Every breath you take
Every time you breathe in you swallow about 60,000 bacteria.

Clean baby
The last time that you could honestly claim to have been clean was just before you were born. It is impossible to completely sterilize yourself even if you bathed in iodine or alcohol.

Blocked Britons
About 40 per cent of Britain's adults are constipated.

Storm warning
The mean average speed at which human wind breaks is about
96 miles per hour.

Bath breeding
Every time you bathe, the number of organisms on your skin
and body actually increases by a factor of three, because the
water frees them from the nooks and crannies on your body and
encourages them to multiply.

Wax teeth
When King George I's mother the Electress Sophia finally lost
her teeth she replaced all her missing dentures with little squares
of wax.

Bigwigs
In the eighteenth century, at the peak of wig wearing in England,
male wigs became so voluminous that you needed to denude ten
long haired men to make just one hairpiece – hence the expression
"bigwig". Horace Walpole's was so thick and heavy that he used
to remove it during debates in the House of Commons because he
couldn't hear through it. Human hair was in such short supply that
wigs were made from the hair of horses, goats and cows.
Barristers' wigs are still made from horse hair today.

Ancient "cures" for baldness
Ancient Egyptians tried to cure hair loss with vipers' oil and
bats' ears.

Bald Caligula
Emperor Caligula was so sensitive about his premature baldness
that he frequently ordered men with good heads of hair to shave
all their hair off out of spite.

Depilatory delousing
The Ancient Egyptians used depilatory devices to completely rid
their heads and bodies of hair, including the insides of their ears
and nostrils. The fashion had more to do with hygiene than
masochism: the Nile valley climate was an ideal breeding
ground for body bugs and lice, and shaving was the only
preventative measure against bodily infestation.

Greasepaint George
King George IV wore heavy make-up. His niece, the young
Princess Victoria, recorded in her diary that she threw up when
she was required to kiss her flatulent uncle because his cheeks
were nearly half an inch thick with greasepaint.

Bad wigs
In ancient Rome, blonde wigs were fashionable for both men
and women. The most sought-after variety on the market was
hair shorn from conquered Germanic natives of Northern
Europe. The wigs were unrealistic and were often kept in place
with a piece of string tied under the chin. Bald Romans who
couldn't afford wigs did the next best thing and had hair painted
on to their skulls instead.

The ear scoop
Apart from the razor-blade, the two most indispensable
implements in a gentleman's toilet routine from Roman times until
the nineteenth century were the ear scoop and the tongue scraper.

Joke of the Day
One snowman to another:
"Funny, I smell carrots
too."

Hair hats

Henry III, King of France, had long, flowing locks but lost them
all when he was quite young because he kept dyeing his hair
with untreated chemicals. Later he went around wearing a velvet
cap which had bunches of hair sewn inside the rim. Before wigs
became fashionable for men in England in the late seventeenth
century, bald men would often sew clumps of hair inside the
rims of their hats.

What cost white teeth?

The first widely used British tooth-cleaning agent was a solution
of nitric acid – it may have been fatal for teeth and gums but it
definitely made your teeth whiter.

Bearded Hadrian

Instead of shaving, Julius Caesar had his facial hairs individually
plucked out with tweezers. Hadrian was the first Roman
Emperor to make beards fashionable: he grew one to hide his
scrofulous skin complaint.

Real poo

Roman women made hair conditioner from bear's grease, deer
bone marrow, rat's heads and excrement.

UFOLOGY
Chasing Venus

On the morning of 17 April 1966, Dale F. Spaur, Deputy Sheriff of Portage County, Ohio, was notified that a UFO had caused a car's engine to stall. He and his assistant drove to the scene, and saw the UFO. As the machine flew away to the east, Spaur drove at top speed after it – sometimes reaching a hundred miles an hour. Forty miles away from the point where he started, Spaur was joined by another police car, driven by Officer Wayne Huston of East Palestine. Huston also saw the UFO. He said it was "shaped something like an ice-cream cone with a sort of partly melted top". The chase continued into Pennsylvania, ending in Conway. Officer Frank Panzanella of Conway told them that he had also been watching the shining object for about ten minutes. All four then saw the UFO rise straight up into the night sky and disappear.

According to Project Blue Book what these four independent observers had actually seen was the planet Venus.

The hair robbers
At the height of the craze for wigs for both men and women, the demand for human hair became so great that it became dangerous to let a child with a good head of hair stray out of sight.

The jaws of death

The fashion for wearing dentures made from real human teeth
went hand in hand with the rise of bodysnatching in the first half
of the nineteenth century. Although people were prepared to
wear the teeth of the dead, they weren't too keen on thinking
about how they got them in the first place. The Irish anatomist,
Professor Macartney of Trinity College, Dublin once silenced a
mob who were protesting about raids by bodysnatchers on their
local burial ground by pointing out to the crowd that many of
them were complaining with mouths full of teeth plundered
from under their very feet.

Teeth transplants

In late-nineteenth-century Britain there was a craze not just for
dentures made from human teeth, but for human teeth
transplants – teeth removed from one set of gums and surgically
implanted into someone else's. Although it was dangerous,
unhygienic, and encouraged poor people to sell their own
perfectly good teeth for pennies, this practice didn't completely
die out until shortly before the First World War.

The fashion for black teeth

In sixteenth-century Italy fashionable women coloured their
teeth. In Russia they always dyed them black.

Girls are made of . . .

Elizabethan women drank puppy dog urine to improve their
complexions.

Apples and puppy dog fat

Queen Elizabeth I wore an attractive hair pomade made from a
mixture of apples and puppy dog fat.

Thought for the Day

Never moon a werewolf.

Mice in their hair

Many eighteenth-century hairstyles became verminous because
they were usually set with rancid lard and stuffed with horse
hair. Many women wore silver or gold wire cages on their heads
at bedtime to prevent mice nesting in their tresses.

Of periwigs and plagues

Although the quality was poor, hair from corpses was widely
used in manufacture of wigs for three hundred years. The bottom
briefly fell out of the periwig business during the Great Plague
of London in 1665. Samuel Pepys recorded that no one dared
buy a new wig for fear that the hair had been cut off the heads
of plague-infected cadavers.

A little of what you fancy

Hashish warriors

Genghis Khan, whose conquests covered most of the known
world, whipped his men into a frenzy before a battle by getting
them high on hashish.

Nutmeg high

About 4,000 different plants can, in some form or other, be used as mind-altering drugs. You can actually get high on nutmeg, but you would need to take at least 20 grams to do it.

 Don't worry, be happy

Find ecstasy in life; the mere sense of living is joy enough.
Emily Dickinson, 1830–86

High-flying reindeer

The Christmas tradition of flying reindeer probably has its origins in a rather less romantic ancient Siberian ritual. At feast times the reindeer herdsmen would spike their drinks with an hallucinogenic substance called fly agaric – a particularly potent drug similar to LSD which passes through the human digestive system relatively undiluted. When the herdsmen relieved themselves in the snow, their urine was lapped up by thirsty reindeer, who then also became "high" on the drug.

Drink up

The Tomb of Mausolus, one of the Seven Wonders of the World but later completely destroyed by earthquake, was built in 353 BC in Turkey by Queen Artemisia on the death of her husband King Mausolus. The original idea was that the king's body was to be placed in the tomb, but there was a last-minute change of plan: the Queen had him cremated, then poured his ashes into a goblet of wine and drank the lot.

Stoned Sioux

The great chief Sitting Bull was regularly stoned on cannabis and wrote detailed accounts of his experiences while under the influence. It may have been the Sioux nation's fondness for pot that ensured the slaughter of Custer and his 7th Cavalry, at the Battle of Little Big Horn, to the last man. The Indians were incensed because Custer's troops had unwittingly trampled through an area where the sacred herb was grown.

The army disease

Although morphine is one of the most highly addictive drugs known – only twenty to twenty-five days' usage of the drug will produce a morphine junkie – it was used until the early twentieth century as a general painkiller for the most benign of ailments, including colds, or minor headaches. At the beginning of the twentieth century the United States had over 3,000 high street stores selling over 50,000 different opium-based drugs over the counter. Morphine and opium were so widely used on the battlefield during the American Civil War – the first as a painkiller and the latter as a recreational drug – that opium addiction became known as the "army disease".

Absinthe antics

The favourite tipple of the working classes and many writers and artists in nineteenth-century Paris was absinthe, an hallucinogenic liquor made from toxic wormwood oil. When it was drunk in large enough quantities absinthe allegedly produced convulsions and brain damage, and was linked with a spate of murders and suicides.

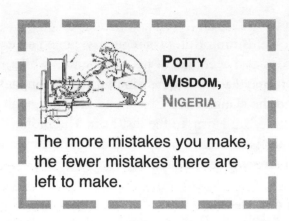
> **POTTY WISDOM,** NIGERIA
>
> The more mistakes you make,
> the fewer mistakes there are
> left to make.

Thirsty Europeans

Europeans constitute just 13 per cent of the world's population,
but consume more than half the world's alcohol.

No man is an island . . .

. . . but Elvis came close. In 1994 a woman from Clapham in
south London asked to be relocated from her council flat
because it was being haunted by the ghost of Elvis Presley. Of
course, the very last thing you need if you want a decent night's
sleep would be Elvis hanging around your fridge in the middle
of the night. Apart from his regular meals, including a supper
which comprised three large cheeseburgers and six banana
splits, he snacked for up to twenty-four hours a day on his very
favourite ice creams – Eskimo Pies and Nutty Buddys.

Druggy royals

Between 1897 and 1914 the British royal family, which at the
time was headed by Queen Victoria, Edward VII and George V
respectively, were regularly supplied with cocaine and heroin.
Record books from a pharmacy in Braemar show that while

staying at Balmoral the royals and their guests were supplied
with cocaine and heroin solutions as well as sleeping pills.
Heroin was believed to be non-addictive and was introduced in
the second half of the nineteenth century to wean people off
opium.

Mother's ruin
The London "gin epidemic" of the mid-eighteenth century
("drunk for a penny, dead drunk for twopence") had a practical
side: gin was considered to be a much safer bet than the water,
and it also had the added attraction of lowering one's sensitivity
to bug bites.

Slit nostrils for smokers
Some Russian Czars deported smokers to Siberia or submitted
them to torture and death. The first Romanov Czar Mikhail
Feodorovich ordered that offenders should have their nostrils
slit.

Curing syphilis
American Indians used cannabis resin to cure syphilis.

Crisis, what crisis?
The last czar of Russia, Nicholas II, spent the final two years of
his reign high on a cocktail of addictive drugs. He took cocaine
for colds, opium and morphine for stomach complaints, and
hallucinogens, which he obtained from a herbalist. Visitors were
shocked by his appearance and remarked on his dull eyes,
dilated pupils, hollow cheeks, vacant smile and his apparent lack
of concern about the impending crisis.

ANIMAL NEWS Hot Fish in Navel

While attempting the enormous project of constructing a dictionary of ancient Sumerian, scholars at the University of Pennsylvania in Philadelphia found that some of the phrases they encountered on ancient tablets remained semantically difficult no matter how they tried to interpret them. After weeks of work one example stubbornly refused to mean anything other than: "He put a hot fish in her navel."

Sunday Times

The Synod of Fools and Jesters

Although alcoholism in Russia was a way of life, few Russians could drink Peter the Great under the table. He was a huge man with a phenomenal capacity to hold his drink in spite of the vast quantities of alcohol he consumed. He created a drinking club known as his Synod of Fools and Jesters and held mock-religious ceremonies designed to celebrate drink – all of these were just excuses for regular drunken orgies. At the head of this company was the Kremlin's second biggest dipsomaniac Nikita Zotov. Peter would pour vodka down the throats of his cronies with a funnel, while Zotov, seated on a high ceremonial chair, threw up on the heads down below. When the Czar's doctors begged him to take spa waters to repair some of the damage done to his body by alcohol, he understood because he also fancied himself as a bit of a medical man. He drank the water, gulping as many as twenty glasses of water one after the other, but always topped it up with alcohol to improve the flavour.

Fully cured
Some of the most sought after varieties of Virginian tobacco were arranged in bunches and left to cure in lavatories so that they would absorb the fumes of human ordure and urine.

Prime addicts
The British Prime Minister George Canning (1827) was addicted to laudanum, an hallucinatory drug derived from opium. His predecessor Lord Liverpool, Prime Minister from 1812, was addicted to ether.

A bedtime drink
Ivan the Terrible was addicted to mercury, and always had a cauldron of it kept by his bedside. Mercury was one of the only recognized cures for syphilis.

Ways to go
Sir Walter Raleigh was a dedicated pipe-smoker who, if he hadn't had his head chopped off, may have become Europe's first lung cancer statistic.

"I cannot tell a lie, I did inhale"
Pot was often grown freely by American eighteenth-century plantation owners and the landed gentry and smoked for pleasure. George Washington's diary of 1765 records that he grew and smoked his own cannabis and, unlike a later President Bill Clinton, knew that there wasn't much point in it unless you inhaled.

HEROES

El Alamein 1942

In North Africa, on 23 and 24 October 1942, General Montgomery's 8th Army of 200,000 men and 1,100 tanks, with commanding air support, attacked Field Marshal Rommel's Italians and the German Afrika Korps of 96,000 men and 500 tanks. Minefields and artillery held up the advance, and after five days the British had lost 10,000 men without achieving a breakthrough. Told to triumph, whatever the cost, Montgomery launched a further attack, which, assisted by RAF assaults, broke the enemy line and exposed their flanks. By 3 November Rommel was in retreat. The Axis forces were then pursued 1,500 miles by the British forces, who drove them from North Africa. Axis casualties were anything up to 10,000 men, with 30,000 taken prisoner. It was Britain's first land victory of the war, and raised shattered national morale.

God's breezes

A nun jailed for smoking cannabis at her convent in Patras, Greece in 1980 claimed it helped her "participate" more in her prayers. Sister Flothee however denied planting and growing cannabis plants: she said it was "God's breezes" which blew seeds into the convent garden.

Monkey gland business

In the 1930s British soccer players were given "monkey gland" extracts to make them play better. The most publicized users were Wolverhampton Wanderers, who soared to the op of the First Division after receiving a course of "monkey gland" treatment. The substance has never been banned, but it is unlikely that it ever really enhanced performance.

Heroin and fire
In the nineteenth century boxers regularly used heroin for its anaesthetic and stimulating properties. Many of the apparently "punch-drunk" boxers were in fact displaying obvious signs of addiction. A popular method used by trainers to keep a fighter alert while he was high on heroin was to run a naked flame down his back.

Anal espresso
In large enough doses, caffeine can be used by athletes as a performance boosting drug. Tests on urine samples at the Seoul Olympics showed that some athletes had dosed themselves with caffeine through the rectum by the use of caffeine-laced suppositories.

Subway underworld
Over an eight-month period in 1992, refuse collectors on the New York subway collected four tons of syringes discarded by drug addicts.

Caffeine capers
The world's most extensively used mind-altering drug is caffeine, although it is almost impossible to take a fatal overdose of it unless you're capable of drinking about 300 cups of coffee in under fifteen minutes.

Confusions of an Opium Eater
Thomas de Quincy, the author of *Confessions of an Opium Eater*, degenerated into a physical wreck thanks to his habit of

quaffing up to 8,000 drops of opium and six or seven glasses of laudanum a day, a habit which caused him to lose his teeth and make his skin take on the appearance of cracked parchment. Although his gift for writing never deserted him, he was incapable of coping with the practicalities of everyday life and was extremely absent-minded; while poring over his manuscripts by candlelight he frequently set fire to his hair. He was also quite hopeless with money. He once approached a friend for a loan of seven shillings and sixpence. By way of security, he offered a screwed up ball of paper which he said was a "document". It turned out to be a £50 note.

Constant craving

Prader-Willi syndrome is a rare brain disorder which condemns the victim to a lifetime's constant craving for food. Sufferers often become so obese that they suffocate in their own flab.

Elvis, Honorary Narcotics Agent

Elvis's favourite reading matter, apart from the Bible, was the *Physician's Desk Reference*. During the last two and a half years of his life, Elvis, appointed "Honorary Narcotics Agent" by Richard Nixon in 1970, received more than 19,000 doses of narcotics, stimulants, sedatives and anti-depressants from his personal physician alone. Dr George Nichopoulos was tried and convicted in 1981 for overprescribing drugs, but as Elvis had dozens of other secret sources, including dentists, the full picture of his drug abuse will never be known. The pathologist who compiled the toxicology report on Presley after his death in 1977 testified that he had never seen so many drugs in one body.

URBAN MYTHS
True or False – you decide

"NO ANSWER"

Rock group the Electric Light Orchestra recorded their first album, released in the UK in late 1971 and simply called *Electric Light Orchestra*. The same album was scheduled for release in America on the United Artists label three months later. But it was given a completely different title: *No Answer*.

This apparently came about because of a misunderstood transcription of a telephone call. When the record company was scheduling the album for release, there was a phone call placed between the two record companies. The aim was for United Artists to find out the name of the album so that they could prepare advance publicity material. However the employee making the call failed to get through and simply noted down "No Answer" as the result of the enquiry. This was unfortunately mistaken for an answer to the question and the company adopted it as the title for the record. By the time the error was discovered it was too late to rectify the situation.

It may not be a coincidence that ELO later recorded the hit "Telephone Line" including lines such as "I'd tell you everything, if you'd pick up that telephone."

A stimulating euphorant

Before it was finally banned in 1906 the use of cocaine was widespread. Shops freely sold cocaine bonbons, cocaine cigarettes, even cocaine ointment. Sigmund Freud endorsed cocaine as a "stimulating euphorant". The popularity of Coca-Cola was helped by the fact that many people believed that the soft drink contained a large shot of the drug.

Philanthropic addict

William Wilberforce, the philanthropist who ensured the abolition of the slave trade, was an opium addict.

Amphetamine soldiers

Japanese servicemen were regularly given amphetamines during the Second World War to keep them awake. In less than ten years the number of known amphetamine addicts in Japan rose from a few to more than 200,000.

Opiate cough mixtures

Although opium is one of the most toxic plant poisons on earth, it was widely used in patent medicines, especially cough mixtures, in the early 1900s. In a five-year period, 1,500 people in England and Wales died as a result of taking opium-based patent medicines.

"Death" cigarettes

A cigarette brand named Death, launched by a Californian company, claimed to be the first "honest smoke": 10 per cent of all revenue is donated to cancer research and the cigarette packs, branded with a skull and crossbones, advised smokers to quit.

Once when sober, once when drunk
The Goths of ancient Germany had a custom of debating all important state matters twice – once sober, and once drunk.

William Pitt, the Drinker
Britain's youngest ever Prime Minister William Pitt "the Younger" was advised as a young man to drink a bottle of port a day for his health. He took it to heart: at his peak he could get through, in a day, six bottles of port, two bottles of madeira and one and a half bottles of claret. He often made speeches in the House of Commons dead drunk and before making an important intervention in debates went behind the Speaker's Chair to throw up. He drank himself to death aged forty-six.

Alexander the Great Drinker
Alexander the Great, the bisexual Macedonian king who ruled an empire stretching from Greece to India, was famed just as much for his marathon drinking sessions as for his military conquests. During one of Alexander's drinking contests thirty-five men died. During another bout he killed one of his closest friends with a spear. Alexander finally dropped dead during a drinking contest at the age of thirty-two; his best friend Hephaestion expired while drinking half a gallon of wine for breakfast.

Do as we say, not as we do
While until recently Britain has some of the strictest licensing laws in Europe, the bars of the House of Commons are and always have been exempt.

Morphine and moonshine
When the US Congress introduced Total Prohibition in 1919, the American medical profession recommended morphine as an

ideal substitute for alcohol. During Prohibition about 35,000 Americans were killed by drinking "moonshine" and other forms of illegal liquor.

The Battle Of Cambrai 1917

HEROES

This was the scene of the world's first massed tank attack. On 20 December, the 434 vehicles of Brigadier-General Elles' Tank Corps, supported by an inadequate number of infantry and 40,000 cavalry, rolled over the Hindenburg Line west of Cambrai in an attempt to break the cycle of trench warfare. By mid-morning they had routed the Germans on a six-mile front, and Cambrai was open for the taking. Indecisive leadership resulted in the cavalry failing to capitalize on the breakthrough. By 30 November, many tanks had broken down; the Germans counter-attacked with a hail of poison gas shells, and the British had to withdraw from the salient they had created. They suffered 40,000 killed and wounded; the Germans lost a similar amount. A year later, Allied success in the Cambrai area, and the influx of American forces, began the startling series of victories that led to the German capitulation.

Bar fall

The poet Lionel Johnson died of injuries sustained from falling off his barstool in 1902.

A bottle a day

In the mid-1700s a quarter of London's population was estimated to be drinking at least one bottle of gin per day.

Wine, more wine!

Selim II, Sultan of the Ottomans from 1566–1574, could drink a
bottle of Cyprus wine without drawing breath. When he ran out
his favourite tipple and one of his advisers suggested he capture
Cyprus to replenish his stocks, the mad Turkish leader eagerly
agreed. His men massacred 30,000 Cypriot Christians in the
process; their leader Bragadino was flayed alive and his skin
stuffed with straw and displayed to the Turkish troops.

Two quarts of martini a day

The actor W. C. Fields was quite happy to be Hollywood's best-
known alcoholic and drank two quarts of martini a day.
Whenever he travelled, he took three trunks with him: one for
his clothes and two for his liquid refreshment.

Two quarts of whisky and forty cans of beer a day

Alice Cooper (né Vincent Furnier) is one of rock and roll's
greatest surviving dipsomaniacs. He went on the wagon after
committing himself to a sanitorium in 1977 when his intake
reached two quarts of whisky and up to forty cans of beer a day.
His band at that time were spending £150,000 a year on
alcoholic beverages.

Forty pints an hour

The publishers Guinness dropped pint-swallowing from their
Book of Records in 1971 because the activities of people who
were swilling up to sixty-five pints of beer an hour by
regurgitating every fourth or fifth pint were not very good for
the company image. The very last record entry was that of Horst
Pretorius of West Germany, who knocked back just under forty
pints of beer in one hour, and kept it all down.

POTTY WISDOM, FRANCE

He who does not eat cheese will go mad.

The oldest profession
In 1981 French magistrates gave an eighty-year-old prostitute a ten-month suspended prison sentence. The Paris court heard that Madame Marie Louise Soccodato had been plying her trade since 1941, although lately business had been dropping off.

Cocaine Führer
In pre-war Nazi Germany cocaine was hugely popular with the rich and powerful – the head of the Luftwaffe Hermann Goering was a notorious cocaine and morphine addict. Some historians have made a connection between the delusions of strength and paranoia suffered by cocaine abusers and similar traits displayed by Nazi leaders: it has even been speculated that Hitler may have been snorting cocaine when he decided to conquer Russia.

No smoking
In the seventeenth century smokers were tortured in Russia and executed in Germany.

Poetic licence
The poet and dramatist W. B. Yeats took mescaline, a powerful hallucinogenic drug derived from a Mexican cactus. Charles Dickens took opium and Samuel Coleridge became addicted to it.

Sometimes a cigar is just a cigar
Sigmund Freud continued to choke his way through twenty large cigars a day even after doctors told him he had cancer of the mouth.

The man who swallowed fifty-eight condoms
In 1992 the Englishman John McGuire was found to have swallowed a record-breaking fifty-eight condoms in an attempt to smuggle half a pound of cannabis resin into Australia. They were discovered after he was admitted to hospital with a suspected burst appendix.

And for my next trick . . .
Cocaine snorters often find that their habit has rotted away the membrane separating their nasal passages. Status Quo's Francis Rossi claimed that after several years of cocaine abuse his favourite party trick to dissuade young people from taking the drug was to pass a handkerchief up one nostril and then down the other.

Kick-starting Brezhnev
The comatose Soviet leader Leonid Brezhnev spent the last ten years of his life as a tranquillizer and sleeping pill junkie. His prolific drug abuse accelerated the ageing process and caused massive damage to his central nervous system. Brezhnev's public appearances were so famous for their lack of animation that they inspired widespread rumours that he was already long dead. His

assistants later admitted that during a state visit to East Germany in 1979 they had to set the drugged President on his feet and propel him forwards as though they were "kick-starting a car".

Food-related deaths

Man bites dog
In 1994 fifteen mourners at a funeral in Nsukka, Nigeria, died after eating the deceased's dog.

The Fat King
Reinaldo de Carvalho, the "Fat King" of Rio de Janeiro's Carnival celebration, died trying to lose weight. He entered a weight-loss clinic in Rio and dropped dead after losing sixty-six pounds in thirty days.

Kneaded to death
In 1994 a forty-seven-year-old Japanese bakery worker, depressed because his wife had left him, took his own life by throwing himself into a giant dough mixer.

Shooting up Vegemite
Australian Paul Cook, a twenty-one-year-old storeman from Sydney, died after injecting himself with his favourite spread Vegemite.

Happy birthday
An Italian, Paolo Ginelli, visited a Naples hotel restaurant in November 1994 to celebrate his eightieth birthday. On his way out the restaurant sign fell on his head and killed him.

Happiness is . . .

Happiness is insanity?

According to some leading psychologists, happiness may be a
form of insanity. Miserable people tend to have a far more
realistic and objective view of life: if you think that people are
talking about you behind your back it's because they really are.

Spring is here

The most popular time to commit suicide is on a Monday or
Tuesday afternoon in the spring.

The man who would not die

Hans Klaus from Kiel, West Germany is the world's most
unsuccessful suicide. He failed in twenty-eight attempts on his
own life, including ten slashed wrists, four poisonings, two
hangings, stabbing, gassing, drowning and drug overdosing. He
finally gave up after throwing himself out of a fourth-floor
window and landing on a passer-by.

The unhappy states of America

In the USA someone attempts suicide every minute of the day.

His and hers

The most common methods of suicide are hanging or
suffocation for males, and poisoning for females.

The difficulty of killing yourself

For each successful suicide, there are fifteen failed attempts.

Early euthanasia

In ancient Athens the local magistrate would keep a supply of poison handy for any elderly, depressed or terminally ill person who wanted to commit suicide: all you had to do was ask permission to drink it.

Revenge

Vera Czermak decided to take her own life when she found out that her husband had been unfaithful to her, and leaped from a third-floor window. She came to later in a hospital bed unable to understand why she wasn't dead. Doctors explained that the now late Mr Czermak had broken her fall.

We'll do it for you

In nineteenth-century Britain, failed suicides were hanged.

Assisted euthanasia

The ancient Britons practised euthanasia by throwing themselves off overhanging rocks: if they were too old to jump someone would give them a shove.

Jugged

Scandinavians practised euthanasia by putting their old people in big earthenware jars and leaving them to die.

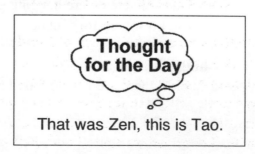

Thought for the Day

That was Zen, this is Tao.

Trampled
Old Ethiopians who wanted to die allowed themselves to be tied to wild bulls.

Trampled 2
In the Congo people used to jump up and down on their elderly or terminally ill relatives until they had finished them off.

Vietnam's legacy
More American veterans of the Vietnamese war have died by suicide since their return than were actually killed in battle.

Obligatory suicide
In Ceos, in Ancient Greece, it was obligatory for people over the age of sixty to commit suicide.

Stoical?
Zeno was the Greek who founded Stoicism, a school of philosophy characterized by impassivity and an indifference to pleasure or pain. He hanged himself at the age of ninety-eight after falling down and wrenching his finger.

Eccentric aristocrats

August Thistlethwayte and the Queen of London Whoredom
August Frederick Thistlethwayte, the grandson of Henry Bathurst, Bishop of Norwich and a relative of Earl Bathurst, enjoyed a large estate in Rossshire, Scotland and a luxurious London home at 15 Grosvenor Square, which he shared with his extravagant wife, the former prostitute Laura Bell, known as

"the Queen of London Whoredom". The marriage lasted four years until Thistlethwayte's death in unusual circumstances. Whenever Thistlethwayte wanted his valet instead of summoning him by the traditional method of ringing a bell, he fired a revolver shot through the ceiling. On 9 August 1887 he was found dead in his bedroom after accidentally shooting himself while attempting to call for his manservant.

The Dancing Marquess

Henry Cyril Paget, 5th Marquess of Anglesey and one of the wealthiest men in Victorian England, devoted his life to unashamedly squandering his very large personal fortune. A flamboyant extrovert, Paget's principle interests were dressing up, collecting and wearing very expensive jewellery, dancing and staging lavish theatrical extravaganzas. He converted the centuries old Paget family chapel into a theatre and from 1901 onwards he staged a series of productions in which casts of up to fifty or sixty were dressed in fantastic jewel-studded costumes. Paget was especially fond of Aladdin; he played the part of Pekoe and during the interval would perform his celebrated "Butterfly Dance" wearing large gossamer-effect wings and huge clusters of jewels. "The Dancing Marquess" was particularly fond of using his beautiful young wife Lilian to showcase his vast collection of jewellery, often all of it simultaneously. On their honeymoon Paget observed his new wife window-shopping in the jewellers Van Cleef and Arpels, purchased the entire window display then made her wear all of it to the races. Marital relations were further strained when he took to waking her in the middle of the night, ordering her to strip naked then covering her with gems. She subsequently sued for divorce on the grounds of non-consummation. Paget died bankrupt aged just twenty-nine in 1905.

Joke of the Day
I always wanted to be
somebody. I should have
been more specific.

Macho Cameron

The Camerons of Scotland, who fought on the side of Bonnie
Prince Charlie in the battle of Culloden, had a reputation for
toughness. One of the best-known Cameron chiefs, Sir Ewan
Cameron of Lochiel was said to have killed the last wolf in
Scotland with his bare hands, was the last to hold out against
Oliver Cromwell and once bit through a Cromwellian officer's
windpipe. Despite his ferocity, Ewan was said to be "the very
model of a Highland gentleman". One winter's day he was out
camping in the Highlands with his grandson, Donald. The
weather took a turn for the worse and as night fell they elected
to set up camp in the open. Sir Ewan noticed that his young
companion had rolled a large snowball to make a pillow for his
head and quickly kicked it away, growling, "I'll have no
effeminacy here, boy."

If at first you don't succeed . . .

Charles Radclyffe, fifth Earl of Derwentwater, was a
gamomaniac – an obsessive whose disorder is characterized by
persistent proposals of marriage. He proposed on fifteen
occasions to the reluctant Countess of Newburgh who became
so annoyed by the constant harassment that she bolted herself
into her home and gave her servants instructions to throw him
off the property on sight. The Earl finally found a way into her

house by climbing on to her roof and lowering himself down the
chimney into her drawing room where, black from soot, he
made his sixteenth marriage proposal. This time his persistence
paid off and she agreed to marry him.

Turkey eggs and port

Apart from the Duke of Wellington, the third Duke of Rutland,
the Marquess of Granby, also a much respected soldier, has
more English public houses and inns named after him than any
other person in history. Rutland's son, the fourth Duke, was
famous however for spectacular overindulgence. He began each
day with a breakfast of six or seven turkey eggs then spent the
rest of the day washing them down with port. He died aged
thirty-three of liver disease.

Have pity on a poor, blind, lame, old lady

Lady Diana Cooper, fabled society beauty and muse of Evelyn
Waugh, was one of the best known English society hostesses of
her day. Whenever the plates on the dinner table were cold Lady
Cooper would warm hers, and everyone else's, by holding them
over her breasts. She always wore a large hat during the day,
concealing a set of rollers underneath and in old age she carried
with her everywhere a small dog in a basket. If she was
somewhere where dogs were not allowed, she simply smuggled
it in, concealed inside a large muff. Her driving skills were
legendary. She regularly ran red lights and parked wherever she
liked, assisted by a message she always left in her windscreen
which read: "Please have pity on a poor, blind, lame, old lady."
At a reception honouring musician Sir Robert Mayer on his
birthday, the elderly Lady Cooper fell into conversation with a
friendly woman who seemed to know her well. Her failing
eyesight prevented her from recognizing her fellow guest, until

she peered more closely at the magnificent diamonds and realized she was talking to the Queen. Lady Cooper curtsied and said, "I'm sorry ma'am. I didn't recognize you without your crown!"

A club too

Lord Birkenhead, appointed Lord Chancellor in 1919, was a regular visitor to the National Liberal Club, which he used exclusively to avail himself of the men's toilet. One day Lord Birkenhead was stopped by an irritated member who complained: "I do wish you wouldn't use this club as a urinal." The chancellor replied, "Oh I see. It's a club as well, is it?"

Hoist by his own petard

Thomas Pitt, the second and last Lord Camelford and cousin of the English prime minister William Pitt, was known for his vast collection of weaponry, especially duelling pistols, and his willingness to pick an argument at the drop of a hat. Throughout his short, violent life he persistently got himself involved in various fights and disputes until 1814, when at the age of twenty-nine he picked a fight with a friend, Captain Best, over a prostitute. The two pistols to be used in the duel were considered to be the best in England. One of them was thought slightly superior to the other, and it was agreed that the duellers should toss a coin to decide the choice of weapons. Best gained the advantage, and at the first discharge, Lord Camelford fell mortally wounded.

Off

The fourth Duke of Marlborough (1739–1817) was so cripplingly shy that he once went for three years at a stretch without uttering a single word. He was jolted out of his silence at the beginning of the fourth year by the imminent arrival of the Frenchwoman Madame de Staël; when informed of her visit he said simply, "I'm off."

URBAN MYTHS
True or False – you decide

THE COCKROACH LETTER

A businessman was woken up on a long-haul flight by a large cockroach crawling on his cheek. He was furious and subsequently complained to the airline.

He received an apology letter from the airline's PR Officer. It went into some detail regarding the airline's strict pest control regulations. It explained that it was close to impossible to guarantee that insects never made it on to an aircraft, but went on to say that they did everything within their power to protect their passengers. They also suggested several possible sources of the contamination – sub-contractors, luggage handlers, an insect in someone's luggage and so on. The PR Officer also offered the businessman a free upgrade to first class on his next flight.

However the good impression created by the apology letter was somewhat undermined by a Post-It note which was still stuck on the letter, presumably left there by the PR Officer's secretary, to whom it had been an instruction. The Post-It note read *"Just send this dork the usual cockroach letter."*

A less common illness

Earl John James Hamilton, the ninth Earl of Abercorn
(1756–1818), was so overbearingly aristocratic that it was said
even the King was afraid to speak to him. Mocked by fellow
aristocratics as "il magnifico", Hamilton wore his ceremonial
Blue Ribbon of the Knights of the Garter at all times, even when
he went hunting, and allowed himself no contact with people of
lesser status. His servants were expected to wear white kid
gloves when they changed his bed linen and his footmen were
expected to dip their hands in a bowl of rose water before
handing him a dish. In 1816 Hamilton's youngest daughter died
of consumption. He was grief-stricken, but too proud to admit
that a member of his family had died of a disease associated
with poverty and the working classes. He persuaded his doctor
to write a letter to *The Times* announcing that the death had been
caused by something "less common".

The Proud Duke

Charles Seymour, sixth Duke of Somerset, was known as "the
proud Duke" because of his obsession with rank and protocol.
Seymour was such a snob that he refused to converse with his
servants except by sign language. The towering walls and spiked
gateways of his estate, Petworth House, were his way of
ensuring that common people were shut out from any view of
his home. Whenever he was obliged to travel, runners were sent
ahead to clear the riff-raff out of the way and he had a number
of private houses built along the route from his country estate to
London, so that whenever he travelled he would not have to
mingle with the lower classes in public inns. The "Proud Duke"
would never even allow his own daughters to sit in his presence.
One who did so, when she thought her father was asleep, was
disinherited.

Crewe's folly

Lord Crewe was so snobbish that he couldn't bear the sight of
his own servants. He laid down a rule that any servant he
encountered at Crewe Hall after 10 a.m. was liable for instant
dismissal. This was possibly why in 1866 no one told him about
the blaze that destroyed most of Crewe Hall until it was too late.

POTTY WISDOM, GHANA

The wise create proverbs for
fools to learn, not to repeat.

Hailing a bus

The friends of a wealthy English Victorian aristocrat once chided
him that he was so out of touch with ordinary people that he had
probably never even ridden on a bus. The gentlemen confessed
that indeed, he had not, and made amends by boarding the first one
that came along. When the conductor asked, "Where to, Guv?", he
replied, "A hundred and thirty-seven, Eton Square."

Curious customs

The nineteenth-century earl Lord Monboddo, reputed to be "the
most learned judge of his day", spent his life convinced that
babies were born with tails and that there was a universal
conspiracy of silence among midwives who cut them off at
birth. Monboddo's faith in his tail theory remained intact even
after witnessing the births of his own children. He concluded

that the crafty midwives had tricked him and destroyed the evidence. In 1785 he travelled from Edinburgh to visit the King's Bench in London and during his visit part of the court roof collapsed, causing lawyers and judges to flee for their lives. Monboddo, however, sat alone, unmoved among the debris and confusion. When asked later why he had not reacted, he replied that he had thought that he was observing some native court ceremony with which he was unfamiliar.

Poets, authors, composers

The worst-ever poet writing in English

William McGonagall (1825–1902) is widely acknowledged as the worst-ever poet in the English language. Many of McGonagall's works were dedicated to Queen Victoria and whenever the queen visited Scotland he went to Balmoral in vain hope of giving his sovereign a recitation of his latest work. Although he never got beyond the palace gates, his persistence paid off when he received a polite note from the Queen's private secretary, Lord Biddulph, suggesting he go home and not trouble Her Majesty again. This near-brush with royalty went to McGonagall's head and he had a new calling card printed, re-styling himself "William McGonagall – Poet To Her Majesty". Serenely unaffected by the laughter that generally greeted his work, he became a cult figure in Dundee, where his perform-ances drew large audiences. McGonagall only once managed to sell a copy of his poems, to a policeman on the gates of Balmoral for twopence, but was also once commissioned to write, for the sum of two guineas, a rhyme to promote Sunlight Soap:

> You can use it with great pleasure and ease
> Without wasting any elbow grease
> And when washing the most dirty clothes
> The sweat won't be dripping from your nose.

His subsequent attempts to sell more poems, including one attempt to crack the American market, were fruitless.

The royal post of Poet Laureate has been held by three greats (Dryden, Wordsworth and Tennyson), several minor talents and a few truly bad poets; of the latter category, Alfred Austin (1835–1913) was the most outstanding. His appointment was blatantly political, he was awarded the laureateship by the British Prime Minister Lord Salisbury, who saw no reason why a failed politician with no track record as a poet shouldn't make a success of the job provided he supported the right party. Although very small, Austin had a towering ego and took his appointment as proof that he was now officially England's greatest wordsmith. His poems, mostly overblown epics expressing his own insensitive, right-wing politics, were universally panned by the critics who followed his career with mounting disbelief, but Austin struck a pose of lofty indifference, continuing to churn out rubbish while lambasting his critics. For example, on the illness of the Prince of Wales:

> Across the wires the electric message came:
> 'He is no better, he is much the same.'

When it was pointed out to him that his poems were riddled with basic grammatical errors, Austin replied, "I dare not alter these things. They come to me from above."

Don't worry, be happy

Happiness comes when your work and words are of benefit to yourself and others.
Buddha, c. 400 BC

The worst-ever American poet

Julia A. Moore, born in 1847 in Plainfield, Michigan, is widely acknowledged as the worst-ever American poet. The eldest of four children, her mother was an invalid and she had to raise the family herself but still found time to write verse, which she described with some degree of understatement as "sentimental". Her inspiration came from the deaths of neighbours, stories she read in newspapers, anecdotes about heroic Civil War deeds or her own childhood memories. Her favourite subject matter, tragic and untimely death, caused critics to note that she rattled off poems "like a Gatling Gun'. In *Little Libbie*, for example:

> While eating dinner, this dear little child
> Was choked on a piece of beef.
> Doctors came, tried their skill awhile,
> But none could give relief.

A reviewer advised, "To meet such steady and unremitting demands on the tear ducts a person should instead be equipped with a water main." Her magnum opus was her collection of poems, *The Sweet Singer of Michigan Salutes The Public*, published in 1876. The critics ironically praised the work as a masterpiece. Mark Twain later claimed it had kept him laughing for the best part of twenty years; she had "the touch that makes an intentionally humorous episode pathetic," Twain noted, "and an intentionally pathetic one funny". She published no more poetry after her second book *A Few Words to the Public* in

1878. Mark Twain later satirized her in *Huckleberry Finn* as
Emmeline Grangerford.

Frank Zappa and the Mothers of Invention
The avant-garde musician Frank Zappa led twenty-five rock
bands up to his death aged fifty-two, but made his name as
leader of the band Mothers of Invention from 1964 to 1978. The
hallmarks of a Mothers concert were the props: stuffed giraffes,
gallows and boxes of rotting vegetables. During one show in
New York Zappa persuaded two US Marines to dismember a
doll on stage by telling them "Pretend this is a gook baby."
There was once an apocryphal story doing the rounds that Zappa
had enlivened a performance by eating faeces on stage. He
denied it: "I never performed this act on stage. The nearest I
ever came to it anywhere was at the Holiday Inn buffet in
Fayetteville, North Carolina in 1973."

Bestseller
During his entire lifetime, Herman Melville's timeless classic of
the sea, *Moby Dick*, sold only fifty copies.

A Swift solution
The Anglo-Irish satirist Jonathan Swift, author of *Gulliver's
Travels*, confessed a hatred for Scottish children and women –
"a sort of species hardly a degree above a monkey". He also
had a reputation for being extremely rude to strangers. His
irritability may have been partly attributable to a health problem
– he suffered from a condition which caused gritty matter to
accumulate in his bowels. One day he was sitting in a coffee
house when he was approached by Dr Arbuthnot, who had no
idea who Swift was. Arbuthnot had just finished writing a letter
and the ink was still wet. He enquired as to whether Swift had

any sand about his person. "No Sir, Swift replied, "but I have the gravel and if you will give me your letter I will piss upon it."

Betjeman's boys
The Poet Laureate Sir John Betjeman once wrote an obscene but unpublished poem about choirboys.

Charlotte Brontë sued
Charlotte Brontë offered to rewrite parts of *Jane Eyre* after the headmaster of the school on which she based the infamous Lowood school threatened to sue.

Dirty Mrs Pepys
Samuel Pepys chronicled his daily life in the minutest of detail, but only once in the nine years he kept his diary does he mention his wife having a bath. He is also said to have sexually harassed his young female employees. The two may be connected.

Tormented about the fundament
Samuel Pepys suffered terribly from flatulence; he wrote in his diary, "Wind doth now and then torment me about the fundament extremely."

Buried upright
The dramatist Ben Jonson asked his patron King Charles I a personal favour – a square foot of his own in Westminster Abbey so that he could be buried there when he died. The king agreed and stuck to his word. Jonson got exactly one square foot and had to be buried upright in it.

Virgil's fly
The poet Virgil spent the equivalent of £50,000 on the funeral of his pet fly.

Nonsense
From childhood the Victorian "nonsense poet" and artist Edward Lear suffered from what he called "the Demon", epilepsy, and "the Morbids" – manic depression – both of which he always maintained were the result of excessive masturbation.

The Tale of the Baker's Daughter
In 1380 the great English poet Geoffrey Chaucer stood accused of rape by Cecile Champaigne, a baker's daughter. Chaucer paid her off and the charges against him were dropped.

Does pornography make you go blind?
Samuel Pepys was an avid reader of pornographic material; he gave up writing his diary because he feared he was losing his eyesight.

Proust's bed
Marcel Proust wrote most of his novels lying in bed in a room lined with cork.

Dying from the top down
The satirist Jonathan Swift dreaded old age and foresaw the prolonged illness and the terrible consequences of dementia. He once told a friend, "I shall die like a tree; I shall die first at the top." This was prophetic. He lost his mind and became obsessed with exercise and dieting, even took to eating his meals while walking round the room. Before he died prematurely senile at seventy-eight his manservant showed him off to members of the public for a fee.

Ives's income campaign

The American composer Charles Ives, hailed as the founding
father of American music when his *Concord Sonata* was first
performed in 1939, spent most of his time and money
advocating an amendment to the US Constitution that would
prevent any American citizen from earning more than $20,000 a
year.

Astonished and surprised

Noah Webster, the great US lexicographer, wrote the seventy-
thousand-word *An American Dictionary of the English
Language*, published in 1828, his country's first ever truly
native dictionary. Webster was a notorious philanderer. One day
his wife found him in bed with the chambermaid. "Noah, I am
surprised," cried the wounded Mrs Webster. He sat up, and
informed her, "No madam, you are astonished. I am surprised."

Gould hands

The Canadian pianist Glenn Gould attained cult status partly
thanks to his bizarre mannerisms as a concert performer; he
lived in morbid fear of draughts and often took to the stage as
though dressed for an arctic expedition, swathed in furs, scarves
and mittens. Gould was a hypochondriac and often travelled
with handfuls of assorted pills in his coat pockets, which
sometimes led to unfortunate results when he was often detained
by suspicious customs officials. He also had a phobia about
shaking hands; he once sued Steinway after a piano salesman
gripped his hand too vigorously.

Scientific Shelley

Percy Bysshe Shelley loathed cats: he once tied one to a kite in
a thunderstorm to see if it would be electrocuted.

Come home, Gilbert
The famous British essayist, novelist, critic, and poet
G. K. Chesterton (1874–1936) was preoccupied with writing to
the exclusion of almost everything else. He was extremely
absent-minded and frequently forgot to keep appointments,
relying on his wife in all practical matters. Once on a lecture
tour he sent her a telegram: "Am in Market Harborough. Where
ought I to be?" She wired back: "Home".

Rat-ravaged writings
The eccentric philosopher Jeremy Bentham hardly ever stopped
writing. He jotted his ideas down on scraps of paper, pinned
them to the walls or the curtains or just left them lying on the
floor. Ideas came so thick and fast that he worked at times
literally knee deep in pieces of paper. Bentham frequently lost
track of what he had written; one day he came across his
important paper on parliamentary reform. He wrote on the
cover, "What can this be? Surely this was never my opinion?"
Bentham kept several pet rats, which he allowed to nibble on
and ruin his writings. After he died it was left to Bentham's
friends and students to piece together and rewrite some of his
most important works from the tattered remains of his rat-
ravaged manuscripts.

H. G. Wells's hat
The author H. G. Wells (1866–1946) was leaving a Cambridge
party when he accidentally picked up a hat that did not belong to
him. Discovering his mistake, he decided not to return the
headgear to its rightful owner, although his name was inside the
brim. The hat fitted Wells comfortably and anyway, he had
grown to like it. He wrote to the former owner: "I stole your hat;
I like your hat; I shall keep your hat. Whenever I look inside it I

shall think of you and your excellent sherry and of the town of
Cambridge. I take off your hat to you."

Odd boy

Percy Grainger, Australia's best known composer through such
classics as *An English Country Garden* and *Danny Boy*, often
slept naked on top of his piano. In 1935 he founded the Grainger
Museum at the University of Melbourne, where he intended to
show his collection of musical souvenirs to the Australian
public, including several life-size papier-mâché models of his
best friends and his collection of whips. His last wish was that
his skeleton should also go on display in the museum. The
request was quietly ignored by the trustees.

He probably wasn't wrong

Samuel Johnson was a hypochondriac who often begged his
wife to lock him in his room and shackle his legs because he
was convinced he was going mad.

POTTY WISDOM, CHINA

Govern a great nation as you
would cook a small fish.

You don't know where it's been

James Joyce, whose most famous novel *Ulysses* was considered so
lewd that the full version was banned from publication in Britain

and the US for nearly twenty years, overcame writer's block by masturbating. One day a fan approached him and said, "Let me shake the hand that wrote *Ulysses*." Joyce thought for a while and replied, "No, best not, it's done lots of other things too."

Marriages made in heaven

Never too late to divorce
The oldest couple ever to be divorced were Simon and Ida Stern, who parted company in Milwaukee, USA in February 1984. He was ninety-seven, she was six years younger.

Centenarian's toyboy
In 2006 a thirty-three-year-old man in northern Malaysia married a 104-year-old woman. According to reports, it was Muhamad Noor Che Musa's first marriage and his wife's twenty-first. Muhamad, an ex-army serviceman, said he found peace and a sense of belonging after meeting Wook Kundor, with whom he said he initially sympathized because she was childless, old and alone, the report said. "I am not after her money, as she is poor," Muhamad reportedly said. "Before meeting Wook, I never stayed in one place for long." He said he hoped to help his new bride to master Roman script while she taught him Islamic religious knowledge. The report did not say if any of Wook's previous twenty husbands are still alive. Malaysian Muslim men are allowed by their religion to take up to four wives at a time, but reports of women who marry more than once are rare.

ANIMAL NEWS Snoopius

Snoopy, the philosophical beagle from the Charlie Brown comic strip, may have assumed a more historical, perhaps even religious significance. Professor Filippo Magi, director of the Vatican's Archaeological Study and Research, reports a strange find at a dig beneath one of Rome's most historic churches: the papal Basilica of St Mary Major. Under the church are the remains of a huge, first-century AD forum, or market, and among the crowded Roman graffiti on its walls is a perfect image of Snoopy the beagle. Some Rome newspapers are reported to be showing a picture of the famous dog lying on the roof of his kennel thinking: "Suspirium! Acetate progredi, heu!" (Sigh! The years roll on, alas!).
Daily Mail

Women, boys and melons
Until about a hundred years ago, it was commonplace for wealthy Egyptian men on their wedding night to pay a servant to consummate the marriage for them: proof of the old Arab saying, "a woman for duty, a boy for pleasure, but a melon for ecstasy".

The Czar's toy soldiers
His wife Catherine the Great may have been one of history's biggest nymphomaniacs, but Czar Peter III spent his entire honeymoon and most of the rest of his married life playing with his toy soldiers under the bedsheets.

346

Thought for the Day

*True love is like a ghost:
everybody talks about it, but
few have seen it.
François La Rochefoucauld,
1613–1680*

Frederick and his whippets

The Prussian King Frederick the Great never once slept with his Elizabeth. It was variously rumoured that as a young man he had suffered such a dire bout of venereal disease that the only cure was castration, or he was simply gay. In his later years he was rumoured to be romantically attached to his pack of Italian whippets.

All night long

Louis XV introduced himself to his new Polish wife Maria by making love to her seven times on their wedding night. He was fifteen years old at the time.

Too embarrassed to enter Poland

The eighteenth-century Saxon-born monarch King Augustus II of Poland was known as Augustus "the Strong" for his exceptional physical size and strength, and for his unquestionable virility. Over a period of fifty years he fathered three hundred and sixty-five bastards and one legitimate heir. He found it so difficult to keep track of his children that he "accidentally" had at least one incestuous relationship with a daughter. It didn't go down very well with his wife Eberdine, who was so embarrassed by his behaviour that she hardly ever set foot in Poland throughout her husband's reign.

MURDER AND MAYHEM

The Original Thugs

The first group of organized serial killers in history were the Hindu "thugs" (pronounced "tugs"), from whom we derive our modern word "thug". When the British annexed India in the late eighteenth century the conquerors noted that the roads were infested with bands of robbers who strangled their victims. It became slowly apparent that the killing was, in fact, a religious ceremony, and that the Thugs killed people – often a whole caravan-load consisting of dozens – as a sacrifice to the black goddess Kali. The bodies were mutilated, then buried. In 1829 a British army captain, William Sleeman, organized the suppression of Thuggee, so that within twenty years it had virtually ceased to exist.

With a holy medal for luck
The brother of the king of France Philippe the Duke of Orléans was one of history's most famous homosexuals, but French court etiquette required that he had to have a full-time,

fully-paid official court mistress. Madame de Grancey was
never actually allowed in his bedroom and spent all of her
time playing cards. Although Philippe's second wife stood at
least eighteen inches taller than him, was considerably more
butch than he was, and frightened the living daylights out
of him the moment he met her, the couple were able – for
dynastical purposes only – to sire three children. Philippe
revealed afterwards that this had only been possible because
he had on each occasion rubbed his penis with a holy medal
for luck.

Honey, I'm emperor
Germany's Kaiser Wilhelm I rowed with his wife Augusta
virtually every day of their married life, which lasted nearly
sixty years. When Wilhelm first became Emperor he couldn't be
bothered to tell her about it: she got the news from one of his
footmen.

She'll do
In rural Turkey it was customary for a mother-in-law to give her
son's prospective bride a body search in a public baths before
she would consent to the marriage.

Soil conditioning
In Java, married farmers sometimes copulate in their fields to
make the soil more fertile.

Wild oats
Before he married her mother, Queen Victoria's father lived
openly for twenty-seven years with a former French-Canadian
prostitute.

URBAN MYTHS
True or False – you decide

THE TYRE REFUND

In 1987, a man walked into the Nordstrom department store in Fairbanks, Alaska with two snow tyres. He put the tyres on the counter, and asked the clerk for his money back. The clerk had only been working there for a few weeks. He simply read the price from the side of the tyres, took $158 from the cash register, and "refunded" the man.

However, the Nordstrom department store chain sells expensive clothing, not car parts. They have never sold a snow tyre and never will. When the clerk's manager confronted him about why he had accepted the snow tyres, even though he knew for a fact that the store did not sell tyres, he replied that the manager had, only the day before, told him that the customer was always right. He had simply been trying to put this principle into practice!

For the love of Eudoxia

Although Peter the Great had long since ditched his first wife Eudoxia and remarried, he suffered understandable pangs of jealousy when he found that Eudoxia had a new man in her life. The following day at precisely 3 pm the Czar had a wooden stake driven up her lover's rectum.

Abstinent Albert

Many Victorian couples abstained from marital relations on
Sundays because sex on the Sabbath was considered improper.
Although Queen Victoria valued a healthy sex life, her husband
Albert wasn't a keen collaborator on any day of the week. He
always went to bed wearing a little all-in-one woollen sleeping
suit, and once said of heterosexual intercourse, "That particular
species of vice disgusts me."

Juana the Mad

The Spanish Queen Juana "The Mad" was driven completely
round the bend by her faithless and mostly absent husband
Philip. When her beloved Philip died aged twenty-eight she
resolved to see more of him in future: she had his body
embalmed and kept it by her side at all times, even at mealtimes
and in bed at night.

"Let me introduce you to my widow"

Leopold II, King of the Belgians took his second wife – a
sixteen-year-old prostitute he'd discovered in a Paris brothel –
when he was seventy-four years old. When the ceremony was
over, he turned to one of the witnesses and said, "Let me
introduce you to my widow"; three days later the king was dead.

Death as the subject of a pop record: the ten all-time tackiest

1. *Seasons in the Sun* – Terry Jacks (1974)
2. *Tell Laura I Love Her* – Ricky Valance (1960)
3. *Terry* – Twinkle (1964)
4. *Old Shep* – Elvis Presley (1960)
5. *Leader of the Pack* – Shangri-Las (1965)
6. *Teen Angel* – Mark Dinning (1960)
7. *Ode to Billie Joe* – Bobby Gentry (1967)

8. *Patches* – Clarence Carter (1970)
9. *Endless Sleep* – Mary Wilde (1958)
10. *Camouflage* – Stan Ridgway (1986)

HEROES

Special Air Service Selection – What Makes a Hero?

Colloquially known as "the Sickeners", the selection tests for the British Special Air Service (SAS) are amongst the toughest for any elite force. The Selection Training Course, based on one designed by Major John Woodhouse in 1950, places an emphasis on both physical and mental strength. Candidates begin with road runs and proceed to a number of rigorous cross-country marches carrying Bergen rucksacks weighing up to 25 kg. The culmination of the Selection Training Course is "The Fan Dance", a 60 km land navigation over the Brecon Beacons in South Wales which has to be completed in 20 hours regardless of weather. By this stage a third of the candidates will have dropped out or been "binned". But this is not the end of the selection process – candidates still have to endure seven weeks of Continuation Training, which includes simulated interrogation by enemy intelligence forces, a five day "escape and evasion" test, where candidates have to live off the land equipped only with a knife and a box of matches, and parachute training. Successful candidates are then finally admitted to "the Regiment".

Eight widowed first ladies

1. Anna Tuthill Symmes Harrison. After she had borne his tenth child her husband William Henry Harrison became the first US president to die in office, from pneumonia, in 1841.
2. Margaret Mackall Smith Taylor. Pipe-smoking wife of

Zachary "Old Rough and Ready" Taylor. Her husband fell ill while taking part in a ceremony in blistering heat at the Washington Monument in July 1850, and died five days later.

3. Mary Todd Lincoln. Husband Abraham was assassinated at Ford's Theatre, Washington on Good Friday, 14 April 1865 by an actor, John Wilkes Booth.

4. Lucretia Rudolph Garfield. Wife of James Garfield, the second president shot in office. His assassin was a lawyer who had been passed over for an important government job.

5. Ida Saxton McKinley. An epileptic who suffered a seizure during her husband William's second inaugural ball. President McKinley was standing in line at the Buffalo Pan-American Exposition in 1901 when he was shot twice by a Polish anarchist, and died eight days later.

6. Florence Harding. Wife of the twenty-ninth US president Warren G. Harding, who died of a heart attack in his third year of office in San Francisco in 1923.

7. Anna Eleanor Roosevelt. Husband Franklin D. Roosevelt died of a cerebral hamorrhage in April 1945 while at Warm Springs, Georgia.

8. Jacqueline Lee Bouvier Kennedy Onassis. Wife of John Fitzgerald Kennedy, the youngest man elected President and the youngest to die in office. On 22 November 1963 he was shot dead as his motorcade passed through Dallas, Texas.

Eight alleged lovers of "the Virgin Queen", Elizabeth I

1. The Duke of Alençon
2. Robert Dudley, Earl of Leicester
3. Robert Devereux, Earl of Essex
4. Sir Christopher Hatton
5. Thomas Heneage

6. Edward Vere, Earl of Oxford
7. Sir William Pickering
8. Sir Walter Raleigh

Ten contemporary cures for bubonic plague

1. Wash the victim in goat urine.
2. Apply the entrails of a newborn puppy to the victim's forehead.
3. Drink menstrual blood.
4. Pierce your testicles.
5. Inhale fumes from a latrine.
6. Commit incest on an altar.
7. Smoke tobacco.
8. Apply dried toad to the bubo.
9. Eat the pus-filled boil of plague victims.
10. Eat a little treacle after rainfall.

 **Joke of the Day**
I've had a perfectly wonderful evening. This wasn't it, though.

No seconds: ten last meals of condemned murderers

1. Ham, eggs, toast and coffee – Gee Jon, Chinese murderer, the first man ever to be executed in the US by lethal gas, at Carson City State Prison in 1924.
2. Hot fudge sundae – Barbara Graham, convicted murderess, executed by lethal gas at San Quentin, California in 1955.
3. Steak and chips followed by peach cobbler desert –

murderer Charlie Brooks, executed by lethal injection at Huntsville, Texas in 1982.

4. Cheez Doodles and Coca-Cola – mass poisoner Margaret Velma Barfield, a fifty-two-year-old grandmother and the first woman ever to die by lethal injection, at central prison, North Carolina in 1962.

5. Hamburger, eggs and potatoes – British killer Gary Gilmore, the first man to be executed in the US for a decade when he was shot dead by firing squad at Utah in 1977.

6. Chocolate – Chauncey Millard, the youngest person ever executed in the state of Utah, killed by firing squad in 1869. The eighteen-year-old was still eating his chocolate bar as he was being shot.

7. A large steak salad, potato pancakes and two helpings of jelly and ice cream – Isadore Zimmerman, a twenty-six-year old convicted of murder, at Sing Sing in 1939. Zimmerman continued to protest his innocence to the last mouthful.

8. A US one-dollar-bill sandwich – Joshua Jones, hanged at Pennsylvania in 1839 for the murder of his wife. While Jones was awaiting execution he sold his body to the prison doctors for ten dollars. He spent nine dollars on delicacies to vary his prison diet. Upon realizing that he still had a dollar bill in his pocket just minutes before his execution, he requested two slices of bread.

9. Two hamburgers and Coca-Cola – Leslie B. Gireth, executed at San Quentin in 1943 for the murder of his girlfriend. Gireth had lost his nerve halfway through a suicide pact with her. His last meal was an exact replica of what she had eaten just before he shot her.

10. Garlic bread, shrimp, french fries, ice cream, strawberries and whipped cream – the heroic last order of Perry Smith

and Richard Eugene Hickock, before their double hanging at Kansas in 1965. They lost their appetites however at the last minute and the meal was untouched.

UFOLOGY
Showers of Space People

Ruth May Weber, of Yucca Valley, California, had a psychic experience involving aliens. She heard a voice telling her that Earth was already inhabited by thousands of space people, who would take over in the event of some great world catastrophe. Later, walking through the streets of her home town, she suddenly saw showers of space people floating down through the air, and then disappearing into the crowd, entirely unnoticed by the citizens of Yucca Valley.

Ten succinct pop critiques
1. The Beatles : "Bad mannered little shits." – Nöel Coward (1964)
2. *Let's Groove*, Earth, Wind & Fire (1981): "Let's not." – Johnny Black, *Smash Hits*
3. *Run to the Hills*, Iron Maiden (1982): "Don't think I wasn't tempted." – Red Starr, *Smash Hits*
4. *All the Way Up*, Belle & the Devotions (1984): "Don't tempt me." – Stephen Gray, *Record Mirror*
5. *The Robots*, Kraftwerk (1978): "Zzzzzzzzzz." – Dean Porsche, *Zig-Zag*

6. *I'm Alive*, ELO (1980): "A blatant lie. Product." – Deanne Parsons, *Smash Hits*
7. *Away From This Town*, Still Life (1982): "And the further the better." – Robin Smith, *Record Mirror*
8. *Like a rock*, Bob Seger (1986): "Exactly, Bob. Prehistoric." – Kevin Murphy, *Sounds*
9. *Wasting Time*, Strangeways (1979): "Yes, mine." – Robin Banks, *Sounds*
10. *Forever Young*, Alphaville (1984): "Should have been strangled at birth." – Morrissey, *Smash Hits*

Dipped in vitriol: ten writers on writers

1. "To me, (Edgar Allen) Poe's prose is unreadable, like Jane Austen's. No, there is a difference. I could read his prose on a salary, but not Jane's." Mark Twain, on Jane Austen
2. "Reading him is like wading through glue."
   Alfred, Lord Tennyson, on Ben Jonson
3. "There are two ways of disliking poetry. One way is to dislike it, the other is to read Pope."
   Oscar Wilde, on Alexander Pope
4. "I don't think Browning was very good in bed. His wife probably didn't care for him very much. He snored and had fantasies about twelve-year-old girls."
   W. H. Auden, on Robert Browning
5. "The work of a queasy undergraduate scratching his pimples."
   Virginia Woolfe, on James Joyce's *Ulysses*
6. "The Hitler of the book racket."
   Percy Wyndham Lewis, on Arnold Bennett
7. "He was dull in company, dull in his closet, dull everywhere . . . he was a mechanical poet."
   Samuel Johnson, on Thomas Gray

8. "A poor creature who has said or done nothing worth a serious man taking the trouble of remembering."
Thomas Carlyle, on Percy Bysshe Shelley
9. "An outstandingly unpleasant man, one who cheated and stole from his friends and peed on their carpets."
Kingsley Amis, on Dylan Thomas.
10. "When his cock wouldn't stand up he blew his head off. He sold himself a line of bullshit and he bought it."
Germaine Greer, on Ernest Hemingway

POTTY WISDOM, NIGERIA

All great truths begin as blasphemies.

Decomposing composers: ten causes of death
1. Johann Sebastian Bach (1685–1750): a stroke, after undergoing an unsuccessful operation on his eye.
2. George Frederic Handel (1685–1759): septicaemia as a consequence of unsterile instruments employed to remove his cataracts.
3. Wolfgang Amadeus Mozart (1756–1791): Bright's disease, a degenerative kidney disease.
4. Franz Schubert (1797–1821): typhoid.
5. Franz Liszt (1811–1886): pneumonia.
6. Peter Ilyich Tchaikovsky (1840–1893): cholera.

7. Johannes Brahms (1833–1897): cancer of the liver.
8. Claude Debussy (1862–1920): cancer of the rectum.
9. Alban Berg (1885–1935): blood poisoning from an infected insect bite.
10. Sergei Rachmaninov (1873–1943): malignant melanoma.

Ten depressed artists
1. Vincent van Gogh, Dutch expressionist: while a voluntary inmate in an asylum at St Rémy, he absconded and shot himself at the scene of his last painting, *Cornfields with Flight of Birds*, aged thirty-seven.
2. Mark Rothko, Russian-American abstract expressionist painter: slashed his wrists in his studio, aged sixty-seven.
3. Arshile Gorky, American abstract expressionist painter: hanged himself in his studio, aged forty-four.
4. Jackson Pollock, American abstract expressionist painter, after several attempts to drown himself, drove his car into a tree, aged forty-four.
5. Virginia Woolf, British writer: filled her pockets with rocks and drowned herself in the river Ouse, aged fifty-nine.
6. Sylvia Plath, American poet: gassed herself in her kitchen oven, aged thirty.
7. Ernest Hemingway, American novelist: blasted himself in the head with a shotgun, aged sixty-one.
8. John Gould Fletcher, American poet and author, drowned himself in a pond, aged sixty-four.
9. Gérard de Nerval, French writer: hanged himself from a sewer grate, aged forty-seven.
10. Hart Crane, American author: travelling from Mexico to the US, jumped from the deck of the *SS Orizaba*, somewhere off the Florida coast, aged thirty-three.

Ten banned authors

1. William Shakespeare: *King Lear* banned in Britain from 1788 to 1820, considered "inappropriate" in the light of King George III's apparent mental illness.
2. Casanova: his *Memoires* were banned by the Pope (1834) and by Mussolini (1935).
3. Thomas Hardy: *Tess of the D'Urbervilles* (1891) and *Jude the Obscure* (1896) thought to be "pornographic" and banned from all British and US libraries.
4. Rudyard Kipling: in 1898 *A Fleet in Being* was banned by the British government on grounds of national security.
5. Charles Darwin: from 1926 to 1937 *On the Origin of Species* was banned in the Soviet Union, Yugoslavia, Greece and by the US state of Tennessee.
6. Arthur Conan Doyle: in 1929 the Soviet Union banned *The Adventures of Sherlock Holmes* for "occultism".
7. James Joyce: upset the Catholic church with graphic accounts of sex and defecation. The full version of *Ulysses* was banned in Britain and the US for nearly twenty years. When the "obscene" *Dubliners* was published in 1922 it was burned on the streets of Dublin.
8. Adolf Hitler: *Mein Kampf* was banned in Czechoslovakia (1932) and Palestine (1937).
9. Ernest Hemingway: in 1939 *A Farewell to Arms* was banned in Ireland for being "immoral and irreligious".
10. D. H. Lawrence: *The Rainbow* and *Lady Chatterley's Lover* were both banned in Britain. During the *Lady Chatterley* trial, prosecution council Mervyn Griffith-Jones asked the jury: "Is it a book that you would even wish your wife or your servants to read?" He also takes the trouble to keep a detailed tally of the novel's profanities, informing the jury that the word "cunt" occurred fourteen times.

Ten writers who died of tuberculosis
 1. John Keats (1795–1821)
 2. Emily Brontë (1818–48)
 3. Anne Brontë (1820–49)
 4. Charlotte Brontë (1816–55)
 5. Robert Louis Stevenson (1850–94)
 6. Anton Chekhov (1860–1904)
 7. Franz Kafka (1883–1924)
 8. D. H. Lawrence (1885–1930)
 9. George Orwell (1903–50)
10. William Somerset Maugham (1874–1965)

Ten famous misanthropes
 1. "Happiness is to vanquish your enemies, to chase them before you, to rob them of their wealth, to see their near and dear bathed in tears, to ride their horses and sleep on the white bellies of their wives and daughters." – Genghis Khan
 2. "If they were drowning to death, I'd put a hose in their mouth." – Ray Kroc, Chairman of McDonald's (1968–84), on his competitors
 3. "It is better to be feared than loved, if you cannot be both." – Niccolo Machiavelli
 4. "The meek shall inherit the Earth, but not its mineral rights." – J. Paul Getty
 5. "Happiness is nothing more than good health and a bad memory." – Albert Schweitzer
 6. "The public be damned – I'm working for my stock-brokers." – William H. Vanderbilt, in reply to a newspaper reporter who asked the railway magnate if the withdrawal of an unprofitable express train was against public interest. (Chicago, 1883)

7. "You can get a lot more done with a kind word and a gun, than with a kind word alone." – Al Capone

8. "Practically everyone but myself is a pusillanimous son of a bitch." – General George S. Patton Jnr

9. "The secret of success is sincerity. Once you can fake that you've got it made." – Jean Giraudoux, French dramatist

10. "Start every day off with a smile; get it over with." – W. C. Fields, US comic actor

To die for: ten last suppers

1. Buddha: died at the age of eighty in 483 BC from an intestinal hemorrhage after eating a very hot curry.

2. King John: fell dead after gorging on peaches and cider, one year after signing Magna Carta.

3. Robert Greene, sixteenth-century English dramatist: expired after consuming too much Rhenish wine and pickled herring at an authors' gala luncheon.

4. Bonnie Parker and Clyde Barrow: enjoyed bacon and tomato sandwiches, in their car, before dying of multiple gunshot wounds.

5. Adolf Hitler: vegetarian ravioli, washed down with arsenic.

6. James Dean: crashed on a glass of milk and an apple.

7. Ernest Hemingway: cleaned his palate by applying a shotgun to his head after dining on New York strip steak, baked potato, Caesar salad and Bordeaux wine.

8. Jimi Hendrix: choked to death after enjoying a tuna sandwich.

9. Diana, Princess of Wales: asparagus and mushroom omelette, Dover sole with vegetable tempura and champagne.

10. First-class menu, RMS *Titanic*, 14 April, 1912:

First Course
Hors d'Oeuvres
Oysters

Second Course
Consommé Olga
Cream of Barley

Third Course
Poached Salmon with Mousseline Sauce, Cucumbers

Fourth Course
Filet Mignons Lili
Sauté of Chicken, Lyonnaise
Vegetable Marrow Farci

Fifth Course
Lamb, Mint Sauce
Roast Duckling, Apple Sauce
Sirloin of Beef, Chateau Potatoes, Green Peas, Creamed Carrots,
Boiled Rice, Parmentier and Boiled New Potatoes.

Sixth Course
Punch Romaine

Seventh Course
Roast Squab and Cress

Eighth Course
Cold Asparagus Vinaigrette

Ninth Course
Pâté de Foie Gras, Celery

Tenth Course
Waldorf Pudding
Peaches in Chartreuse Jelly
Chocolate and Vanilla Éclairs
French Ice Cream

Twelve eponymous illnesses

1. James Parkinson: Parkinson's disease (1817)
2. William Stokes and Robert Adams: Stokes-Adams attack (1826)
3. Sir Charles Bell: Bell's palsy (1828)
4. Thomas Hodgkin: Hodgkin's disease (1832)
5. Sir Dominic Corrigan: Corrigan's pulse (1832)
6. Prosper Menière: Menière's disease (1850)
7. Guillaume Dupuytren: Dupuytren's contraction (1851)
8. Thomas Addison: Addison's disease (1855)
9. John Hughlings Jackson: Jacksonian epilepsy (1875)
10. Sergei Korsakoff: Korsakoff's syndrome (1887)
11. Max Wilms: Wilms' tumour (1899)
12. Alois Alzheimer: Alzheimer's disease (1907)

URBAN MYTHS
True or False – you decide

COCA-COLA CAN BE USED AS A SPERMICIDE

Various commodities such as honey and sodium bicarbonate, acidic fruit juices and oils have been used as spermicides in the past. In 1985, three Harvard research scientists were made aware that Coca-Cola is said to be used for this purpose in some third world countries and also that the drink was widely used as a contraceptive aid in the USA in years gone by.

The soft drink's spermicidal capabilities had never been investigated, so Dr Sharee Umpierre and her colleagues tested a few varieties of Coke in their lab. They found Diet Coke to be the most effective spermicide while Coke in its original formula also served the purpose. New Coke was the least effective of the three.

The sperm-killing experiment involved test tubes containing small samples of preserved sperm into which they poured small amounts of each variety of Coke. All of them proved spermicidal to some degree. A Coca-Cola spokesman said the company hadn't seen the new report, but followed up by saying that "our position is we do not promote any of our products for any medical use."

Ten musical bans

1. Fourth century BC: Plato called for a ban on contemporary music from the Greek republic because it led to low morals.

2. 1936: Adolf Hitler banned the playing of Mendelssohn because the composer was Jewish.

3. 1958: Jerry Lee Lewis stepped off a plane in London arm-in-arm with his wife Myra, who he revealed was also his cousin and "about thirteen". Britain was aghast when it turned out that the rocker was a serial bigamist who first married at the age of fourteen. His tour was cancelled and he was banned from playing in Britain.

4. 1962: *Speedy Gonzales*, a novelty single by the US crooner Pat Boone was removed from playlists because it was considered offensive to Mexicans.

5. 1963: *Dominique* by The Singing Nun was banned in Springfield, Massachusetts by station WHYN because it was "degrading to Catholics".

6. 1966: The Beatles's *A Day in the Life* was widely banned because of perceived drug references.

7. 1968: Communist party leader Chairman Mao Tse-Tung banned *The Sound Of Music* in China because it was a blatant example of capitalist pornography.

8. 1969: *Je T'Aime . . . Moi Non Plus* by Jane Birkin and Serge Gainsbourg was banned by US and European radio stations for content of an explicit sexual nature.

9. 1970: The Rolling Stones released their new single *Cocksucker Blues*, a successful ploy to get them out of a contractual obligation.

10. 1971: The Malawian dictator Dr Hastings Banda banned the song *Delilah* made famous by the Welsh singer Tom Jones, in deference to a favourite mistress of the same name.

Thought for the Day

Love is a sport in which the
hunter must contrive to have
the quarry in pursuit.
Jean Kerr, 1923–2000

Ten unsung siblings

1. Bleda the Hun, elder brother of Attila
2. Paula Hitler, younger sister of Adolf
3. Maria Ulyanova, younger sister of Lenin
4. Caspar van Beethoven, unmusical brother of Ludwig
5. Gebhard Himmler, elder brother of Heinrich
6. Henrietta Marx, younger sister of Karl
7. Feodor the not remotely Terrible, younger brother of Ivan
8. Pierre d'Arc, younger brother of Joan
9. Mao Zemin, little brother of Mao Zedong
10. Omm Omar Hussein, little sister of Saddam

 Don't worry, be happy

Some cause happiness wherever they go; others whenever
they go.
Oscar Wilde, 1854–1900

Ten royal sobriquets
1. Constantine the Copronymous, Byzantine emperor, so named because at his christening in AD 718 the baby Constantine defecated in the baptismal font.
2. Loius the Stammerer, ninth-century king of France.
3. Pepin the Hunchback, ninth-century Frankish prince.
4. Alfonso the Fat, thirteenth-century king of Portugal.
5. Pedro the Cruel, fourteenth-century king of Castile.
6. Stephen the Fop, fourteenth-century Bavarian duke.
7. Queen Juana the Mad, sixteenth-century Castillian queen.
8. Otto the Idle, twelfth-century Germanic king.
9. Henry the Impotent, fifteenth-century king of Castile.
10. Selim the Grim, sixteenth-century Sultan of Turkey, so-called for his penchant for wholesale slaughter of sibling rivals to the throne.

Ten nationalities yet to be insulted by the Duke of Edinburgh*
1. Germans
2. Greeks
3. Danes
4. Argentinians
5. Russians
6. Mongolians
7. Japanese
8. Finns
9. Spaniards
10. Sudanese

*Doing his bit for race relations in 1986, Prince Philip, the Duke of Edinburgh, advised a British student in Beijing, "Don't stay here too long or you'll go back with slitty eyes," and later described

Beijing as "ghastly". During a 1976 tour in Hong Kong – unaware that his microphone was on – he told a photographer, "Fuck off or I'll have you shot." At an official function in Chile he was introduced to Dr Salvador Allende, soon to become the country's president, and found fault with Dr Allende's attire (Allende was wearing an ordinary suit instead of the required white tie and tails). Allende explained that his people were very poor and that as their representative it would be inappropriate for him to dress expensively. Philip replied, "And if they had told you to wear a bathing costume, I suppose you'd have come dressed in one." On the same tour of South America he told the fascist dictator of Paraguay, General Alfredo Stroessner, a protector of Nazi war criminals, "It's a pleasant change to be in a country that isn't ruled by its people." On a tour of Canada he reminded his British Commonwealth hosts, "We don't come here for our health, you know," and, visiting an Aboriginal cultural park in Queensland, Australia, demanded to know, "What's it all about? Do you still throw spears at each other?" Other victims of his "dry sense of humour" include: the Dutch ("What a po-faced lot the Dutch are."); the French ("Isn't it a pity Louis XVI was sent to the guillo-tine?"); Panamanians (on a trip to Panama he shouted at his official police escort who had sounded a siren, "Switch that bloody thing off, you silly fucker!"); Hungarians ("Most of them are pot-bellied."); and the Scots ("They drink too much."). At least the Duke is very even-handed; in 1966 he reminded his wife's loyal subjects, "You know, British women can't cook," and in 1995 enquired of a Scottish driving intructor, "How do you keep the natives off the booze long enough to pass the test?" Philip has been dubbed "the best argument for republicanism since George III".

POTTY WISDOM, BULGARIA

If you do what people tell you, you will be fishing hares in the sea and hunting fish in the woods.

Ten uninspiring presidents

1. John Quincy Adams (1825–29): ". . . a disgusting man to do business with, coarse and dirty and clownish in his address and stiff and abstracted in his opinions, which are drawn from books exclusively." – William Henry Harrison
2. Andrew Jackson (1829–37): "A barbarian who could not write a sentence of grammar and hardly could spell his own name."– John Quincy Adams
3. Warren G. Harding (1921–23): "He writes the worst English I have ever encountered. It reminds me of a string of wet sponges . . . of tattered washing on the line . . . of stale bean soup, of college yells, of dogs barking idiotically through endless nights. It is so bad that a sort of grandeur creeps into it. It drags itself out of a dark abyss of pish, and crawls insanely up the topmost pinnacle of posh. It is rumble and bumble. It is flap and doodle. It is balder and dash." – H. L. Mencken
4. Calvin Coolidge (1923–29): "He slept more than any other president, whether by day or night. Nero fiddled, but Coolidge only snored." – H. L. Mencken

5. Franklin D. Roosevelt (1933–45): "Had every quality that morons esteem in their heroes. He was the first American to plumb the real depths of vulgar stupidity." – H. L. Mencken
6. Dwight D. Eisenhower (1953–61): "This fellow don't know any more about politics than a pig knows about Sunday." – Harry S. Truman
7. Lyndon Baines Johnson (1963–69): "How does one tell the President of the United States to stop picking his nose and lifting a leg to fart in front of the camera and using "chickenshit" in every other sentence?" – Stuart Rosenberg, TV Director
8. Gerald Ford (1974–77): "In the Bob Hope Golf Classic the participation of President Gerald Ford was more than enough to remind you that the nuclear button was at one stage at the disposal of a man who might have either pressed it by mistake or else pressed it deliberately to obtain room service." – Clive James, Australian writer
9. Ronald Reagan (1981–89): "In a disastrous fire in Ronald Reagan's library, both books were destroyed. And the real tragedy is that he hadn't finished colouring them." – Jonathan Hunt, US journalist
10. George W. Bush (2000–): "Apparently Arnold (Schwarzenegger) was inspired by President Bush, who proved you can be a successful politician in this country even if English is your second language." – Conan O'Brien, US TV presenter

Miscellany

Clean queen
Although London's tap water is good enough for just under seven million of her subjects, the Queen never cleans her teeth in it, let alone ever drinks it.

Would you buy used furniture from this man?
Al Capone's business card described him as a used furniture dealer.

Ballgrabbing mugger
A Canadian woman who grabbed the testicles of elderly men before stealing their wallets was finally apprehended in October 1999. Michelle Lawes, thirty-five, attacked more than a dozen men between the ages of sixty and eighty-three. Her ploy was to ask her victims for a cigarette then grab them between the legs while she searched for their wallets. A Toronto police spokesman explained, "It was basically a type of distraction."

Why we know him as Picasso
Picasso's full name was Pablo Diego José Francisco de Paula Juan Nepomuceno Maria de los Remedios Cipriano de la Santissima Trinidad Ruiz y Picasso.

Full of it
The great Aztec emperor Montezuma had a nephew, Cuitlahac, whose name meant "plenty of excrement".

He came on well, though
Einstein didn't talk properly until after his ninth birthday. His
parents thought he was mentally retarded.

A memento
The Persian king Cambyses II had a finely tuned sense of poetic
justice. When one of his judges was found guilty of corruption,
Cambyses had him flayed then had the judge's old seat
re-upholstered with his skin. Then he appointed the dead judge's
son to sit in judgment where his father had previously sat.

Priorities
It takes more water to make one rubber car tyre than it does to
keep a thirsty child alive for six months.

Berlin's unlucky elephant
The very first bomb dropped by the Allies on Berlin during
World War II killed the only elephant in Berlin Zoo.

The perfect sandcastle
Scientists claim to have discovered the secret of building the
perfect sandcastle: according to researchers from the
Massachusetts Institute of Technology (MIT) in the United
States, the formula you should use is to mix eight parts sand to
one part water.

A traditional welcome
In 2006 a Maori cultural performer who head-butted a Dutch
tourist, breaking his nose, was told to do 150 hours' community
work. He said he thought the man was laughing at him during a
traditional indigenous welcome to New Zealand.

The most discerning gourmet
The catfish has over 27,000 taste buds – more than any other animal.

Brain in a jar
When Albert Einstein died in 1955 his body was cremated, but his brain was preserved in a glass jar. It was Albert's dying wish that his best bit should be saved in case post-mortem analysis should shed new light on the rare gift of human genius. It didn't.

The forgotten corpse
In 1994 a Croatian, Stanislav Kovac, was knocked down and killed by a car on a business trip to Botrop, Germany. Local undertaker Rudolf Dauer subsequently completed a 560-mile trip from Botrop to the funeral in Zagreb, only to have to explain to bereaved relatives that he had forgotten to bring the corpse with him.

Clearly crazy
Frederick Armstrong was convicted in 1993 of stabbing an eighty-one-year-old preacher to death and cutting off his head before stunned onlookers, including a few police officers, at a funeral home in Baton Rouge, USA. Armstrong's defence attorney appealed against the verdict on the grounds that their client was obviously insane at the time. "A rational man," reasoned Armstrong's lawyer, "does not decapitate a man's head in the presence of a police officer."

The names of the three wise monkeys
The names of the three wise monkeys are: Mizaru (see no evil), Mikazaru (hear no evil), and Mazaru (speak no evil).

The Furrier
A 1911 mail order in the USA netted hundreds of thousands of
dollars with the promise of a miracle cure that could turn blacks
into whites. The most outrageous American mail order con of all
time, however, began in 1946 and lasted for a decade. William
Johnson, a semi-literate miner from Kentucky, decided to cash in
on a rumour sweeping America that Adolf Hitler had been
smuggled out of Europe after World War II and was alive and well
and living in North America. Johnson posed as the Führer, who
was now settled in Kentucky with some of his Nazi chiefs of staff,
and planning to take over the USA. He made a public appeal for
cash to help his cause, and right-wing Americans and fascists of
German extraction sent him a steady stream of postal orders as he
elaborated on his dastardly plans for space ships, "invisible ships"
and underground hoards of ammunition. The fact that he often
signed his name as "The Furrier" didn't stop the American public
from sending him tens of thousands of dollars.

A very shy tortoise
The highest amount ever paid for a deceased tortoise was the
£49 forked out by a Mrs D. Cobb in 1992. When she became
suspicious about her pet's apparent inactivity, a sales
representative from the Reptile Kingdom, Luton, explained to
her that it was it was "probably shy".

Sometimes a fern is more than a fern
Sigmund Freud had a morbid fear of ferns.

Sterilization of "defectives"
By the 1920s, at least thirty-one American states were legally
sterilizing people who they classified as "defectives" in an
attempt to purify the genetic composition of their population. In

1927 the US Supreme Court upheld eugenic sterilization laws on the grounds that the offspring of people of limited intelligence, the mentally ill and members of what they defined as "criminal classes" had no right to exist because they would be an unfair burden on decent, law-abiding, tax-paying Americans. Although the stigma of the obvious Nazi connotation led some US states to repeal their laws after the Second World War, twenty-one of them retained their sterilization laws until as late as the 1980s.

"I'm feeling a bit 'possessed by the gods'"
The word "giddy" is derived from the Anglo-Saxon word "gyddig" meaning "possessed by the gods".

Uncopyrightable
The only fifteen-letter word that can be spelled without repeating a letter is "uncopyrightable".

Saudi Arabia and the United Kingdom
Apart from Saudi Arabia, the United Kingdom is the only country in the world without a written constitution.

Having the Englishes
In France, menstruation is known as *avoir les anglais* ("to have the Englishes").

Unfair fight
The slaves sent into the Roman amphitheatres to fight wild animals often had their teeth removed and their arms broken to ensure that they didn't damage the Emperor's expensive menagerie.

376

ANIMAL NEWS Zebra Cross

San Francisco police were recently called in to apprehend a zebra making its escape from the Marine World zoo down a neighbouring six-lane freeway. After a high-speed chase – up to 45 mph – the animal was finally cornered, but if the cops thought that was the end of it they were in for a shock. The irate zebra kicked in two doors on a squad car, smashed a mudguard, climbed on the bonnet and chewed the steering wheel. It also bit two animal handlers before it could be returned to captivity.
Daily Mail

Bullfighting ban

Bullfighting in Spain would probably have been banned years ago if it weren't for the entertainment of foreign – more often than not, British – tourists. Opinion polls show that about 93 per cent of the population of Spain either no longer support bullfighting, or abhor it and want to see it abolished. In the last 225 years in which figures have been available for bullfights taking place in Spain and South America, fifty-eight matadors and mounted bullfighters have died. During this same period 1.3 million bulls have been cruelly put to death, and over 40,000 horses have been either crushed to death or disembowelled in Spain alone. The bull is usually unwilling to fight, and has to be either goaded into action with stimulants, or injected with sedatives if it becomes too frisky. There are a variety of traditional tricks to make sure that the bull doesn't pose a genuine threat to the matador, including: plugging one nostril with cotton wool to interfere with the bull's breathing and ensure that it tires quickly; pouring laudanum into the bull's ears; and sticking a darning needle through the bull's testicles.

Thelma Pickles
John Lennon's first girlfriend was named Thelma Pickles.

Early Antabuse
The Ottoman Sultan Suliman I used to cure persistent drunks by pouring molten lead down their throats.

A realist
The eighteenth-century English painter Benjamin West had the body of an executed murderer crucified to see how it hung.

"Bomber" Harris
Sir Arthur "Bomber" Harris's thousand-bomber raids on German cities during World War II, designed in his own words "to do maximum damage and destruction to populated areas", once made even Churchill blanch. During the area-bombing of Cologne in May 1942 the entire city was so completely devastated by fire that late arrivals couldn't find anything left to bomb; one bomb-aimer who complained to his pilot that he couldn't find anywhere left to drop his load was told by his pilot, "Well start a bloody fire somewhere where it's not burning."

Bad science
Vivisection claims the lives of 20 million animals worldwide every year. The National Cancer Institute has to date tested "cures" on half a million animals, with a success rate of only 0.00001 per cent.

Near-human apes
In 1980 the Chinese attempted to impregnate female
chimpanzees with human sperm to develop a near-human hybrid
"for economic and technical purposes". Dr Qi Yongxiang in the
city of Shenyang said the "near-human ape" would do menial
tasks and provide substitutes for human transplant organs. The
Chinese authorities said that as the creature produced would be
classed as animal, there need be no qualms about killing it.

The tongue is mightier than the biceps
Proportionate to its size, the strongest muscle in the body is the
tongue.

Debeaking chickens
Factory-reared chickens often have their beaks removed to stop
them from attacking, or even eating each other. Mechanical
"debeaking machines" use hot blades to cut through a highly
sensitive area of tissue around the chicken's mouth. In some
parts of the US, the beaks are burned off.

Killed by a diaper
In 1854 a single child's nappy killed 616 people in Soho,
London. The outbreak of Asiatic Cholera took its toll after water
used to wash the infected nappy entered the public drinking
supply from a leaking cesspool in Broad Street.

Anesthesia, our daughter
Anesthesia was once a fashionable Christian name for baby
girls. It became popular after Queen Victoria inhaled chloroform
to help her through the birth of her seventh child.

Horsehair dartboards
The original pub dartboards were made of horsehairs.

Tasteful
The Forum novelties company of Elmont, New York, dominates the bad taste field of the American mail order novelty gift business. Their catalogue includes Potty Pot Shots toilet bowl targets for men to urinate on, the Shove-It desk set, including an executive anus-shaped pen-holder, a plastic mould to make penis-shaped ice cubes, penis-shaped ice cream cones, a rubber hot-dog bap holding a two-headed rubber penis, the Shit Head Hat made from lifelike rubber turds, Deluxe Doggy Doo ("so real it fools other dogs") the Party Pooper, a rubber turd shaped to hang off the toilet seat to make it look as though it missed the target, and an imitation soiled nappy "just like the real thing".

The king is dead
The word "Checkmate" in chess comes from the Persian phrase, "Shah mat", which means "the king is dead".

Pine head
Pinocchio is Italian for "pine head".

The most miserly person who ever lived was an American woman, Henrietta Howland Green. Although the total extent of her wealth was never revealed, she was known to have kept a balance of nearly $31.5 million in one bank alone. Her son had to have his leg amputated because she spent too long searching for a free clinic and she ate cold porridge because she was too mean to heat it. She lived mostly on onion and eggs, and wore old newspapers when her petticoats wore out. She died aged eighty-one in 1916, leaving an estate worth $95 million.

URBAN MYTHS
True or False – you decide

MARLBORO CIGARETTES ARE FUNDED BY THE KU KLUX KLAN

There is a widespread belief that the Philip Morris Company, which makes Marlboro cigarettes, is owned by or connected to the Ku Klux Klan. This theory is generally supported by certain aspects of the packaging. Looked at from a certain angle, the red and white design can be made to appear as a series of "K"s. There are three spots on the inside of the packet which are said to represent the Klansman's eyes, or to represent the races of heaven and earth in Klan mythology.

Regardless of the details, one common theme in this belief is the idea that Philip Morris, the founder of the company, was a member of the Klan, and that this is the source of the connection. This would have come as something of a surprise to the real Philip Morris, a London tobacconist who set up the company in the mid-nineteenth century in London. By the time his company spread its operations to the US in the early part of the twentieth century, Morris had died, but the company he founded continues to bear his name to this day.

Whether or not the packaging of Marlboro represents anything other than basic product design is another question, but given the fact that the story of Philip Morris's Klan membership is so far from the truth, it seems most likely that there is no truth to any other part of this elaborate urban legend.

Ice, ice, ice
Supposedly, the Inuit have hundreds of words for ice but none for hello.

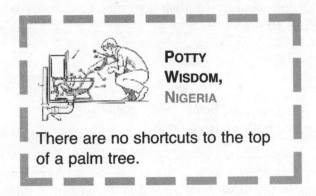

POTTY WISDOM, NIGERIA

There are no shortcuts to the top of a palm tree.

Another miserly Briton
The affluent eighteenth-century farm-owner Daniel Dancer of Harrow Weald was believed to be the most miserly Briton of his time. Although he inherited a fortune, rather than use any fuel he would heat his food by sitting on it.

Many Mohammeds
The most common name in the world is Mohammed.

Funny money
The word "pound" is abbreviated "lb", because Libra means "pound" in Latin as well as "scales". The abbreviation for British Pound Sterling comes from the same source: an "L" for Libra, with a stroke through it to indicate that the word has been abbreviated. The same was true for the Italian lira which uses the same abbreviation ("lira" coming from Libra). British currency, before it went metric, was always quoted as

"pounds/shillings/pence", abbreviated as "L/s/d" (*libra*/*solidus*/*denarius*).

The watershed
Under sixteenth-century English law, men could only beat their wives before 10 pm.

Tails!
If you toss a coin 10,000 times, on average it will fall heads up about 4,950 times. The heads side weighs slightly more, so it ends up on the bottom more often.

The Web of Babel
After English, the most widely used languages on the Internet are German, Japanese, French, Spanish, Swedish, Italian, Portuguese, Dutch, Norwegian, Finnish, Czech, Danish, Russian and Malay.

A jiffy
A "jiffy" is an actual unit of time for 1/100th of a second.

Hell
Ninety per cent of us believe in divine retribution.

Ow!
There are many more male hypochondriacs than female.

Kneeless babies
Babies are born without knee caps. They don't appear until the child reaches two to six years of age.

Brass monkey business
The saying "it's so cold out there it could freeze the balls off a
brass monkey" probably originated in the English Civil War.
The cannonballs were stacked in a pyramid formation called a
brass monkey. When it became extremely cold outside they
would crack and break off.

Spacemen don't cry
In space, no one can see you cry: without gravity tears don't
flow.

I heard that!
Men can read smaller print than women, but women have better
hearing.

Mrs Fagin
The Koh-i-Noor diamond is one of several stolen gems which
now form part of the British Crown Jewels. It was seized from
India after the defeat of the Maharajah of the Punjab at Lahore,
and presented to Queen Victoria in 1851. The huge diamond,
regarded as India's most fabulous treasure, was the largest in the
world at that time. In 1854 when the Maharajah visited
Buckingham Palace, Queen Victoria demonstrated breathtaking
tactlessness when she casually showed it off to its rightful
owner. The Maharajah took the massive insult with dignity, but
thereafter always referred to Queen Victoria as "Mrs Fagin".
India still regards the diamond as their national treasure, and to
this day considers that Queen Elizabeth II is the recipient of
stolen property.

Of cocks and roosters
The word "rooster" was invented to describe male chickens because Americans were too embarrassed to contemplate using the word "cock".

Whips and sonic booms
The tip of a bullwhip moves so fast that it breaks the sound barrier. The "crack" of a whip is actually a tiny sonic boom.

 ## Don't worry, be happy
Pleasure comes from the outside, happiness from the inside.

Cinderella's fur slippers
Cinderella's slippers were originally made out of fur. The story was changed in the 1600s by a translation error.

Now do you believe us?
In 1943 a unit of Gurkha soldiers fighting in the British army in Burma made a series of commando raids along the coast of Japanese-held Arakan. When they returned and claimed to have killed over one hundred of the enemy, the Gurkhas were understandably miffed when British officers treated their story with undisguised scepticism. They made sure no one doubted their word when they returned from the next raid loaded down with sacks full of Japanese heads.

By these balls I swear . . .
In ancient Rome, men traditionally took an oath by grabbing their testicles with the right hand.

Thought for the Day

A lover . . . tries to stand
in well with the pet dog
of the house.
Molière, 1622–73

Boots, legs and all

The lack of good boots has been the perennial problem of
marching armies down the centuries. In the Second World War
German soldiers on the Russian front found their boots were far
less capable of keeping their feet dry through the freezing winter
than those of their Soviet opponents, so the resourceful Germans
found a practical way to strip the frozen dead soldiers of their
footwear. They collected frozen bodies and sawed their legs off
at the knee. Legs and boots were then placed in an oven until
they were sufficiently thawed out for the boots to be removed.

Mad Dadd

The best-known and most remarkable works of the Victorian artist
Richard Dadd were completed in Bedlam where he was serving a
life sentence for the murder of his father Robert. In 1842 Dadd
accompanied his patron Sir Thomas Phillips on a Grand Tour of
Europe and the Middle East, and during the trip Dadd first began
to experience headaches and "sun stroke". In Rome, Dadd
experienced an uncontrollable urge to attack the Pope during one
of his public appearances. It appeared that Dadd had become
convinced that he was being called upon by God to do battle with

the devil, who could assume any shape he desired, including the
Pontiff. In spite of fixation Dadd continued working in Newman
Street, London, living on hard-boiled eggs and beer. Dadd's father
Robert meanwhile had Alexander Sutherland of St Luke's
Hospital examine his son, and Sutherland concluded that the artist
was clinically insane. Dadd's brother George was at this time also
showing signs of mental illness. In 1843 Robert Dadd
accompanied Richard on a trip to Cobham, and during this trip
Dadd attacked and killed his father with a knife and razor. Dadd
fled to Dover and boarded a ship for Calais, then set off in the
direction of Paris, but on the way drew attention to himself by
attempting to cut the throat of a fellow traveller. He was finally
detained in Montereau where he confessed to the murder of his
father. In July 1844, shortly after Dadd's twenty-seventh birthday,
he was sent to Bethlem Hospital's criminal lunatic department.
Dadd remained in Bedlam for almost twenty years during which
period he completed his famous works *The Fairy Feller's Master-
Stroke*, *Contradiction*, *Oberon and Titania*, and *Portrait of a
Young Man*. In 1864 Dadd was moved to the brand-new lunatic
asylum at Broadmoor, near London and two years later died of
lung disease.

The Star-Spangled Banner
The words "United States" and "America" are never once
mentioned in "The Star-Spangled Banner". The US Congress
didn't make the song the official anthem of the USA until 1931
– 117 years after it was written.

Mind your Ps and Qs
The expression "Mind your Ps and Qs" came from the days of
"hot metal" mechanical printing, when text was created by
arranging individual letters on to a plate and locking them into

place. All of the letters were placed in bins – all the As in one bin, all the Bs in another bin, and so on. There were two cases of bins for each letter, one case contained capitals – the upper case – the others were in the lower case. As the printing process forced the letters to be arranged upside down to the viewer and the letters were in mirror writing, it was very easy to confuse an upside-down, backwards p with an upside-down, backwards q.

Ods niggers noggers

The 1623 Profane Oaths Act made swearing illegal in England. The popular oaths of the day, the colourful "gog's malt", the suggestive "cat's nouns", or the extremely naughty "a turd i' your teeth" could earn you a shilling fine or a good whipping. Most people took no notice and carried on swearing, and so in 1745 the law was beefed up with stiffer penalties. By this time most people were saying "stap me vitals" or possibly even "ods niggers noggers" to the Act, which curiously enough lay neglected and ignored on the statute books for over 200 years until it was repealed in 1967.

Breeding

To meet the rules of breed standards for show purposes, many pedigree dogs are bred to the point of deformity. Pekinese bitches are often incapable of whelping properly and have to be delivered by Caesarean section. They also often suffer from cleft palates, chronic breathing and eyesight problems. Cavalier King Charles Spaniels suffer spinal disc and heart problems, and West Highland Whites are prone to eye and skin disease. Many Dalmatians are also born deaf as a result of in-breeding, and many breeds have deformed kneecaps. Large breeds like Dobermanns, Labradors and Great Danes often suffer from spinal deformity.

Alarm beds and enema sticks

When Prince Albert unveiled his plan for a Crystal Palace to house
the Great Exhibition of 1851, experts confidently predicted that
the London sparrows who perched on it would crush the whole
structure with the combined weight of their droppings. Exhibits on
show included an "alarm bed" which catapulted the sleeper bodily
across the room at a chosen hour and a physician's walking stick
the handle of which doubled as an enema.

Orville's eggs

The aviator Orville Wright numbered the eggs that his chickens
produced so he could eat them in the precise order they were
laid. He also had a morbid fear of public appearances. When
President Franklin Roosevelt went to Wright's home town,
Dayton, to campaign for re-election, Orville was invited to lunch
with him. He could hardly refuse the invitation, but later when
he found himself in the back of the President's touring car being
driven though cheering crowds, at the first opportunity he
hopped out, thanked the President for lunch, then walked home.

Because it felt so good

In 1996, Phillip Johnson, thirty-two, was hospitalized after
shooting himself in the left shoulder with his .22-calibre rifle "to
see how it felt". Twelve months later an ambulance crew was
again called to Johnson's home, where he was bleeding from
another left-shoulder gunshot. According to the local newspaper,
Johnson said the earlier shooting felt so good he had to do it again.

Florence Nightingale and her pet owl

The Crimean War heroine Florence Nightingale was a
hypochondriac who lived every day to the ripe old age of ninety
complaining that she was ill. To her death she refused to believe

in the existence of bacteria and kept a miniature pet owl in her pocket which she took with her everywhere.

US Society for Prevention of Cruelty to Mushrooms

The US Society for Prevention of Cruelty to Mushrooms has 300 members dedicated to the protection of poisonous and edible mushrooms from abuse. President Brad Brown says that the remit of the society also extends to protecting vegetables, "and any other neglected or mistreated forms of life, regardless of age, race, sex, religion or other stereotypical attributes".

Good Queen Bess

In 1603 in London alone, 30,000 of Queen Elizabeth's subjects died of the plague. "Good Queen Bess" responded to the national crisis by fleeing with her court to Windsor Castle, where she had a gallows set up and threatened to hang anyone who tried to follow her.

That's where it got to

In 1994 a Swedish man with impaired hearing made a complete recovery after doctors removed a forty-seven-year-old bus ticket from his ear.

Pet Cemetery

To circumvent a French law which bans the burial of animals in human cemeteries, in 1977 Helene Lavanent and Yvette Soltane booked themselves graves in a pet cemetery so that they could be buried with their dogs.

A nose of gold

The great sixteenth-century Danish astronomer Tycho Brahe
was not a man you would want to get into an argument with.
High-handed and hot-tempered, he fought duels, kept a mistress
who bore him eight children, employed a dwarf as a jester, had a
pet elk (which died after breaking a leg while going downstairs
drunk), dabbled in alchemy and tyrannized the local peasantry.
Brahe's other claim to fame was that he wore an artificial nose
made from silver and gold, his own having been sliced off in a
duel. It happened in 1566 while the 20-year-old Tycho was
studying at the University of Rostock in Germany. Attending a
dance at a professor's house, he got into a quarrel with one
Manderup Parsbjerg over some fine point of mathematics. They
decided to take it outside in the form of a duel conducted in
pitch darkness with swords. Reconstructive surgery not being an
option, Tycho concealed the loss of face as best he could with
an artificial bridge made of precious metals. Apparently he
carried some glue with him at all times to keep the nose firmly
in place. Brahe is thought to have died when he contracted a
urinary infection while attending a banquet hosted by a baron in
Prague in which he drank extensively but felt that etiquette
prevented him from leaving the table to relieve himself before
the host left. His tomb was reopened in 1901 and his remains
were examined by medical experts. The nasal opening of the
skull was rimmed with green, a sign of exposure to copper.

Byron the Rottweiler

In 1984 a Texan hairdresser was upset when her pet Rottweiler
killed and ate her four-week-old daughter, but mortified when
she was told that the animal would have to be put down. She
told newspaper reporters, "I can always have another baby, but I
can't replace my dog Byron."

391

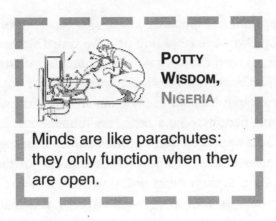

POTTY WISDOM, NIGERIA

Minds are like parachutes:
they only function when they
are open.

Taking an air bath

Benjamin Franklin, American founding father, inventor,
statesman and philosopher, known for discovering electricity
through his experiments with lightning and for his sparkling wit,
was a plump little man who liked to sit stark naked in front of
his open window; some call it indecent exposure, he called it
"taking an air bath".

Caramba

No one is quite sure why, but the English language uses the
sexual act as a basis for its lexicon of swear words more than
any other. In Germany most swearing is profoundly anal: nearly
every German joke there is to be told leads inexorably to a
punchline containing the lynchpin expletives *scheiss* (shit),
dreck (crap) or *leck mich im arsch* (lick my arse). Scatological
themes pepper the whole German culture, and as a result the
German sense of humour, to British or French ears, sounds very
ponderous and lacking in subtlety. Italy has a massive
vocabulary of profanities, most of them based around religious
themes, usually referring to God and the Virgin Mary. Most lose

a little in translation, especially *porco Dio* (that pig of a God), the confusing *Dio cane* (that dog of a God) or *Dio serpente* (that snake of a God), and the very odd *Dio canarino* (that canary of a God) and *Dio scapa da lett senza scarpi* (God escaped from bed without shoes). Mussolini once launched a campaign to try to persuade his people to be a little less foul-mouthed, and a series of notices appeared all over the country ordering *Non bestemmiare per l'onore d'Italia* (Do not swear for the honour of Italy). All that these notices did, however, was encourage people to invent a new crop of oaths directed at Il Duce and his ****ing notices. The Spaniards are skilled and enthusiastic swearers, their oaths tending towards long-winded anal references, as in the popular *cago en la leche de tu madre* (I shit on your mother's milk), or ingenious combinations of religion and scatology, as in *me cago en Dios* (I shit on God) and *me cago en todos los santos* (I shit on all the saints), an invitation to a triple-whammy thunderbolt if ever there was one. The all-time Spanish No. 1 oath however is still the multi-purpose *caramba*, which doesn't appear to have any meaning at all.

Natural selection?
Although Charles Darwin was the first person to shed light on the dangers of inbreeding he wasn't quite bright enough to avoid marrying his own first cousin Emma. There were signs of eccentricity on both sides of a family which was already dangerously interlinked. His grandmother and great-grandfather were unstable drunks, his uncle Erasmus was insane and committed suicide, and his brother Erasmus was a chronic and neurotic invalid. His grandfather, yet another Erasmus, who had a terrible stammer, was considered a leading expert on the treatment of the mentally ill, and had whirling beds and gyrating chairs fitted into most of the country's lunatic asylums so that

patients could be rotated until blood poured out of their ears, eyes and noses. Charles Darwin himself was also a stammerer and a morose hypochondriac: he suffered from fainting fits and would take to his bed for months on end.

Cat's eyes
In parts of Malaysia cats are often killed by scalding, then their eyes are gouged out and eaten raw. They say it's very good for your eyesight.

The war at home
Since 1979 there have been more children killed by guns on the streets of the US than there were American troops killed in Vietnam.

Shoes and food
The cost of a pair of fashion sports shoes as worn by the average Western teenager would feed a starving family of four in the developing world for six months.

Spying plants
Documents released under the US Freedom of Information Act reveal that the CIA once trained cats to carry bombs, used otters to plant underwater explosives and spent hundreds of thousands of dollars on research into whether or not plants could be used to spy on people.

Pleased to meet you
In sixteenth-century England it was conventional for men to greet female guests, providing they were related, by fondling their breasts.

LEGAL NEWS

Legal News: Pulp Snow White
A school in Florida has banned its pupils from reading
the fairy tale *Snow White* after Christian parents
complained of its "graphic violence".
Midweek

The Black Death
The bubonic plague never actually went away. There are several
cases of plague reported every year, and parts of western USA
are still regarded as plague risk areas. The last major outbreak of
bubonic plague took place in eastern Siberia in 1910, killing
60,000 people in seven months. It was spread by a fur trapper
who had picked it up from the skin of an infected marmot – a
rodent the skin of which is sold as a substitute for sable. As
recently as 1966 there were over a thousand confirmed cases,
and at least 500 plague deaths in Vietnam.

A very large jar
When Alexander the Great died his body was preserved in a
large jar of honey.

Hollywood cruelty
Before Hollywood film-makers were forced to submit to the
"Cruelty to Animals" code enforced by the American Humane
Association (AHA), animals were routinely maimed and
slaughtered in the name of popular entertainment. In Schaffner's
film *Patton* a donkey was clubbed to death, two calves were
killed and two mules died. When an explosive device tied to a
horse's chest went off, the film crew were alleged to have taken
a lunch break while the horse died in agony. In the $20 million
flop *Heaven's Gate* at least five horses were killed, one of them
literally blown apart, because the writer/director Michael

Cimono wanted "real blood" and banned the AHA from his set. In Sergei Dandarchuk's *Waterloo* starring Rod Steiger, *Variety* magazine reported on "ditches clogged with dead horses". In *Pat Garrett and Billy the Kid* many horses died immediately or had to be put down later because of the injuries they suffered, and live chickens were buried up to their necks in the sand and used for target practice. In Francis Ford Coppola's *Apocalypse Now* a live water buffalo was hacked to death. Ingmar Bergman once wanted to kill a live horse on the set, but when the actor David Carradine vehemently protested Bergman had it killed off the set and filmed the still warm carcass. Bergman was also alleged to have killed three other horses, including one which was burned alive, and once had a dog strangled.

Bonnie and Clyde's grisly end
The legendary bank robbers Bonnie and Clyde were eating bacon and tomato sandwiches when they were ambushed by a posse of patrolmen led by a Texas Ranger and perforated by seventy-seven bullets, splattering bits of brain all over the upholstery. Local souvenir hunters scoured the car for trophies, even cutting off locks of Bonnie Parker's hair. One was stopped by a coroner as he tried to saw off one of Clyde Barrow's ears.

A maggot under my tongue
As a warm maggot is a happy wriggling maggot, a fisherman will often keep a couple under his tongue to keep them at an ambient temperature. Hence the saying, "Old fishermen never die, they just smell that way."

No beardies
When the wealthy Englishman Henry Budd died in 1862 he left an estate to each of his two sons on the condition that they did

not wear moustaches. Moustachioed Walt Disney hated beards so much that he would not allow bearded men to work for him. Margaret Thatcher wouldn't allow bearded men into her Cabinet.

Making a prophecy come true

Success can give academics a dangerously inflated view of their own self importance. Take the sixteenth-century Italian polymath Girolamo Cardano. His reputation as a mathematician alone was such that he was consulted by Leonardo da Vinci on questions of geometry. As a sideline Cardano also earned international fame as the most successful astrologer of his day and was hired to draw up horoscopes for the crowned heads of Europe, including England's young King Edward VI. He predicted his own death, down to the very hour, at the age of seventy-five. When the time arrived and Cardano found himself in robust good health, he committed suicide rather than be proven wrong.